AF324236

CONTENTS

INTRODUCTION

Features of the Nuwave Air Fryer

Nuwave air fryer, is the same as other brand air fryers, which utilize extremely hot flowing air to crisp and cook the food quickly. The NuWave Air Fryer comes with an advanced digital display that includes a digital timer with a built-in automatic shutoff function. Unlike other analog air fryers, the NuWave Air Fryer has an advanced LCD display that tells you the exact temperature that your meals are being cooked at. There is no need to mess around with the analog dial or guess the cooking temperature. With the advanced NuWave Air Fryer, it takes the guesswork out of cooking with its easy one-touch digital controls. With the NuWave Air Fryer, all of your favorite fried foods taste the way they should, without any extra fat. With no oily mess to soak and scrub, the NuWave Air Fryer is the new and healthy way to enjoy fried foods without any of the guilt. The NuWave Air Fryer can even save you money while saving you calories. No more wasting money on fast food or supplies for deep-frying at home. Instead, you can efficiently air-fry your favorite foods with less fat and calories but with the same great taste!

What makes the NuWave Air Fryer stand out from competitors?

There are a few distinct things that make the NuWave Air Fryer so popular. First of all, its 6-quart capacity is a little higher than most other brands, which only have around a 4-quart capacity. After comparing it to other air fryer machines, users concluded that its design lets it fry more evenly, with items getting browned regardless of where in the basket they are placed. The biggest benefit of the NuWave Air Fryer over other air fryers is its versatility. The basket, rotisserie, muffin trays and grill trays let you do more than just fry food in the Air Fryer. It has far more presets and manual control options, so you can cook just about anything you want. At the same time, this versatility does not mean the machine gets complicated. The display is simple enough to figure out even if you're new to air frying.

How do you use the NuWave Air Fryer?

The Air Fryer works by exposing food to blasts of super-high, heated air. This cooks food while crisping up the outside. Users who cook regularly with the air fryer say they love the ability to get fried foods without having to deal with added calories and messy cleanup. In addition to frying foods, the NuWave Air Fryer can also be used to grill or rotisserie foods. The possibilities for cooking with the NuWave Air Fryer are endless. You can use it for wings, donuts, hash browns, roasted chicken, kale chips, pizzas and more. Cooking food is as easy as gathering your ingredients, putting them inside the fryer and clicking a few buttons.

Nuwave Air Fryer FAQ's

Where can I cook with my NuWave Brio Digital Air Fryer?

The NuWave Brio can be used anywhere with a standard electrical outlet and potential for 900, 1500, or 1800 watts of power. Place the NuWave Brio on a flat, level surface, such as a countertop or tabletop when operating. Always ensure the NuWave Brio has at least 3 inches between the back vent and a wall or any potential obstruction.

How do I clean the NuWave Brio Digital Air Fryer?

The Base Tray, Fry Pan Basket, Fry Pan Basket Net and all accessories for the NuWave Brio can be cleaned in the dishwasher, top rack only. These parts can also be hand washed simply by wiping them down with a damp cloth.

What type of accessories can I use with the NuWave Brio Digital Air Fryer?

In addition to the accessories that are designed specifically for the NuWave Brio, any items that are oven-safe and small enough to fit comfortably inside the 6-quart basket can be used with the NuWave Brio. Items such as aluminum foil, metal and some glass pans and even frozen entrée trays are safe for use in the NuWave Brio. Additionally, any cooking utensils that can be used in a conventional oven can be used in the NuWave Brio.

Nuwave Air Fryer VS Traditional Deep Frying

Nuwave Brio Healthy Digital Air Fryer

Precise temperature control. The Brio's temperature range is 100°F to 400°F, adjustable in precise 5°F increments. Enclosed cooking chamber. The Brio keeps the heat inside and stays cool outside, making it safe for the whole family. No oil required. By using little or no oil to cook, the Brio makes fried food healthier. Built-in safety features. The Brio won't cook if the air fry basket isn't properly placed. Pre-Heat feature. By pre-heating the Brio, you can ensure crispier results and faster cooking times. Easy to clean. Since nearly all of the Brio's parts easily separate and are dishwasher-safe, clean-up is a breeze. Easy to use. The Brio features an intuitive touch screen digital interface.

Traditional Deep Frying

Imprecise cooking temperature. You are forced to guess at the oil temperature, which often results in over- or under-cooking your food. Unreliable containment. Stovetop frying leaves you susceptible to hot oil splatters, burns, and a greasy mess. Extra Fat and Calories. Soaking fried foods in oil leaves you with fattening, greasy food that has up to 70% more calories than air fried foods. Burn and fire hazard. Deep frying on a stove can result in burns or even grease fires if you're not careful. Long Prep Time. Unless you're frying with fancy, expensive equipment, you may have to wait a long time before the oil is hot enough for frying. Difficult to clean. Cleaning grease stains can be a tremendous hassle, especially from clothing. Harder to use. Because you are forced to fiddle with the knobs on your old stove, it's hard to know whether you've set the right temperature or how long your food should stay in the oil.

APPETIZERS AND SIDE DISHES

1. Cinnamon Mixed Nuts

Servings:4
Cooking Time: 25 Minutes
Ingredients:
- ½ cup pecans
- ½ cup walnuts
- ½ cup almonds
- A pinch cayenne pepper
- 2 tbsp sugar
- 2 tbsp egg whites
- 2 tsp cinnamon

Directions:
1. In a bowl, mix the cayenne pepper, sugar, and cinnamon; set aside. In another bowl, beat the egg whites and mix in the pecans, walnuts,and almonds. Add in the spice mixture and stir well.
2. Lightly grease the frying basket with baking tray. Pour in the nuts mixture. Select Toast function, adjust the temperature to 360 F, and press Start. Toast for 10 minutes, then stir the nuts using a wooden vessel, and toast further for 10 minutes. Pour the nuts in a bowl and let cool.

2. Kale Chips

Servings: 4
Cooking Time: 20 Minutes
Ingredients:
- 4 cups stemmed kale
- ½ tsp. salt
- 2 tsp. avocado oil

Directions:
1. Take a large bowl, toss kale in avocado oil and sprinkle with salt. Place into the air fryer basket.
2. Adjust the temperature to 400 Degrees F and set the timer for 5 minutes. Kale will be crispy when done. Serve immediately.
- **Nutrition Info:** Calories: 25; Protein: 0.5g; Fiber: 0.4g; Fat: 2.2g; Carbs: 1.1g

3. Healthy Asparagus Potatoes

Servings: 4
Cooking Time: 35 Minutes
Ingredients:
- 9 oz asparagus, cut into 2-inch pieces
- 2 lbs potatoes, cut into quarters
- 1/4 cup balsamic vinegar
- 2 tbsp olive oil

Directions:
1. Fit the oven with the rack in position
2. In a large bowl, add potatoes, balsamic vinegar, olive oil, and salt and toss well.
3. Spread potatoes in baking pan.
4. Set to bake at 390 F for 25 minutes. After 5 minutes place the baking pan in the preheated oven.
5. Add asparagus and stir well and bake for 15 minutes more.
6. Season with pepper and salt.
7. Serve and enjoy.
- **Nutrition Info:** Calories 232 Fat 7.3 g Carbohydrates 38.3 g Sugar 3.9 g Protein 5.2 g Cholesterol 0 mg

4. Creamy Broccoli Casserole

Servings: 6
Cooking Time: 30 Minutes
Ingredients:
- 16 oz frozen broccoli florets, defrosted and drained
- 1/2 tsp onion powder
- 10.5 oz can cream of mushroom soup
- 1 cup cheddar cheese, shredded
- 1/3 cup almond milk
- For topping:
- 1 tbsp butter, melted
- 1/2 cup cracker crumbs

Directions:
1. Fit the oven with the rack in position
2. Add all ingredients except topping ingredients into the 1.5-qt casserole dish.
3. In a small bowl, mix together cracker crumbs and melted butter and sprinkle over the casserole dish mixture.
4. Set to bake at 350 F for 35 minutes. After 5 minutes place the casserole dish in the preheated oven.
5. Serve and enjoy.
- **Nutrition Info:** Calories 203 Fat 13.5 g Carbohydrates 11.9 g Sugar 3.6 g Protein 6.9 g Cholesterol 26 mg

5. Lemon-garlic Kale Salad

Servings: 8
Cooking Time: 10 Minutes
Ingredients:
- 2 cups sliced almonds
- 1/3 cup lemon juice
- 1 teaspoon salt
- 1-1/2 cups olive oil
- 4 cloves crushed garlic
- 12 ounces kale, stems removed

Directions:
1. Set toaster oven to toast and toast almonds for about 5 minutes.
2. Combine lemon juice and salt in a small bowl, then add olive oil and garlic; mix well and set aside.
3. Slice kale into thin ribbons; place in a bowl and sprinkle with almonds.

4. Remove garlic from dressing, then add desired amount of dressing to kale and toss.
5. Add additional dressing if necessary, and serve.
- **Nutrition Info:** Calories: 487, Sodium: 312 mg, Dietary Fiber: 3.7 g, Total Fat: 49.8 g, Total Carbs: 10.2 g, Protein: 6.5 g.

6. Bacon Croquettes

Servings: 8
Cooking Time: 8 Minutes
Ingredients:
- 1 pound sharp cheddar cheese block
- 1 pound thin bacon slices
- 1 cup all-purpose flour
- 3 eggs
- 1 cup breadcrumbs
- Salt, as required
- ¼ cup olive oil

Directions:
1. Cut the cheese block into 1-inch rectangular pieces.
2. Wrap 2 bacon slices around 1 piece of cheddar cheese, covering completely.
3. Repeat with the remaining bacon and cheese pieces.
4. Arrange the croquettes in a baking dish and freeze for about 5 minutes.
5. In a shallow dish, place the flour.
6. In a second dish, crack the eggs and beat well.
7. In a third dish, mix together the breadcrumbs, salt, and oil.
8. Coat the croquettes with flour, then dip into beaten eggs and finally, coat with the breadcrumbs mixture.
9. Press "Power Button" of Air Fry Oven and turn the dial to select the "Air Fry" mode.
10. Press the Time button and again turn the dial to set the cooking time to 8 minutes.
11. Now push the Temp button and rotate the dial to set the temperature at 390 degrees F.
12. Press "Start/Pause" button to start.
13. When the unit beeps to show that it is preheated, open the lid.
14. Arrange the croquettes in "Air Fry Basket" and insert in the oven.
15. Serve warm.
- **Nutrition Info:** Calories 723 Total Fat 51.3 g Saturated Fat 21.3 g Cholesterol 183 mg Sodium 1880 mg Total Carbs 23.3 g Fiber 1 g Sugar 1.3 g Protein 40.6 g

7. Green Bean Casserole(1)

Servings: 4
Cooking Time: 20 Minutes
Ingredients:
- 1 lb. fresh green beans, edges trimmed
- ½ oz. pork rinds, finely ground
- 1 oz. full-fat cream cheese
- ½ cup heavy whipping cream.
- ¼ cup diced yellow onion
- ½ cup chopped white mushrooms
- ½ cup chicken broth
- 4 tbsp. unsalted butter.
- ¼ tsp. xanthan gum

Directions:
1. In a medium skillet over medium heat, melt the butter. Sauté the onion and mushrooms until they become soft and fragrant, about 3–5 minutes.
2. Add the heavy whipping cream, cream cheese and broth to the pan. Whisk until smooth. Bring to a boil and then reduce to a simmer. Sprinkle the xanthan gum into the pan and remove from heat
3. Chop the green beans into 2-inch pieces and place into a 4-cup round baking dish. Pour the sauce mixture over them and stir until coated. Top the dish with ground pork rinds. Place into the air fryer basket
4. Adjust the temperature to 320 Degrees F and set the timer for 15 minutes. Top will be golden and green beans fork tender when fully cooked. Serve warm.
- **Nutrition Info:** Calories: 267; Protein: 3.6g; Fiber: 3.2g; Fat: 23.4g; Carbs: 9.7g

8. Air Fry Garlic Baby Potatoes

Servings: 4
Cooking Time: 20 Minutes
Ingredients:
- 1 lb baby potatoes, cut into quarters
- 1/2 tsp granulated garlic
- 1 tbsp olive oil
- 1/2 tsp dried parsley
- 1/4 tsp salt

Directions:
1. Fit the oven with the rack in position 2.
2. In a mixing bowl, toss baby potatoes with oil, garlic, parsley, and salt.
3. Transfer potatoes in air fryer basket then place air fryer basket in baking pan.
4. Place a baking pan on the oven rack. Set to air fry at 350 F for 20 minutes.
5. Serve and enjoy.
- **Nutrition Info:** Calories 97 Fat 3.6 g Carbohydrates 14.4 g Sugar 0.1 g Protein 3 g Cholesterol 0 mg

9. Flavored Mashed Sweet Potatoes

Servings: 8
Cooking Time: 9 Minutes
Ingredients:
- 3 pounds sweet potatoes, peeled and chopped
- Salt and ground black pepper, to taste
- 2 garlic cloves

- ½ teaspoon dried parsley
- ½ teaspoon dried rosemary
- ¼ teaspoon dried sage
- ½ teaspoon dried thyme
- 1½ cups water
- ½ cup Parmesan cheese, grated
- 2 tablespoon butter
- ¼ cup milk

Directions:
1. Place the potatoes and garlic in the Instant Pot, add 1 ½ cups of water to the Instant Pot, cover and cook for 10 minutes in the manual setting.
2. Relieve the pressure, drain the water, transfer the potatoes and garlic to a bowl and mix them using a hand mixer.
3. Add butter, cheese, milk, salt, pepper, parsley, sage, rosemary and thyme and mix well. Divide between plates and serve.
- **Nutrition Info:** Calories: 240, Fat: 1, Fiber: 8.2, Carbohydrate: 34, Proteins: 4.5

10. Butternut Squash Croquettes

Servings:4
Cooking Time: 17 Minutes
Ingredients:
- $^1/_3$ butternut squash, peeled and grated
- $^1/_3$ cup all-purpose flour
- 2 eggs, whisked
- 4 cloves garlic, minced
- 1½ tablespoons olive oil
- 1 teaspoon fine sea salt
- $^1/_3$ teaspoon freshly ground black pepper, or more to taste
- $^1/_3$ teaspoon dried sage
- A pinch of ground allspice

Directions:
1. Line the air fryer basket with parchment paper. Set aside.
2. In a mixing bowl, stir together all the ingredients until well combined.
3. Make the squash croquettes: Use a small cookie scoop to drop tablespoonfuls of the squash mixture onto a lightly floured surface and shape into balls with your hands. Transfer them to the basket.
4. Put the air fryer basket on the baking pan and slide into Rack Position 2, select Air Fry, set temperature to 345ºF (174ºC), and set time to 17 minutes.
5. When cooking is complete, the squash croquettes should be golden brown. Remove from the oven to a plate and serve warm.

11. Broccoli Olives Tomatoes

Servings: 4
Cooking Time: 10 Minutes
Ingredients:

- 4 cups broccoli florets
- 1/2 tsp lemon zest, grated
- 2 garlic cloves, minced
- 1 tbsp olive oil
- 1 tsp dried oregano
- 10 olives, pitted and sliced
- 1 tbsp fresh lemon juice
- 1 cup cherry tomatoes
- 1/4 tsp salt

Directions:
1. Fit the oven with the rack in position
2. Add broccoli, garlic, oil, tomatoes, and salt in a large bowl and toss well.
3. Spread broccoli mixture onto the baking pan.
4. Set to bake at 450 F for 15 minutes. After 5 minutes place the baking pan in the preheated oven.
5. Meanwhile, mix together oregano, olives, lemon juice, and lemon zest in a mixing bowl.
6. Add roasted vegetables to the bowl and toss well.
7. Serve and enjoy.
- **Nutrition Info:** Calories 86 Fat 5.1 g Carbohydrates 9.4 g Sugar 2.9 g Protein 3.2 g Cholesterol 0 mg

12. Baked Sweet Potatoes

Servings: 6
Cooking Time: 35 Minutes
Ingredients:
- 4 large sweet potatoes, peel and cut into cubes
- 8 sage leaves
- 1 tsp honey
- 2 tsp vinegar
- 1/2 tsp paprika
- 2 tbsp olive oil
- 1/2 tsp sea salt

Directions:
1. Fit the oven with the rack in position
2. Add sweet potato, oil, sage, and salt in a baking dish and mix well.
3. Set to bake at 375 F for 40 minutes. After 5 minutes place the baking dish in the preheated oven.
4. Transfer roasted sweet potatoes into the large bowl and toss with honey, vinegar, and paprika.
5. Serve and enjoy.
- **Nutrition Info:** Calories 92 Fat 5.1 g Carbohydrates 12 g Sugar 1.2 g Protein 0.8 g Cholesterol 0 mg

13. Air-fried Herb Mushrooms

Servings: 2
Cooking Time: 25 Minutes
Ingredients:

- 1 lbs mushrooms, wash, dry, and cut into quarter
- 1 tbsp white vermouth
- 1 tsp herb de Provence
- 1/4 tsp garlic powder
- 1/2 tbsp olive oil

Directions:

1. Fit the oven with the rack in position 2.
2. Add all ingredients to the bowl and toss well.
3. Transfer mushrooms in the air fryer basket then place the air fryer basket in the baking pan.
4. Place a baking pan on the oven rack. Set to air fry at 350 F for 25 minutes.
5. Serve and enjoy.
- **Nutrition Info:** Calories 99 Fat 4.5 g Carbohydrates 8.1 g Sugar 4 g Protein 7.9 g Cholesterol 0 mg

14. Parsley Mushroom Pilaf

Servings:4
Cooking Time: 35 Minutes
Ingredients:

- 2 tbsp olive oil
- 2 cups heated vegetable stock
- 1 cups long-grain rice
- 1 onion, chopped
- 2 garlic cloves, minced
- 2 cups cremini mushrooms, chopped
- Salt and black pepper to taste
- 1 tbsp fresh parsley, chopped

Directions:

1. Preheat on AirFry function to 400 F. Heat olive oil in a frying pan over medium heat. and sauté mushrooms, onion, and garlic for 5 minutes until tender. Stir in rice for 1-2 minutes.
2. Pour in the vegetable stock. Season with salt and pepper. Transfer to a baking dish and place in your oven. Press Start and cook for 20 minutes. Serve sprinkled with chopped parsley.

15. Paprika Potatoes

Servings: 4
Cooking Time: 30 Minutes
Ingredients:

- 1 lb baby potatoes, quartered
- 1/4 tsp rosemary, crushed
- 1/2 tsp thyme
- 2 tbsp paprika
- 2 tbsp coconut oil, melted
- 1 tbsp olive oil
- Pepper
- Salt

Directions:

1. Fit the oven with the rack in position

2. Place potatoes in a baking dish and sprinkle with paprika, rosemary, thyme, pepper, and salt.
3. Drizzle with oil and melted coconut oil.
4. Set to bake at 425 F for 35 minutes. After 5 minutes place the baking dish in the preheated oven.
5. Serve and enjoy.
- **Nutrition Info:** Calories 165 Fat 10.9 g Carbohydrates 16.2 g Sugar 0.4 g Protein 3.4 g Cholesterol 0 mg

16. Apple & Cinnamon Chips

Servings:2
Cooking Time: 25 Minutes
Ingredients:

- 1 tsp sugar
- 1 tsp salt
- 1 whole apple, sliced
- ½ tsp cinnamon
- Confectioners' sugar for serving

Directions:

1. Preheat your oven to 400 F on Bake function. In a bowl, mix cinnamon, salt, and sugar. Add in the apple slices and toss to coat. Transfer to a greased baking tray. Press Start and set the time to 10 minutes. When ready, dust with sugar and serve chilled.

17. Tasty Saffron Risotto

Servings: 10
Cooking Time: 10 Minutes
Ingredients:

- 2 tablespoons extra virgin olive oil
- ½ cup onion, peeled and chopped
- 2 tablespoons hot milk
- ½ teaspoon saffron threads, crushed
- 1½ cups Arborio rice
- 3½ cups vegetable stock
- Salt, to taste
- 1 cinnamon stick
- ⅓ cup dried currants
- 1 tablespoon honey
- ⅓ cup almonds, chopped

Directions:

1. In a bowl, mix the milk with the saffron, mix and set aside. Put the Instant Pot in the sauté mode, add the oil and heat.
2. Add the onion, mix and cook for 5 minutes. Add rice, broth, saffron and milk, honey, salt, almonds, cinnamon stick and blackcurrant. Stir, cover the Instant Pot and cook over rice for 5 minutes.
3. Relieve the pressure, add rice to the rice, discard the cinnamon stick, divide it between the plates and serve.

- **Nutrition Info:** Calories: 260, Fat: 7, Fiber: 2, Carbohydrate: 41, Sugar: 1.5, Proteins: 3.9

18. Spicy Brussels Sprouts(1)

Servings: 2
Cooking Time: 15 Minutes
Ingredients:
- 1/2 lb Brussels sprouts, trimmed and halved
- 1 tbsp chives, chopped
- 1/4 tsp cayenne
- 1/2 tsp chili powder
- 1/2 tbsp olive oil
- Pepper
- Salt

Directions:
1. Fit the oven with the rack in position
2. Add all ingredients into the large bowl and toss well.
3. Spread Brussels sprouts in baking pan.
4. Set to bake at 370 F for 20 minutes. After 5 minutes place the baking pan in the preheated oven.
5. Serve and enjoy.
- **Nutrition Info:** Calories 82 Fat 4.1 g Carbohydrates 10.9 g Sugar 2.6 g Protein 4 g Cholesterol 0 mg

19. Baked Apple Sweet Potatoes

Servings: 2
Cooking Time: 30 Minutes
Ingredients:
- 2 large sweet potatoes, diced
- 2 tsp cinnamon
- 2 large green apples, diced
- 2 tbsp maple syrup
- 1 tbsp olive oil

Directions:
1. Fit the oven with the rack in position
2. In a large bowl, add sweet potatoes, oil, cinnamon, and apples and toss well.
3. Spread sweet potatoes mixture in baking pan.
4. Set to bake at 400 F for 35 minutes. After 5 minutes place the baking pan in the preheated oven.
5. Drizzle with maple syrup and serve.
- **Nutrition Info:** Calories 352 Fat 7.6 g Carbohydrates 74 g Sugar 35.7 g Protein 2.2 g Cholesterol 0 mg

20. Spicy Tortilla Chips

Servings: 4
Cooking Time: 5 Minutes
Ingredients:
- ½ teaspoon ground cumin
- ½ teaspoon paprika
- ½ teaspoon chili powder
- ½ teaspoon salt
- Pinch cayenne pepper
- 8 (6-inch) corn tortillas, each cut into 6 wedges
- Cooking spray

Directions:
1. Lightly spritz the air fryer basket with cooking spray.
2. Stir together the cumin, paprika, chili powder, salt, and pepper in a small bowl.
3. Place the tortilla wedges in the basket in a single layer. Lightly mist them with cooking spray. Sprinkle the seasoning mixture on top of the tortilla wedges.
4. Put the air fryer basket on the baking pan and slide into Rack Position 2, select Air Fry, set temperature to 375ºF (190ºC), and set time to 5 minutes.
5. Stir the tortilla wedges halfway through the cooking time.
6. When cooking is complete, the chips should be lightly browned and crunchy. Remove from the oven. Let the tortilla chips cool for 5 minutes and serve.

21. Parmesan Dill Pickles

Servings:4
Cooking Time: 20 Minutes
Ingredients:
- 3 cups dill pickles, sliced, drained
- 2 eggs
- 2 tsp water
- 1 cup grated Parmesan cheese
- 1 ½ cups breadcrumbs, smooth
- Black pepper to taste

Directions:
1. Add the breadcrumbs and black pepper to a bowl and mix well. In another bowl, crack the eggs and beat with the water. Add the Parmesan cheese to third bowl.
2. Preheat on AirFry function to 400 F. Dredge the pickle slices in the egg mixture, then in breadcrumbs, and finally in the Parmesan cheese. Place them in the fryer oven. Press Start.AirFry for 8-10 minutes until crispy. Serve with cheese dip.

22. Homemade French Fries

Servings:2
Cooking Time: 25 Minutes
Ingredients:
- 2 russet potatoes, cut into strips
- 2 tbsp olive oil
- Salt and black pepper to taste

Directions:
1. In a bowl, toss the strips with olive oil and season with salt and pepper. Arrange them on the frying basket. Select AirFry function, adjust the temperature to 400 F, and press

Start. Cook for 18-22 minutes. Check for crispiness and serve with aioli, ketchup, or crumbled feta cheese.

23. Simple Roasted Asparagus

Servings: 4
Cooking Time: 10 Minutes
Ingredients:
- 1 bunch asparagus
- 4 tablespoons olive oil
- Salt and pepper to taste

Directions:
1. Start by preheating toaster oven to 425°F.
2. Wash the asparagus and cut off the bottom inch.
3. Toss the asparagus in olive oil and lay flat on a baking sheet.
4. Sprinkle salt and pepper over asparagus.
5. Roast in the oven for 10 minutes.
- **Nutrition Info:** Calories: 127, Sodium: 1 mg, Dietary Fiber: 0.7 g, Total Fat: 14.0 g, Total Carbs: 1.3 g, Protein: 0.7 g.

24. Party Chicken Wings

Servings: 3
Cooking Time: 20 Minutes
Ingredients:
- 15 chicken wings
- Salt and black pepper to taste
- ⅓ cup chili sauce
- ⅓ cup butter
- ½ tbsp vinegar

Directions:
1. Preheat on Air Fry function to 360 F. Season the wings with salt and pepper. Add them to the greased basket and fit in the baking tray. Cook for 15 minutes. Toss every 5 minutes. Once ready, remove them to a bowl.
2. Melt the butter in a saucepan over low heat. Add in the vinegar and hot sauce. Stir and cook for a minute. Turn the heat off. Pour the sauce over the chicken. Toss to coat thoroughly. Transfer the chicken to a serving platter. Serve with a side of celery strips and blue cheese dressing.

25. Avocado, Tomato, And Grape Salad With Crunchy Potato Croutons

Servings: 2
Cooking Time: 10 Minutes
Ingredients:
- Potato croutons:
- 1 medium-small russet potato
- 2 cloves garlic
- 1 tablespoon extra light olive oil
- 1 tablespoon nutritional yeast
- 1/2 teaspoon garlic powder
- 1/2 teaspoon onion powder
- 1/2 teaspoon dried thyme
- 1/2 teaspoon dried rosemary
- 1/2 teaspoon dried oregano
- 1/2 teaspoon chili powder
- 1/4 teaspoon Himalayan sea salt
- 1/3 teaspoon cayenne pepper
- Pinch red pepper flakes
- Black pepper to taste
- Salad:
- 1 cup grape tomatoes
- Small handful dried cranberries
- Small handful green grapes
- 2-3 sprigs cilantro
- 1 avocado
- 2 tablespoons extra-virgin olive oil
- 1 tablespoon nutritional yeast
- 1 tablespoon lemon juice
- 1/2 teaspoon pure maple syrup
- 1/4 teaspoon salt
- Few sprinkles ground pepper
- Small handful toasted pecans

Directions:
1. Peel and cut potatoes into 1-inch cubes.
2. Place potatoes in water with a pinch of salt for 1 hour.
3. When the hour has passed, preheat the toaster oven to 450°F.
4. Drain potatoes and dry them on multiple layers of paper towels, then return to bowl.
5. Peel and mince garlic, then add to bowl.
6. Add rest of crouton ingredients to the bowl and stir together.
7. Lay potatoes mixture across a greased baking sheet in a single layer and bake for 35 minutes, flipping halfway through.
8. Combine oil, yeast, syrup, lemon juice, salt and pepper together to create salad dressing.
9. Slice tomatoes in half and put in a bowl with cranberries and grapes.
10. Chop cilantro and add to bowl. Scoop out avocado and cut it into smaller pieces and add to bowl.
11. Drizzle dressing and mix well. Add potatoes and mix again, top with pecans and serve.
- **Nutrition Info:** Calories: 1032, Sodium: 560 mg, Dietary Fiber: 22.8 g, Total Fat: 84.9 g, Total Carbs: 64.2 g, Protein: 17.0 g.

26. Preparation Time: 20 Minutes

Servings: 2
Cooking Time: 20 Minutes
Ingredients:
- 2 bell peppers, tops and seeds removed
- Salt and pepper, to taste
- 2/3 cup cream cheese
- 2 tablespoons mayonnaise
- 1 tablespoon fresh celery stalks, chopped

Directions:

1. Arrange the peppers in the lightly greased cooking basket. Cook in the preheated Air Fryer at 400 degrees F for 15 minutes, turning them over halfway through the cooking time.
2. Season with salt and pepper.
3. Then, in a mixing bowl, combine the cream cheese with the mayonnaise and chopped celery. Stuff the pepper with the cream cheese mixture and serve.

- **Nutrition Info:** 378 Calories; 38g Fat; 6g Carbs; 5g Protein; 1g Sugars; 6g Fiber

27. Bok Choy And Butter Sauce(3)

Servings: 4
Cooking Time: 20 Minutes
Ingredients:

- 2 bok choy heads; trimmed and cut into strips
- 1 tbsp. butter; melted
- 2 tbsp. chicken stock
- 1 tsp. lemon juice
- 1 tbsp. olive oil
- A pinch of salt and black pepper

Directions:
1. In a pan that fits your air fryer, mix all the ingredients, toss, introduce the pan in the air fryer and cook at 380°F for 15 minutes.
2. Divide between plates and serve as a side dish

- **Nutrition Info:** Calories: 141; Fat: 3g; Fiber: 2g; Carbs: 4g; Protein: 3g

28. Marinara Chicken Breasts

Servings: 2
Cooking Time: 20 Minutes
Ingredients:

- 2 chicken breasts, ½ inch thick
- 1 egg, beaten
- ½ cup breadcrumbs
- A pinch of salt and black pepper
- 2 tbsp marinara sauce
- 2 tbsp Grana Padano cheese, grated
- 2 slices mozzarella cheese

Directions:
1. Dip the breasts into the egg, then into the crumbs, and arrange on the Air fryer baking sheet. Cook for 6-8 minutes at 400 F on Air Fry function. Turn over and drizzle with marinara sauce, Grana Padano and mozzarella cheeses. Cook for 5 more minutes. Serve.

29. Pineapple & Mozzarella Tortillas

Servings: 2
Cooking Time: 15 Minutes
Ingredients:

- 2 tortillas
- 8 ham slices
- 8 mozzarella slices
- 8 thin pineapple slices
- 2 tbsp tomato sauce
- ½ tsp dried parsley

Directions:
1. Preheat on Air Fry function to 330 F. Spread the tomato sauce onto the tortillas. Arrange 4 ham slices on each tortilla. Top the ham with the pineapple and sprinkle with mozzarella and parsley. Cook for 10 minutes and enjoy.

30. Rosemary Chickpeas

Servings:4
Cooking Time: 20 Minutes
Ingredients:

- 2 (14.5-ounce) cans chickpeas, rinsed
- 2 tbsp olive oil
- 1 tsp dried rosemary
- ½ tsp dried thyme
- ¼ tsp dried sage
- ¼ tsp salt

Directions:
1. In a bowl, mix together chickpeas, oil, rosemary, thyme, sage, and salt. Transfer to a baking pan. Select Bake function, adjust the temperature to 380 F, and press Start. Cook for 15 minutes.

31. Crispy Eggplant Slices

Servings: 4
Cooking Time: 8 Minutes
Ingredients:

- 1 medium eggplant, peeled and cut into ½-inch round slices
- Salt, as required
- ½ cup all-purpose flour
- 2 eggs, beaten
- 1 cup Italian-style breadcrumbs
- ¼ cup olive oil

Directions:
1. In a colander, add the eggplant slices and sprinkle with salt. Set aside for about 45 minutes.
2. With paper towels, pat dry the eggplant slices.
3. In a shallow dish, place the flour.
4. Crack the eggs in a second dish and beat well.
5. In a third dish, mix together the oil, and breadcrumbs.
6. Coat each eggplant slice with flour, then dip into beaten eggs and finally, coat with the breadcrumbs mixture.
7. Press "Power Button" of Air Fry Oven and turn the dial to select the "Air Fry" mode.
8. Press the Time button and again turn the dial to set the cooking time to 8 minutes.

9. Now push the Temp button and rotate the dial to set the temperature at 390 degrees F.
10. Press "Start/Pause" button to start.
11. When the unit beeps to show that it is preheated, open the lid.
12. Arrange the eggplant slices in "Air Fry Basket" and insert in the oven.
13. Serve warm.
- **Nutrition Info:** Calories 332 Total Fat 16.6 g Saturated Fat 2.8 g Cholesterol 82 mg Sodium 270 mg Total Carbs 38.3 g Fiber 5.7 g Sugar 5.3 g Protein 9.1 g

32. Charred Green Beans With Sesame Seeds

Servings:4
Cooking Time: 8 Minutes
Ingredients:
- 1 tablespoon reduced-sodium soy sauce or tamari
- ½ tablespoon Sriracha sauce
- 4 teaspoons toasted sesame oil, divided
- 12 ounces (340 g) trimmed green beans
- ½ tablespoon toasted sesame seeds

Directions:
1. Whisk together the soy sauce, Sriracha sauce, and 1 teaspoon of sesame oil in a small bowl until smooth. Set aside.
2. Toss the green beans with the remaining sesame oil in a large bowl until evenly coated.
3. Place the green beans in the air fryer basket in a single layer.
4. Put the air fryer basket on the baking pan and slide into Rack Position 2, select Air Fry, set temperature to 375ºF (190ºC), and set time to 8 minutes.
5. Stir the green beans halfway through the cooking time.
6. When cooking is complete, the green beans should be lightly charred and tender. Remove from the oven to a platter. Pour the prepared sauce over the top of green beans and toss well. Serve sprinkled with the toasted sesame seeds.

33. Crispy Sausage Bites

Servings: 12
Cooking Time: 15 Minutes
Ingredients:
- Nonstick cooking spray
- 2 lbs. spicy pork sausage
- 1 ½ cups Bisquick
- 4 cups sharp cheddar cheese, grated
- ½ cup onion, diced fine
- 2 tsp pepper
- 2 tsp garlic, diced fine

Directions:
1. Lightly spray baking pan with cooking spray.

2. In a large bowl, combine all ingredients. Form into 1-inch balls and place on baking pan, these will need to be cooked in batches.
3. Set oven to bake on 375°F for 20 minutes. After 5 minutes, place baking pan in position 2 and cook 12-15 minutes or until golden brown. Repeat with remaining sausage bites. Serve immediately.
- **Nutrition Info:** Calories 432, Total Fat 32g, Saturated Fat 13g, Total Carbs 14g, Net Carbs 14g, Protein 22g, Sugar 1g, Fiber 0g, Sodium 803mg, Potassium 286mg, Phosphorus 298mg

34. Sunday Calamari Rings

Servings:4
Cooking Time: 20 Minutes
Ingredients:
- 1 lb calamari (squid), cut in rings
- ¼ cup flour
- 2 large beaten eggs
- 1 cup breadcrumbs

Directions:
1. Coat the calamari rings with the flour and dip them in the eggs. Then, roll in the breadcrumbs. Refrigerate for 2 hours. Line them in the frying basket and spray with cooking spray.
2. Select AirFry function, adjust the temperature to 380 F, and press Start. Cook for 14 minutes. Serve with garlic mayo and lemon wedges.

35. Parmesan Zucchini Chips

Servings: 4
Cooking Time: 20 Minutes
Ingredients:
- 1 oz. pork rinds.
- ½ cup grated Parmesan cheese.
- 2 medium zucchini
- 1 large egg.

Directions:
1. Slice zucchini in ¼-inch-thick slices. Place between two layers of paper towels or a clean kitchen towel for 30 minutes to remove excess moisture
2. Place pork rinds into food processor and pulse until finely ground. Pour into medium bowl and mix with Parmesan
3. Beat egg in a small bowl.
4. Dip zucchini slices in egg and then in pork rind mixture, coating as completely as possible. Carefully place each slice into the air fryer basket in a single layer, working in batches as necessary.
5. Adjust temperature to 320 Degrees F and set the timer for 10 minutes. Flip chips halfway through the cooking time. Serve warm.

- **Nutrition Info:** Calories: 121; Protein: 9.9g; Fiber: 0.6g; Fat: 6.7g; Carbs: 3.8g

36. Spicy Broccoli With Hot Sauce

Servings:6
Cooking Time: 14 Minutes
Ingredients:
- Broccoli:
- 1 medium-sized head broccoli, cut into florets
- 1½ tablespoons olive oil
- 1 teaspoon shallot powder
- 1 teaspoon porcini powder
- ½ teaspoon freshly grated lemon zest
- ½ teaspoon hot paprika
- ½ teaspoon granulated garlic
- $^1/_3$ teaspoon fine sea salt
- $^1/_3$ teaspoon celery seeds
- Hot Sauce:
- ½ cup tomato sauce
- 1 tablespoon balsamic vinegar
- ½ teaspoon ground allspice

Directions:
1. In a mixing bowl, combine all the ingredients for the broccoli and toss to coat. Transfer the broccoli to the air fryer basket.
2. Put the air fryer basket on the baking pan and slide into Rack Position 2, select Air Fry, set temperature to 360ºF (182ºC), and set time to 14 minutes.
3. Meanwhile, make the hot sauce by whisking together the tomato sauce, balsamic vinegar, and allspice in a small bowl.
4. When cooking is complete, remove the broccoli from the oven and serve with the hot sauce.

37. Healthy Parsnip Fries

Servings:3
Cooking Time: 20 Minutes
Ingredients:
- 4 large parsnips, sliced
- ¼ cup flour
- ¼ cup olive oil
- ¼ cup water
- A pinch of salt

Directions:
1. Preheat on AirFry function to 390 F. In a bowl, mix the flour, olive oil, water, and parsnip slices. Mix well and toss to coat.
2. Arrange the fries on the frying basket and place in the oven. Press Start and cook for 15 minutes. Serve with yogurt and garlic paste.

38. Balsamic Keto Vegetables

Servings: 3
Cooking Time: 20 Minutes
Ingredients:
- 1/2-pound cauliflower florets
- 1/2-pound button mushrooms, whole
- 1 cup pearl onions, whole
- Pink Himalayan salt and ground black pepper, to taste
- 1/4 teaspoon smoked paprika
- 1 teaspoon garlic powder
- 1/2 teaspoon dried thyme
- 1/2 teaspoon dried marjoram
- 3 tablespoons olive oil
- 2 tablespoons balsamic vinegar

Directions:
1. Toss all ingredients in a large mixing dish.
2. Roast in the preheated Air Fryer at 400 degrees F for 5 minutes. Shake the basket and cook for 7 minutes more.
3. Serve with some extra fresh herbs if desired.
- **Nutrition Info:** 170 Calories; 14g Fat; 7g Carbs; 2g Protein; 5g Sugars; 9g Fiber

39. Cauliflower And Barley Risotto

Servings: 4
Cooking Time: 1 Hour
Ingredients:
- 1 cauliflower head, separated into florets
- 4 tablespoons extra virgin olive oil
- Salt and ground black pepper, to taste
- ½ cup Parmesan cheese, grated
- 2 garlic cloves, peeled and minced
- 1 cup pearled barley
- 2 tablespoons fresh parsley, chopped
- 1 tablespoon butter
- 1 yellow onion, peeled and chopped
- 3 cups chicken stock
- 2 thyme sprigs

Directions:
1. Spread the cauliflower florets in an upholstered pan, add 3 tablespoons of oil, salt and pepper, mix to coat, place in the oven at 425 degrees Fahrenheit and bake for 20 minutes, turning every 10 minutes.
2. Remove the cauliflower from the oven, sprinkle with ¼ cup of cheese and cook for 5 minutes. Put the Instant Pot in the sauté mode, add 1 tablespoon of oil and heat.
3. Add the onion, mix and cook for 5 minutes. Add the garlic, mix and cook for 1 minute. Add the broth, thyme and barley, mix, cover the Instant Pot and cook for 25 minutes in the Manual setting.
4. Release the pressure, uncover the Instant Pot, mix the barley, throw away the thyme, add the butter, the rest of the cheese, the cauliflower, salt, pepper and parsley. Mix the risotto, divide it between the plates and serve.
- **Nutrition Info:** Calories: 350, Fat: 16, Fiber: 10, Carbohydrate: 25, Proteins: 14.6

40. Bread Cheese Sticks

Servings:6
Cooking Time: 5 Minutes
Ingredients:
- 6 (6 oz) bread cheese
- 2 tbsp butter, melted
- 2 cups panko crumbs

Directions:
1. With a knife, cut the cheese into equal-sized sticks. Brush each stick with butter and dip into the panko crumbs. Arrange the sticks in a single layer on the basket tray. Select AirFry function, adjust the temperature to 390 F, and press Start. Cook for 10-12 minutes. Serve warm.

41. Homemade Cheesy Sticks

Servings: 12
Cooking Time: 5 Minutes
Ingredients:
- 6 (6 oz) bread cheese
- 2 tbsp butter
- 2 cups panko crumbs

Directions:
1. Put the butter in a bowl and melt in the microwave for 2 minutes; set aside. With a knife, cut the cheese into equal-sized sticks. Brush each stick with butter and dip into panko crumbs. Arrange the sticks in a single layer in the basket. Fit in the baking tray and cook in the at 390 F for 10 minutes on Air Fry function. Flip halfway through. Serve warm.

42. Paprika Pickle Chips

Servings:3
Cooking Time: 20 Minutes
Ingredients:
- 36 sweet pickle chips
- 1 cup buttermilk
- 3 tbsp smoked paprika
- 2 cups flour
- ¼ cup cornmeal
- Salt and black pepper to taste

Directions:
1. Preheat on Air Fryer function to 400 F. In a bowl, mix flour, paprika, pepper, salt, and cornmeal. Place pickles in buttermilk and let sit for 5 minutes. Drain and dip in the spice mixture. Place them in the cooking basket. Cook for 10 minutes until brown and crispy.

43. Polenta Sticks

Servings: 4
Cooking Time: 6 Minutes
Ingredients:
- 1 tablespoon oil
- 2½ cups cooked polenta
- Salt, to taste
- ¼ cup Parmesan cheese

Directions:
1. Place the polenta in a lightly greased baking pan.
2. With a plastic wrap, cover and refrigerate for about 1 hour or until set.
3. Remove from the refrigerator and cut into desired sized slices.
4. Sprinkle with salt.
5. Press "Power Button" of Air Fry Oven and turn the dial to select the "Air Fry" mode.
6. Press the Time button and again turn the dial to set the cooking time to 6 minutes.
7. Now push the Temp button and rotate the dial to set the temperature at 350 degrees F.
8. Press "Start/Pause" button to start.
9. When the unit beeps to show that it is preheated, open the lid.
10. Arrange the pan over the "Wire Rack" and insert in the oven.
11. Top with cheese and serve.
- **Nutrition Info:** Calories 397 Total Fat 5.6g Saturated Fat 1.3 g Cholesterol 4mg Sodium 127 mg Total Carbs 76.2 g Fiber 2.5 g Sugar 1 g Protein 9.1 g

44. Pineapple Pork Ribs

Servings: 4
Cooking Time: 30 Minutes
Ingredients:
- 2 lb cut spareribs
- 7 oz salad dressing
- 1 (5-oz) can pineapple juice
- 2 cups water
- Salt and black pepper to taste

Directions:
1. Preheat your to 390 F on Bake function. Sprinkle the ribs with salt and pepper and place them in a greased baking dish. Cook for 15 minutes. Prepare the sauce by combining the salad dressing and the pineapple juice. Serve the ribs drizzled with the sauce.

45. Yogurt Masala Cashew

Servings: 2
Cooking Time: 25 Minutes
Ingredients:
- 8 oz Greek yogurt
- 2 tbsp mango powder
- 8¾ oz cashew nuts
- Salt and black pepper to taste
- 1 tsp coriander powder
- ½ tsp masala powder
- ½ tsp black pepper powder

Directions:
1. Preheat on Air Fry function to 350 F. In a bowl, mix all powders, salt, and pepper. Add

in cashews and toss to coat thoroughly. Place the cashews in your Air Fryer baking pan and cook for 15 minutes, shaking every 5 minutes. Serve.

46. Baked Cauliflower & Pepper

Servings: 4
Cooking Time: 30 Minutes
Ingredients:
- 1 cauliflower head, cut into florets
- 1/2 cup fresh dill, chopped
- 12/ onion, sliced
- 1 red bell pepper, cut into 1-inch pieces
- 2 tsp olive oil
- 2 tbsp white wine vinegar
- 3 tbsp balsamic vinegar
- Pepper
- Salt

Directions:
1. Fit the oven with the rack in position
2. Add all ingredients into the zip-lock bag. Seal the bag and shake well and place in the fridge for 1 hour.
3. Pour marinated cauliflower mixture in the baking dish.
4. Set to bake at 450 F for 35 minutes. After 5 minutes place the baking dish in the preheated oven.
5. Serve and enjoy.
- **Nutrition Info:** Calories 86 Fat 2.7 g Carbohydrates 15.3 g Sugar 6.2 g Protein 2.8 g Cholesterol 0 mg

47. Easy Crunchy Garlic Croutons

Servings: 4
Cooking Time: 20 Minutes
Ingredients:
- 2 cups bread, cubed
- 2 tbsp butter, melted
- Garlic salt and black pepper to taste

Directions:
1. In a bowl, toss the bread cubes with butter, garlic salt, and pepper until well-coated. Place the cubes in the Air Fryer basket and fit in the baking tray. Cook in the oven for 12 minutes at 380 F on Air Fry function or until golden brown and crispy.

48. Chili Beef Sticks

Servings:3
Cooking Time: 10 Minutes
Ingredients:
- 1 lb ground beef
- 3 tbsp sugar
- A pinch garlic powder
- A pinch chili powder
- Salt to taste
- 1 tsp liquid smoke

Directions:

1. Place the meat, sugar, garlic powder, chili powder, salt, and liquid smoke in a bowl. Mix well. Mold out 4 sticks with your hands, place them on a plate, and refrigerate for 2 hours.
2. Select Bake function, adjust the temperature to 360 F, and press Start. Cook for 15 minutes.

49. Brussels Sprouts & Sweet Potatoes

Servings: 6
Cooking Time: 15 Minutes
Ingredients:
- 1 lb sweet potatoes, peeled and diced into 1/2-inch cubes
- 1 lb Brussels sprouts, remove stem & into quartered
- 2 tbsp olive oil
- 1 tsp chili powder
- Pepper
- Salt

Directions:
1. Fit the oven with the rack in position 2.
2. Add Brussels sprouts, sweet potatoes, chili powder, olive oil, pepper, and salt into the mixing bowl and toss well.
3. Transfer Brussels sprouts & sweet potato mixture in air fryer basket then place air fryer basket in baking pan.
4. Place a baking pan on the oven rack. Set to air fry at 380 F for 15 minutes.
5. Serve and enjoy.
- **Nutrition Info:** Calories 163 Fat 5.1 g Carbohydrates 28.2 g Sugar 2 g Protein 3.8 g Cholesterol 0 mg

50. Vegetable And Egg Salad

Servings: 4
Cooking Time: 20 Minutes
Ingredients:
- 1/3-pound Brussels sprouts
- 1/2 cup radishes, sliced
- 1/2 cup mozzarella cheese, crumbled
- 1 red onion, chopped
- 4 eggs, hardboiled and sliced
- Dressing:
- 1/4 cup olive oil
- 2 tablespoons champagne vinegar
- 1 teaspoon Dijon mustard
- Sea salt and ground black pepper, to taste

Directions:
1. Start by preheating your Air Fryer to 380 degrees F.
2. Add the Brussels sprouts andradishes to the cooking basket. Spritz with cooking spray and cook for 15 minutes. Let it cool to room temperature about 15 minutes.
3. Toss the vegetables with cheese and red onion.

4.   Mix all ingredients for the dressing and toss to combine well. Serve topped with the hardboiled eggs.
- **Nutrition Info:** 298 Calories; 23g Fat; 5g Carbs; 15g Protein; 6g Sugars; 6g FiberSimple Stuffed Bell Peppers

51.   Cheesy Squash Casserole

Servings: 6
Cooking Time: 30 Minutes
Ingredients:
- 2 lbs yellow summer squash, cut into chunks
- 1/2 cup liquid egg substitute
- 3/4 cup cheddar cheese, shredded
- 1/4 cup mayonnaise
- 1/4 tsp salt

Directions:
1.   Fit the oven with the rack in position
2.   Add squash in a saucepan then pour enough water in a saucepan to cover the squash. Bring to boil.
3.   Turn heat to medium and cook for 10 minutes or until tender. Drain well.
4.   In a large mixing bowl, combine together squash, egg substitute, mayonnaise, 1/2 cup cheese, and salt.
5.   Transfer squash mixture into a greased baking dish.
6.   Set to bake at 375 F for 35 minutes. After 5 minutes place the baking dish in the preheated oven.
7.   Sprinkle remaining cheese on top.
8.   Serve and enjoy.
- **Nutrition Info:** Calories 130 Fat 8.2 g Carbohydrates 7.7 g Sugar 3.5 g Protein 8 g Cholesterol 18 mg

52.   Grandma's Chicken Thighs

Servings: 2
Cooking Time: 30 Minutes
Ingredients:
- 1 pound chicken thighs
- ½ tsp salt
- ¼ tsp black pepper
- ¼ tsp garlic powder

Directions:
1.   Season the thighs with salt, pepper, and garlic powder. Arrange thighs, skin side down, on the Air Fryer basket and fit in the baking tray. Cook until golden brown, about 20 minutes at 350 F on Bake function. Serve immediately.

53.   Chicken Wings In Alfredo Sauce

Servings:4
Cooking Time: 30 Minutes
Ingredients:
- 1 ½ pounds chicken wings
- Salt to taste
- ½ cup Alfredo sauce

Directions:
1.   Preheat on AirFry function to 390 F. Season the wings with salt. Arrange them on the frying basket without touching. Press Start and cook for 20-22 minutes until no longer pink in the center. Remove to a large bowl and coat well with the sauce. Serve.

54.   Lemon-thyme Bruschetta

Servings: 10
Cooking Time: 7 Minutes
Ingredients:
- 1 baguette
- 8 ounces ricotta cheese
- 1 lemon
- Salt
- Freshly cracked black pepper
- Honey
- 8 sprigs fresh thyme

Directions:
1.   Start by preheating toaster oven to 425°F.
2.   Thinly slice baguette, and zest lemon.
3.   Mix ricotta and lemon zest together and season with salt and pepper.
4.   Toast the baguette slices for 7 minutes or until they start to brown.
5.   Spread ricotta mix over slices.
6.   Drizzle with honey and top with thyme, then serve.
- **Nutrition Info:** Calories: 60, Sodium: 71 mg, Dietary Fiber: 0.6 g, Total Fat: 2.0 g, Total Carbs: 7.6 g, Protein: 3.5 g.

55.   Browned Ricotta With Capers And Lemon

Servings: 4 To 6
Cooking Time: 8 Minutes
Ingredients:
- 1½ cups whole milk ricotta cheese
- 2 tablespoons extra-virgin olive oil
- 2 tablespoons capers, rinsed
- Zest of 1 lemon, plus more for garnish
- 1 teaspoon finely chopped fresh rosemary
- Pinch crushed red pepper flakes
- Salt and freshly ground black pepper, to taste
- 1 tablespoon grated Parmesan cheese
- In a mixing bowl, stir together the ricotta cheese, olive oil, capers, lemon zest, rosemary, red pepper flakes, salt, and pepper until well combined.

Directions:
1.   Spread the mixture evenly in the baking pan.
2.   Slide the baking pan into Rack Position 2, select Air Fry, set temperature to 380ºF (193ºC), and set time to 8 minutes.

3. When cooking is complete, the top should be nicely browned. Remove from the oven and top with a sprinkle of grated Parmesan cheese. Garnish with the lemon zest and serve warm.

56. Mashed Squash

Servings: 4
Cooking Time: 20 Minutes
Ingredients:

- 2 acorn squashes, cut into halves and seeded
- ½ cup water
- ¼ teaspoon baking soda
- 2 tablespoons butter
- Salt and ground black pepper, to taste
- ½ teaspoon fresh nutmeg, grated
- 2 tablespoons brown sugar

Directions:

1. Sprinkle the pumpkin halves with salt, pepper and baking soda and place them in the steam basket of the Instant Pot.
2. Add water to the Instant Pot, cover and cook for 20 minutes in manual configuration. Relieve the pressure, take the pumpkin and set it on a plate to cool. Scrape the flesh of the pumpkin and place it in a bowl.

3. Add salt, pepper, butter, sugar and nutmeg and mash with a potato masher. Mix well and serve.
- **Nutrition Info:** Calories: 140, Fat: 1, Fiber: 0.5, Carbohydrate: 10.5, Proteins: 1.7

57. Air Fried Green Tomatoes(1)

Servings: 4
Cooking Time: 20 Minutes
Ingredients:

- 2 medium green tomatoes
- ⅓ cup grated Parmesan cheese.
- ¼ cup blanched finely ground almond flour.
- 1 large egg.

Directions:

1. Slice tomatoes into ½-inch-thick slices. Take a medium bowl, whisk the egg. Take a large bowl, mix the almond flour and Parmesan.
2. Dip each tomato slice into the egg, then dredge in the almond flour mixture. Place the slices into the air fryer basket
3. Adjust the temperature to 400 Degrees F and set the timer for 7 minutes. Flip the slices halfway through the cooking time. Serve immediately
- **Nutrition Info:** Calories: 106; Protein: 6.2g; Fiber: 1.4g; Fat: 6.7g; Carbs: 5.9g

BREAKFAST RECIPES

58. Raspberries Oatmeal

Servings: 4
Cooking Time: 30 Minutes
Ingredients:

- 1 ½ cups coconut; shredded
- ½ cups raspberries
- 2 cups almond milk
- ¼ tsp. nutmeg, ground
- 2 tsp. stevia
- ½ tsp. cinnamon powder
- Cooking spray

Directions:

1. Grease the air fryer's pan with cooking spray, mix all the ingredients inside, cover and cook at 360°F for 15 minutes. Divide into bowls and serve
- **Nutrition Info:** Calories: 172; Fat: 5g; Fiber: 2g; Carbs: 4g; Protein: 6g

59. Delicious Pumpkin Bread

Servings: 12
Cooking Time: 55 Minutes
Ingredients:

- 2 eggs
- 1/4 cup olive oil
- 1/2 cup milk
- 1 cup of sugar
- 1 cup pumpkin puree
- 1 tsp cinnamon
- 1/2 tsp baking soda
- 2 tsp baking powder
- 2 cups flour
- 1/2 tsp salt

Directions:

1. Fit the oven with the rack in position
2. In a bowl, mix flour, baking soda, salt, and baking powder.
3. In a separate bowl, whisk eggs with oil, milk, sugar, and pumpkin puree.
4. Add flour mixture into the egg mixture and mix until well combined.
5. Pour mixture into the greased loaf pan.
6. Set to bake at 350 F for 60 minutes. After 5 minutes place the loaf pan in the preheated oven.
7. Slice and serve.
- **Nutrition Info:** Calories 198 Fat 5.4 g Carbohydrates 35.3 g Sugar 17.9 g Protein 3.6 g Cholesterol 28 mg

60. Croissant With Ham, Mushroom And Egg

Servings: 1
Cooking Time: 8 Minutes
Ingredients:

- 1 store-bought Croissant
- 3 slices honey shaved ham
- 4 honey cherry tomato, halved
- 4 small button mushrooms, quartered
- 1 Egg
- 1.8 oz. shredded cheddar cheese
- Handful salad greens
- 1/2 Rosemary Sprig, roughly diced (optional)

Directions:

1. Grease a baking dish lightly with margarine.
2. Arrange the ingredients in two layers, placing the cheese in the middle and top layer. Create a space in the center of the ham mixture, break egg in it.
3. Sprinkle some black pepper, salt and rosemary over the mixture and place on the Air fryer basket along with the croissant.
4. Baked in preheated 325°F temperature for 8 minutes. (Take out the croissant from the air fryer basket after 4 minutes).
5. Serve croissant and cheesy baked egg on plate along with some salad greens.
- **Nutrition Info:** Calories 111 Carbohydrates 0.3 g Sugar 0.3 g Protein 6 g Cholesterol 21 mg

61. Air Fried Philly Cheesesteaks

Servings:2
Cooking Time: 20 Minutes
Ingredients:

- 12 ounces (340 g) boneless rib-eye steak, sliced thinly
- ½ teaspoon Worcestershire sauce
- ½ teaspoon soy sauce
- Kosher salt and ground black pepper, to taste
- ½ green bell pepper, stemmed, deseeded, and thinly sliced
- ½ small onion, halved and thinly sliced
- 1 tablespoon vegetable oil
- 2 soft hoagie rolls, split three-fourths of the way through
- 1 tablespoon butter, softened
- 2 slices provolone cheese, halved

Directions:

1. Combine the steak, Worcestershire sauce, soy sauce, salt, and ground black pepper in a large bowl. Toss to coat well. Set aside.
2. Combine the bell pepper, onion, salt, ground black pepper, and vegetable oil in a separate bowl. Toss to coat the vegetables well.
3. Place the steak and vegetables in the air fryer basket.
4. Put the air fryer basket on the baking pan and slide into Rack Position 2, select Air Fry, set temperature to 400ºF (205ºC) and set time to 15 minutes.

5. When cooked, the steak will be browned and vegetables will be tender. Transfer them onto a plate. Set aside.
6. Brush the hoagie rolls with butter and place in the basket.
7. Select Toast and set time to 3 minutes. Return to the oven. When done, the rolls should be lightly browned.
8. Transfer the rolls to a clean work surface and divide the steak and vegetable mix between the rolls. Spread with cheese. Transfer the stuffed rolls to the basket.
9. Select Air Fry and set time to 2 minutes. Return to the oven. When done, the cheese should be melted.
10. Serve immediately.

62. Baked Apple Breakfast Oats

Servings: 1
Cooking Time: 15 Minutes
Ingredients:
- 1/3 cup vanilla Greek yogurt
- 1/3 cup rolled oats
- 1 apple
- 1 tablespoon peanut butter

Directions:
1. Preheat toaster oven to 400°F and set it on the warm setting.
2. Cut apples into chunks approximately 1/2-inch-thick.
3. Place apples in an oven-safe dish with some space between each chunk and sprinkle with cinnamon.
4. Bake in the oven for 12 minutes.
5. Combine yogurt and oats in a bowl.
6. Remove the apples from the oven and combine with the yogurt.
7. Top with peanut butter for a delicious and high-protein breakfast.
- **Nutrition Info:** Calories: 350, Sodium: 134 mg, Dietary Fiber: 8.1 g, Total Fat: 11.2 g, Total Carbs: 52.5 g, Protein: 12.7 g.

63. Healthy Tofu Omelet

Servings: 2
Cooking Time: 29 Minutes
Ingredients:
- ¼ of onion, chopped
- 12-ounce silken tofu, pressed and sliced
- 3 eggs, beaten
- 1 tablespoon chives, chopped
- 1 garlic clove, minced
- 2 teaspoons olive oil
- Salt and black pepper, to taste

Directions:
1. Preheat the Air fryer to 355 ºF and grease an Air fryer pan with olive oil.
2. Add onion and garlic to the greased pan and cook for about 4 minutes.

3. Add tofu, mushrooms and chives and season with salt and black pepper.
4. Beat the eggs and pour over the tofu mixture.
5. Cook for about 25 minutes, poking the eggs twice in between
6. Dish out and serve warm.
- **Nutrition Info:** Calories: 248 Cal Total Fat: 15.9 g Saturated Fat: 0 g Cholesterol: 0 mg Sodium: 155 mg Total Carbs: 6.5 g Fiber: 0 g Sugar: 3.3 g Protein: 20.4 g

64. Perfect Chicken Casserole

Servings: 8
Cooking Time: 30 Minutes
Ingredients:
- 8 eggs
- 1 cup mozzarella cheese, shredded
- 8 oz can crescent rolls
- 1 1/2 cups basil pesto
- 3/4 lb chicken breasts, cooked & shredded
- Pepper
- Salt

Directions:
1. Fit the oven with the rack in position
2. Spray a 9*13-inch baking dish with cooking spray and set aside.
3. In a bowl, mix shredded chicken and pesto and set aside.
4. In a separate bowl, eggs, pepper, and salt.
5. Roll out the crescent roll into the prepared baking dish. Top with shredded chicken.
6. Pour egg mixture over chicken and top with shredded mozzarella cheese.
7. Set to bake at 350 F for 35 minutes. After 5 minutes place the baking dish in the preheated oven.
8. Serve and enjoy.
- **Nutrition Info:** Calories 266 Fat 14.3 g Carbohydrates 11.7 g Sugar 2.4 g Protein 21 g Cholesterol 203 mg

65. Aromatic Potato Hash

Servings: 4
Cooking Time: 42 Minutes
Ingredients:
- 2 teaspoons butter, melted
- 1 medium onion, chopped
- ½ of green bell pepper, seeded and chopped
- 1½ pound russet potatoes, peeled and cubed
- 5 eggs, beaten
- ½ teaspoon dried thyme, crushed
- ½ teaspoon dried savory, crushed
- Salt and black pepper, to taste

Directions:
1. Preheat the Air fryer to 390 ºF and grease an Air fryer pan with melted butter.

2. Put onion and bell pepper in the Air fryer pan and cook for about 5 minutes.
3. Add the potatoes, thyme, savory, salt and black pepper and cook for about 30 minutes.
4. Meanwhile, heat a greased skillet on medium heat and stir in the beaten eggs.
5. Cook for about 1 minute on each side and remove from the skillet.
6. Cut it into small pieces and transfer the egg pieces into the Air fryer pan.
7. Cook for about 5 more minutes and serve warm.
- **Nutrition Info:** Calories: 229 Cal Total Fat: 7.6 g Saturated Fat: 0 g Cholesterol: 0 mg Sodium: 103 mg Total Carbs: 30.8 g Fiber: 0 g Sugar: 4.2 g Protein: 10.3 g

66. Hash Browns

Servings: 3
Cooking Time: 18 Minutes
Ingredients:
- 1 tsp flour
- 1 ½ pound potatoes peeled
- ½ shallot
- ½ tsp Cajun seasoning
- 1 egg white
- ½ tsp black pepper
- 1 tsp coconut oil

Directions:
1. Keep the peeled potatoes in a bowl of water and mix them with Cajun seasoning as well as flour. Grate the potatoes and pour some cold water with a little salt to reduce the starch content. Set this mixture aside.
2. Grate the shallot and set it aside, strain your potatoes using a fine strainer or cheesecloth. Ensure all the water has been strained out of the potatoes.
3. Mix the ingredients in a bowl except the potatoes and ensure that they are well combined. Add the potatoes and mix them thoroughly. Form several patties.
4. Place your instant air fryer at 400 degrees Fahrenheit. Once the fryer indicates add food, add the patties on the pan. Flip every time the panel indicates turn food.
5. Serve while hot.
- **Nutrition Info:** Calories 145 Fat 9g, Carbohydrates 15g, Proteins 1g, Sodium: 1990 Mg.

67. Chicken Breakfast Muffins

Servings: 12
Cooking Time: 15 Minutes
Ingredients:
- 10 eggs
- 1/3 cup green onions, chopped
- 1 cup chicken, cooked and chopped
- 1/4 tsp pepper

- 1 tsp sea salt

Directions:
1. Fit the oven with the rack in position
2. Spray 12-cups muffin tin with cooking spray and set aside.
3. In a large bowl, whisk eggs with pepper and salt.
4. Add remaining ingredients and stir well.
5. Pour egg mixture into the greased muffin tin.
6. Set to bake at 400 F for 20 minutes, after 5 minutes, place the muffin tin in the oven.
7. Serve and enjoy.
- **Nutrition Info:** Calories 71 Fat 4 g Carbohydrates 0.5 g Sugar 0.3 g Protein 8 g Cholesterol 145 mg

68. Stuffed Poblanos

Servings: 4
Cooking Time: 30 Minutes
Ingredients:
- ½ lb. spicy ground pork breakfast sausage
- 4 large poblano peppers
- 4 large eggs.
- ½ cup full-fat sour cream.
- 4 oz. full-fat cream cheese; softened.
- ¼ cup canned diced tomatoes and green chiles, drained
- 8 tbsp. shredded pepper jack cheese

Directions:
1. In a medium skillet over medium heat, crumble and brown the ground sausage until no pink remains. Remove sausage and drain the fat from the pan. Crack eggs into the pan, scramble and cook until no longer runny
2. Place cooked sausage in a large bowl and fold in cream cheese. Mix in diced tomatoes and chiles. Gently fold in eggs
3. Cut a 4"–5" slit in the top of each poblano, removing the seeds and white membrane with a small knife. Separate the filling into four and spoon carefully into each pepper. Top each with 2 tbsp. pepper jack cheese
4. Place each pepper into the air fryer basket. Adjust the temperature to 350 Degrees F and set the timer for 15 minutes.
5. Peppers will be soft, and cheese will be browned when ready. Serve immediately with sour cream on top.
- **Nutrition Info:** Calories: 489; Protein: 22.8g; Fiber: 3.8g; Fat: 35.6g; Carbs: 12.6g

69. Mixed Berry Dutch Baby Pancake

Servings:4
Cooking Time: 14 Minutes
Ingredients:
- 1 tablespoon unsalted butter, at room temperature

- 1 egg
- 2 egg whites
- ½ cup 2% milk
- ½ cup whole-wheat pastry flour
- 1 teaspoon pure vanilla extract
- 1 cup sliced fresh strawberries
- ½ cup fresh raspberries
- ½ cup fresh blueberries

Directions:
1. Grease the baking pan with the butter.
2. Using a hand mixer, beat together the egg, egg whites, milk, pastry flour, and vanilla in a medium mixing bowl until well incorporated.
3. Pour the batter into the pan.
4. Slide the baking pan into Rack Position 1, select Convection Bake, set temperature to 330ºF (166ºC) and set time to 14 minutes.
5. When cooked, the pancake should puff up in the center and the edges should be golden brown
6. Allow the pancake to cool for 5 minutes and serve topped with the berries.

70. Delicious Broccoli Quiche

Servings: 8
Cooking Time: 45 Minutes
Ingredients:
- 2 eggs
- 2 1/2 cups broccoli, cooked & chopped
- 8 oz cheddar cheese, shredded
- 1/2 cup onion, chopped
- 1 1/2 cups milk
- 1 tsp baking powder
- 1 cup flour
- 1 tsp salt

Directions:
1. Fit the oven with the rack in position
2. In a large bowl, mix flour, baking powder, and salt and set aside.
3. In a separate bowl, whisk eggs. Add onion and stir well.
4. Pour egg mixture into the flour mixture and stir to combine.
5. Stir in broccoli and cheese.
6. Pour egg mixture into the greased 9-inch pie dish.
7. Set to bake at 350 F for 50 minutes. After 5 minutes place the pie dish in the preheated oven.
8. Serve and enjoy.
- **Nutrition Info:** Calories 223 Fat 11.7 g Carbohydrates 17.5 g Sugar 3.1 g Protein 12.4 g Cholesterol 74 mg

71. Breakfast Potatoes

Servings: 4
Cooking Time: 35 Minutes
Ingredients:

- 2 lbs potatoes, scrubbed and cut into 1/2-inch cubes
- 1 tsp garlic powder
- 1 tbsp olive oil
- 1/2 tsp sweet paprika
- Pepper
- Salt

Directions:
1. Fit the oven with the rack in position
2. Place potato cubes on the parchment-lined baking pan.
3. Drizzle with oil and season with paprika, garlic powder, pepper, and salt. Toss potatoes well.
4. Set to bake at 425 F for 40 minutes, after 5 minutes, place the baking pan in the oven.
5. Serve and enjoy.
- **Nutrition Info:** Calories 190 Fat 3.8 g Carbohydrates 36.3 g Sugar 2.8 g Protein 4 g Cholesterol 0 mg

72. Easy Cheesy Breakfast Casserole

Servings: 8
Cooking Time: 30 Minutes
Ingredients:
- 6 eggs, lightly beaten
- 8 oz can crescent rolls
- 2 cups cheddar cheese, shredded
- 1 lb breakfast sausage, cooked

Directions:
1. Fit the oven with the rack in position
2. Spray a 9*13-inch baking dish with cooking spray and set aside.
3. Spread crescent rolls in the bottom of the prepared baking dish and top with sausage, egg, and cheese.
4. Set to bake at 350 F for 35 minutes. After 5 minutes place the baking dish in the preheated oven.
5. Serve and enjoy.
- **Nutrition Info:** Calories 465 Fat 34.6 g Carbohydrates 11.8 g Sugar 2.4 g Protein 24.2 g Cholesterol 200 mg

73. Sweet Potato And Black Bean Burritos

Servings: 6 Burritos
Cooking Time: 30 Minutes
Ingredients:
- 2 sweet potatoes, peeled and cut into a small dice
- 1 tablespoon vegetable oil
- Kosher salt and ground black pepper, to taste
- 6 large flour tortillas
- 1 (16-ounce / 454-g) can refried black beans, divided
- 1½ cups baby spinach, divided
- 6 eggs, scrambled
- ¾ cup grated Cheddar cheese, divided

- ¼ cup salsa
- ¼ cup sour cream
- Cooking spray

Directions:
1. Put the sweet potatoes in a large bowl, then drizzle with vegetable oil and sprinkle with salt and black pepper. Toss to coat well.
2. Place the potatoes in the air fryer basket.
3. Put the air fryer basket on the baking pan and slide into Rack Position 2, select Air Fry, set temperature to 400ºF (205ºC) and set time to 10 minutes.
4. Flip the potatoes halfway through the cooking time.
5. When done, the potatoes should be lightly browned. Remove the potatoes from the oven.
6. Unfold the tortillas on a clean work surface. Divide the black beans, spinach, air fried sweet potatoes, scrambled eggs, and cheese on top of the tortillas.
7. Fold the long side of the tortillas over the filling, then fold in the shorter side to wrap the filling to make the burritos.
8. Wrap the burritos in the aluminum foil and put in the pan.
9. Put the air fryer basket on the baking pan and slide into Rack Position 2, select Air Fry, set temperature to 350ºF (180ºC) and set time to 20 minutes.
10. Flip the burritos halfway through the cooking time.
11. Remove the burritos from the oven and spread with sour cream and salsa. Serve immediately.

74. Pea And Potato Samosas With Chutney

Servings: 16 Samosas
Cooking Time: 22 Minutes
Ingredients:
- Dough:
- 4 cups all-purpose flour, plus more for flouring the work surface
- ¼ cup plain yogurt
- ½ cup cold unsalted butter, cut into cubes
- 2 teaspoons kosher salt
- 1 cup ice water
- Filling:
- 2 tablespoons vegetable oil
- 1 onion, diced
- 1½ teaspoons coriander
- 1½ teaspoons cumin
- 1 clove garlic, minced
- 1 teaspoon turmeric
- 1 teaspoon kosher salt
- ½ cup peas, thawed if frozen
- 2 cups mashed potatoes
- 2 tablespoons yogurt

- Cooking spray
- Chutney:
- 1 cup mint leaves, lightly packed
- 2 cups cilantro leaves, lightly packed
- 1 green chile pepper, deseeded and minced
- ½ cup minced onion
- Juice of 1 lime
- 1 teaspoon granulated sugar
- 1 teaspoon kosher salt
- 2 tablespoons vegetable oil

Directions:
1. Put the flour, yogurt, butter, and salt in a food processor. Pulse to combine until grainy. Pour in the water and pulse until a smooth and firm dough forms.
2. Transfer the dough on a clean and lightly floured working surface. Knead the dough and shape it into a ball. Cut in half and flatten the halves into 2 discs. Wrap them in plastic and let sit in refrigerator until ready to use.
3. Meanwhile, make the filling: Heat the vegetable oil in a saucepan over medium heat.
4. Add the onion and sauté for 5 minutes or until lightly browned.
5. Add the coriander, cumin, garlic, turmeric, and salt and sauté for 2 minutes or until fragrant.
6. Add the peas, potatoes, and yogurt and stir to combine well. Turn off the heat and allow to cool.
7. Meanwhile, combine the ingredients for the chutney in a food processor. Pulse to mix well until glossy. Pour the chutney in a bowl and refrigerate until ready to use.
8. Make the samosas: Remove the dough discs from the refrigerator and cut each disc into 8 parts. Shape each part into a ball, then roll the ball into a 6-inch circle. Cut the circle in half and roll each half into a cone.
9. Scoop up 2 tablespoons of the filling into the cone, press the edges of the cone to seal and form into a triangle. Repeat with remaining dough and filling.
10. Spritz the air fryer basket with cooking spray. Arrange the samosas in the pan and spritz with cooking spray.
11. Put the air fryer basket on the baking pan and slide into Rack Position 2, select Air Fry, set temperature to 360ºF (182ºC) and set time to 15 minutes.
12. Flip the samosas halfway through the cooking time.
13. When cooked, the samosas will be golden brown and crispy.
14. Serve the samosas with the chutney.

75. Sweet Banana Bread Pudding

Servings:4

Cooking Time: 18 Minutes

Ingredients:

- 2 medium ripe bananas, mashed
- ½ cup low-fat milk
- 2 tablespoons maple syrup
- 2 tablespoons peanut butter
- 1 teaspoon vanilla extract
- 1 teaspoon ground cinnamon
- 2 slices whole-grain bread, torn into bite-sized pieces
- ¼ cup quick oats
- Cooking spray

Directions:

1. Spritz the baking pan with cooking spray.
2. In a large bowl, combine the bananas, milk, maple syrup, peanut butter, vanilla extract and cinnamon. Use an immersion blender to mix until well combined.
3. Stir in the bread pieces to coat well. Add the oats and stir until everything is combined.
4. Transfer the mixture to the baking pan. Cover with the aluminum foil.
5. Put the baking pan into Rack Position 2, select Air Fry, set temperature to 375ºF (190ºC) and set time to 18 minutes.
6. After 10 minutes, remove the foil and continue to cook for 8 minutes.
7. Serve immediately.

76. Tomato, Basil & Mozzarella Breakfast

Servings: 1
Cooking Time: 10 Minutes

Ingredients:

- 2 slices of bread
- 4 tomato slices
- 4 mozzarella slices
- 1 tbsp olive oil
- 1 tbsp chopped basil
- Salt and black pepper to taste

Directions:

1. Preheat on Toast function to 350 F. Place the bread slices in the toaster oven and toast for 5 minutes. Arrange two tomato slices on each bread slice. Season with salt and pepper.

77. Easy Egg Bites

Servings: 6
Cooking Time: 30 Minutes

Ingredients:

- 5 eggs
- 3 bacon slices, cooked & chopped
- 4 tbsp cottage cheese
- 1/2 cup cheddar cheese, shredded
- 1/4 tsp pepper
- 1/4 tsp salt

Directions:

1. Fit the oven with the rack in position

2. Spray 6-cups muffin tin with cooking spray and set aside.
3. Add all ingredients except bacon into the blender and blend for 30 seconds.
4. Pour egg mixture into the prepared muffin tin then divide cooked bacon evenly in all egg cups.
5. Set to bake at 325 F for 35 minutes. After 5 minutes place muffin tin in the preheated oven.
6. Serve and enjoy.
- **Nutrition Info:** Calories 151 Fat 10.9 g Carbohydrates 0.9 g Sugar 0.4 g Protein 11.8 g Cholesterol 158 mg

78. Baja Fish Tacos

Servings: 6 Tacos
Cooking Time: 17 Minutes

Ingredients:

- 1 egg
- 5 ounces (142 g) Mexican beer
- ¾ cup all-purpose flour
- ¾ cup cornstarch
- ¼ teaspoon chili powder
- ½ teaspoon ground cumin
- ½ pound (227 g) cod, cut into large pieces
- 6 corn tortillas
- Cooking spray
- Salsa:
- 1 mango, peeled and diced
- ¼ red bell pepper, diced
- ½ small jalapeño, diced
- ¼ red onion, minced
- Juice of half a lime
- Pinch chopped fresh cilantro
- ¼ teaspoon salt
- ¼ teaspoon ground black pepper

Directions:

1. Spritz the air fryer basket with cooking spray.
2. Whisk the egg with beer in a bowl. Combine the flour, cornstarch, chili powder, and cumin in a separate bowl.
3. Dredge the cod in the egg mixture first, then in the flour mixture to coat well. Shake the excess off.
4. Arrange the cod in the basket and spritz with cooking spray.
5. Put the air fryer basket on the baking pan and slide into Rack Position 2, select Air Fry, set temperature to 380ºF (193ºC) and set time to 17 minutes.
6. Flip the cod halfway through the cooking time.
7. When cooked, the cod should be golden brown and crunchy.
8. Meanwhile, combine the ingredients for the salsa in a small bowl. Stir to mix well.

9. Unfold the tortillas on a clean work surface, then divide the fish on the tortillas and spread the salsa on top. Fold to serve.

79. Sweet Berry Pastry

Servings:3
Cooking Time: 20 Minutes
Ingredients:
- 3 pastry dough sheets
- 2 tbsp strawberries, mashed
- 2 tbsp raspberries, mashed
- ¼ tsp vanilla extract
- 2 cups cream cheese, softened
- 1 tbsp honey

Directions:
1. Preheat oven on Bake function to 375 F. Spread the cream cheese on the dough sheets. In a bowl, combine berries, honey, and vanilla. Divide the mixture between the pastry sheets. Pinch the ends of the sheets to form puff. Place in the oven and cook for 15 minutes.

80. Sweet Breakfast Casserole

Servings: 4
Cooking Time: 30 Minutes
Ingredients:
- 3 tablespoons brown sugar
- 4 tablespoons margarine
- 2 tablespoons white sugar
- 1/2 tsp. cinnamon powder
- 1/2 cup flour
- For the casserole:
- 2 eggs
- 2 tablespoons white sugar
- 2 and 1/2 cups white flour
- 1 tsp. baking soda
- 1 tsp. baking powder
- 2 eggs
- 1/2 cup milk
- 2 cups margarine milk
- 4 tablespoons margarine
- Zest from 1 lemon, grated
- 1 and 2/3 cup blueberries

Directions:
1. In a bowl, mix eggs with 2 tablespoons white sugar, 2 and 1/2 cups white flour, baking powder, baking soda, 2 eggs, milk, margarine milk, 4 tablespoons margarine, lemon zest and blueberries, stir and pour into a pan that fits your air fryer.
2. In another bowls, mix 3 tablespoons brown sugar with 2 tablespoons white sugar, 4 tablespoons margarine, 1/2 cup flour and cinnamon, stir until you obtain a crumble and spread over blueberries mix.
3. Place in preheated air fryer and bake at 300 °F for 30 minutes.
4. Divide among plates and serve for breakfast.

- **Nutrition Info:** Calories 101 Fat 9.4 g Carbohydrates 0.3 g Sugar 0.2 g Protein 7 g Cholesterol 21 mg

81. Creamy Vanilla Berry Mini Pies

Servings: 4
Cooking Time: 20 Minutes
Ingredients:
- 4 pastry dough sheets
- 2 tbsp mashed strawberries
- 2 tbsp mashed raspberries
- ¼ tsp vanilla extract
- 2 cups cream cheese, softened
- 1 tbsp honey

Directions:
1. Preheat fryer on Bake function to 375 F. Divide the cream cheese between the dough sheets and spread it evenly. In a small bowl, combine the berries, honey, and vanilla. Spoon the mixture into the pastry sheets. Pinch the ends of the sheets to form puff. Place the puffs in a lined baking dish. Place the dish in the toaster oven and cook for 15 minutes. Serve chilled.

82. Eggplant Hoagies

Servings: 3 Hoagies
Cooking Time: 12 Minutes
Ingredients:
- 6 peeled eggplant slices (about ½ inch thick and 3 inches in diameter)
- ¼ cup jarred pizza sauce
- 6 tablespoons grated Parmesan cheese
- 3 Italian sub rolls, split open lengthwise, warmed
- Cooking spray

Directions:
1. Spritz the air fryer basket with cooking spray.
2. Arrange the eggplant slices in the pan and spritz with cooking spray.
3. Put the air fryer basket on the baking pan and slide into Rack Position 2, select Air Fry, set temperature to 350ºF (180ºC) and set time to 10 minutes.
4. Flip the slices halfway through the cooking time.
5. When cooked, the eggplant slices should be lightly wilted and tender.
6. Divide and spread the pizza sauce and cheese on top of the eggplant slice
7. Put the air fryer basket on the baking pan and slide into Rack Position 2, select Air Fry, set temperature to 375ºF (190ºC) and set time to 2 minutes.
8. When cooked, the cheese will be melted.
9. Assemble each sub roll with two slices of eggplant and serve immediately.

83. Bacon And Hot Dogs Omelet

Servings: 2
Cooking Time: 10 Minutes
Ingredients:
- 4 eggs
- 1 bacon slice, chopped
- 2 hot dogs, chopped
- 2 small onions, chopped
- 2 tablespoons milk
- Salt and black pepper, to taste

Directions:
1. Preheat the Air fryer to 325 ºF and grease an Air Fryer pan.
2. Whisk together eggs and stir in the remaining ingredients.
3. Stir well to combine and place in the Air fryer.
4. Cook for about 10 minutes and serve hot.
- **Nutrition Info:** Calories: 418 Cal Total Fat: 31.5 g Saturated Fat: 0 g Cholesterol: 0 mg Sodium: 1000 mg Total Carbs: 9.7 g Fiber: 0 g Sugar: 5.6 g Protein: 23.4 g

84. Cheddar Omelet With Soy Sauce

Servings:1
Cooking Time: 15 Minutes
Ingredients:
- 2 eggs
- 2 tbsp cheddar cheese, grated
- 1 tsp soy sauce
- ½ onion, sliced
- ¼ tsp pepper
- 1 tbsp olive oil

Directions:
1. Preheat on Bake function to 350 F. Whisk the eggs along with the pepper and soy sauce. Place the onion in a greased baking dish and pour over the egg mixture. Press Start and cook for 12-14 minutes. Top with the grated cheddar cheese and serve sliced.

85. Zucchini Breakfast Casserole

Servings: 8
Cooking Time: 50 Minutes
Ingredients:
- 12 eggs
- 2 small zucchinis, shredded
- 1 lb ground sausage
- 3 tomatoes, sliced
- 3 tbsp coconut flour
- 1/4 cup coconut milk
- 1/4 tsp pepper
- 1/2 tsp salt

Directions:
1. Fit the oven with the rack in position
2. Cook sausage in a pan until lightly brown.
3. Transfer sausage to a large mixing bowl.
4. Add coconut flour, milk, eggs, zucchini, pepper, and salt. Stir well.
5. Add eggs and whisk until well combined.
6. Pour bowl mixture into the greased casserole dish and top with tomato slices.
7. Set to bake at 350 F for 55 minutes, after 5 minutes, place the casserole dish in the oven.
8. Serve and enjoy.
- **Nutrition Info:** Calories 330 Fat 25 g Carbohydrates 5.7 g Sugar 2.7 g Protein 20.8 g Cholesterol 293 mg

86. Zucchini Fritters

Servings: 4
Cooking Time: 7 Minutes
Ingredients:
- 10½ ounces zucchini, grated and squeezed
- 7 ounces Halloumi cheese
- ¼ cup all-purpose flour
- 2 eggs
- 1 teaspoon fresh dill, minced
- Salt and black pepper, to taste

Directions:
1. Preheat the Air fryer to 360 ºF and grease a baking dish.
2. Mix together all the ingredients in a large bowl.
3. Make small fritters from this mixture and place them on the prepared baking dish.
4. Transfer the dish in the Air Fryer basket and cook for about 7 minutes.
5. Dish out and serve warm.
- **Nutrition Info:** Calories: 250 Cal Total Fat: 17.2 g Saturated Fat: 0 g Cholesterol: 0 mg Sodium: 330 mg Total Carbs: 10 g Fiber: 0 g Sugar: 2.7 g Protein: 15.2 g

87. Cinnamon Sweet Potato Chips

Servings: 6 To 8 Slices
Cooking Time: 8 Minutes
Ingredients:
- 1 small sweet potato, cut into ⅜ inch-thick slices
- 2 tablespoons olive oil
- 1 to 2 teaspoon ground cinnamon

Directions:
1. Add the sweet potato slices and olive oil in a bowl and toss to coat. Fold in the cinnamon and stir to combine.
2. Lay the sweet potato slices in a single layer in the air fryer basket.
3. Put the air fryer basket on the baking pan and slide into Rack Position 2, select Air Fry, set temperature to 390ºF (199ºC), and set time to 8 minutes.
4. Stir the potato slices halfway through the cooking time.
5. When cooking is complete, the chips should be crisp. Remove the pan from the oven. Allow to cool for 5 minutes before serving.

88. Nutritious Cinnamon Oat Muffins

Servings: 12
Cooking Time: 30 Minutes
Ingredients:

- 2 cups oat flour
- 1/3 cup coconut oil, melted
- 1/2 cup maple syrup
- 1 cup applesauce
- 1 tsp cinnamon
- 2 tsp baking powder
- 1 tsp vanilla
- 1/4 tsp salt

Directions:

1. Fit the oven with the rack in position
2. Line 12-cups muffin tin with cupcake liners and set aside.
3. In a bowl, add applesauce, cinnamon, vanilla, oil, maple syrup, and salt and stir to combine.
4. Add baking powder and oat flour and stir well.
5. Pour batter into the prepared muffin tin.
6. Set to bake at 350 F for 35 minutes, after 5 minutes, place the muffin tin in the oven.
7. Serve and enjoy.
- **Nutrition Info:** Calories 158 Fat 7.1 g Carbohydrates 22.2 g Sugar 9.9 g Protein 2 g Cholesterol 0 mg

89. Turkey, Leek, And Pepper Hamburger

Servings:4
Cooking Time: 20 Minutes
Ingredients:

- 1 cup leftover turkey, cut into bite-sized chunks
- 1 leek, sliced
- 1 Serrano pepper, deveined and chopped
- 2 bell peppers, deveined and chopped
- 2 tablespoons Tabasco sauce
- ½ cup sour cream
- 1 heaping tablespoon fresh cilantro, chopped
- 1 teaspoon hot paprika
- ¾ teaspoon kosher salt
- ½ teaspoon ground black pepper
- 4 hamburger buns
- Cooking spray

Directions:

1. Spritz the baking pan with cooking spray.
2. Mix all the ingredients, except for the buns, in a large bowl. Toss to combine well.
3. Pour the mixture in the baking pan.
4. Slide the baking pan into Rack Position 1, select Convection Bake, set temperature to 385ºF (196ºC) and set time to 20 minutes.
5. When done, the turkey will be well browned and the leek will be tender.
6. Assemble the hamburger buns with the turkey mixture and serve immediately.

90. Broccoli Asparagus Frittata

Servings: 6
Cooking Time: 20 Minutes
Ingredients:

- 6 eggs
- 1/2 cup onion, diced & sautéed
- 1 cup asparagus, chopped & sautéed
- 1 cup broccoli, chopped & sautéed
- 3 bacon slices, cooked & chopped
- 1/3 cup parmesan cheese, grated
- 1/2 cup milk
- 1/2 tsp pepper
- 1 tsp salt

Directions:

1. Fit the oven with the rack in position
2. In a mixing bowl, whisk eggs with milk, cheese, pepper, and salt.
3. Add onion, asparagus, broccoli, and bacon and stir well.
4. Pour egg mixture into the greased baking dish.
5. Set to bake at 350 F for 25 minutes. After 5 minutes place the baking dish in the preheated oven.
6. Serve and enjoy.
- **Nutrition Info:** Calories 154 Fat 9.9 g Carbohydrates 4.6 g Sugar 2.4 g Protein 12.4 g Cholesterol 179 mg

91. Tomatta Spinacha Frittata

Servings: 4
Cooking Time: 30 Minutes
Ingredients:

- 3 tablespoons olive oil
- 10 large eggs
- 2 teaspoons kosher salt
- 1/2 teaspoon black pepper
- 1 (5-ounce) bag baby spinach
- 1 pint grape tomatoes
- 4 scallions
- 8 ounces feta cheese

Directions:

1. Preheat toaster oven to 350°F.
2. Halve tomatoes and slice scallions into thin pieces.
3. Add oil to a 2-quart oven-safe pan, making sure to brush it on the sides as well as the bottom. Place the dish in toaster oven.
4. Combine the eggs, salt, and pepper in a medium mixing bowl and whisk together for a minute.
5. Add spinach, tomatoes, and scallions to the bowl and mix together until even.
6. Crumble feta cheese into the bowl and mix together gently. Remove the dish from the oven and pour in the egg mixture.
7. Put the dish back into the oven and bake for 25–30 minutes, or until the edges of the frittata are browned.

- **Nutrition Info:** Calories: 448, Sodium: 515 mg, Dietary Fiber: 2.3 g, Total Fat: 35.4 g, Total Carbs: 9.3 g, Protein: 25.9 g.

92. Almond & Berry Oat Bars

Servings:6
Cooking Time: 35 Minutes + Cooling Time
Ingredients:
- 3 cups rolled oats
- ½ cup ground almonds
- ½ cup flour
- 1 tsp baking powder
- 1 tsp ground cinnamon
- 3 eggs, lightly beaten
- ½ cup canola oil
- ⅓ cup milk
- 2 tsp vanilla extract
- 2 cups mixed berries

Directions:
1. Spray a baking pan with cooking spray. In a bowl, add oats, almonds, flour, baking powder, and cinnamon in a bowl and stir well. In another bowl, whisk eggs, oil, milk, and vanilla.
2. Stir wet ingredients into oat mixture. Fold in the berries. Pour the mixture in the pan and place in the . Cook for 25 minutes at 330 F on Bake function. Let cool before slicing into bars.

93. Parsley Onion & Feta Tart

Servings: 4
Cooking Time: 30 Minutes
Ingredients:
- 3 ½ pounds Feta cheese
- Black pepper to taste
- 1 whole onion, chopped
- 2 tbsp parsley, chopped
- 1 egg yolk
- 5 sheets frozen filo pastry

Directions:
1. Cut each of the 5 filo sheets into three equal-sized strips. Cover the strips with oil. In a bowl, mix onion, pepper, feta, salt, egg yolk, and parsley.
2. Make triangles using the cut strips and add a little bit of the feta mixture on top of each triangle. Place the triangles in a greased baking sheet and cook for 5 minutes at 400 F on Bake function. Serve sprinkled with green onions.

94. Ultimate Breakfast Burrito

Servings: 8
Cooking Time:: 20 Minute
Ingredients:
- 16 ounces cooked bacon ends and pieces
- 16 eggs
- 1 tablespoon butter
- 8 hash brown squares
- 8 large soft flour tortillas
- 2 diced jalapeños
- 2 cups shredded sharp cheddar

Directions:
1. Place bacon on a baking sheet in toaster oven. Bake at 450°F until it reaches desired level of crispiness and set aside.
2. Whisk together eggs in a bowl and set aside.
3. Melt butter into a sauce pan and mix in eggs until they are starting to cook but not fully hardened.
4. While eggs are cooking, microwave and cool hash brown squares.
5. Roll out tortillas and top them with hash browns, bacon, jalapeños, and cheese.
6. Wrap up the burritos and place them seam-down on a baking sheet.
7. Bake at 375°F for 15–20 minutes.
- **Nutrition Info:** Calories: 698, Sodium: 1821 mg, Dietary Fiber: 3.4 g, Total Fat: 43.7 g, Total Carbs: 32.9 g, Protein: 42.1 g.

95. Mozzarella Endives And Tomato Salad

Servings: 4
Cooking Time: 20 Minutes
Ingredients:
- 2 endives, shredded
- ½ pound cherry tomatoes, halved
- 1 tablespoon olive oil
- 4 eggs, whisked
- Salt and black pepper to the taste
- 1 teaspoon sweet paprika
- ½ cup mozzarella, shredded

Directions:
1. Preheat the air fryer with the oil at 350 degrees F, add the tomatoes, endives and the other ingredients except the mozzarella and toss.
2. Sprinkle the mozzarella on top, cook for 20 minutes, divide into bowls and serve for breakfast.
- **Nutrition Info:** calories 229, fat 13, fiber 3, carbs 4, protein 7

96. Strawberry Basil Muffins

Servings: 12
Cooking Time: 20 Minutes
Ingredients:
- 3 tbsp. almonds
- ¾ cup + 2 tbsp. flour, divided
- ½ cup + 2 tbsp. brown sugar, divided
- ½ tsp salt, divided
- ¼ cup + 2 tbsp. coconut oil, melted
- 1 cup white whole-wheat flour
- 2 tsp baking powder
- 1 tsp baking soda
- 1 ¼ cup buttermilk, low fat
- 1 egg
- 1 tsp vanilla
- 1 ½ cups strawberries, chopped
- ¼ cup fresh basil, chopped

Directions:
1. Place rack in position 1 of the oven. Line 2 6-cup muffin tins with paper liners.

2. Place almonds, 2 tablespoons flour, 2 tablespoons brown sugar, and ¼ teaspoon salt in the food processor or blender. Pulse until finely ground. Transfer to a small bowl and stir in 2 tablespoons oil until combined.
3. In a large bowl, combine remaining flour, whole wheat flour, baking powder, baking soda, and remaining salt together.
4. In a separate large bowl, whisk together, remaining brown sugar, oil, buttermilk, juice, egg and vanilla until thoroughly combined.
5. Make a well in the dry ingredients and add wet ingredients, stir just until combined.
6. Fold in berries and basil. Divide evenly between prepared pans. Sprinkle almond topping over muffins.
7. Set oven to bake on 400°F for 25 minutes. After 5 minutes, add muffin tins, one at a time, to oven and bake 18-20 minutes or until muffins pass the toothpick test. Let cool in pan 10 minutes, then transfer to wire rack to cool completely.
- **Nutrition Info:** Calories 209, Total Fat 7g, Saturated Fat 6g, Total Carbs 30g, Net Carbs 28g, Protein 4g, Sugar 14g, Fiber 2g, Sodium 239mg, Potassium 231mg, Phosphorus 140mg

97. Vanilla Granola

Servings:4
Cooking Time: 40 Minutes
Ingredients:
- 1 cup rolled oats
- 3 tablespoons maple syrup
- 1 tablespoon sunflower oil
- 1 tablespoon coconut sugar
- ¼ teaspoon vanilla
- ¼ teaspoon cinnamon
- ¼ teaspoon sea salt

Directions:
1. Mix together the oats, maple syrup, sunflower oil, coconut sugar, vanilla, cinnamon, and sea salt in a medium bowl and stir to combine. Transfer the mixture to the baking pan.
2. Slide the baking pan into Rack Position 1, select Convection Bake, set temperature to 248ºF (120ºC) and set time to 40 minutes.
3. Stir the granola four times during cooking.
4. When cooking is complete, the granola will be mostly dry and lightly browned.
5. Let the granola stand for 5 to 10 minutes before serving.

98. Crispy Tilapia Tacos

Servings:4
Cooking Time: 5 Minutes
Ingredients:
- 2 tablespoons milk
- $^1/_3$ cup mayonnaise
- ¼ teaspoon garlic powder
- 1 teaspoon chili powder
- 1½ cups panko bread crumbs
- ½ teaspoon salt
- 4 teaspoons canola oil
- 1 pound (454 g) skinless tilapia fillets, cut into 3-inch-long and 1-inch-wide strips
- 4 small flour tortillas
- Lemon wedges, for topping
- Cooking spray

Directions:
1. Spritz the air fryer basket with cooking spray.
2. Combine the milk, mayo, garlic powder, and chili powder in a bowl. Stir to mix well. Combine the panko with salt and canola oil in a separate bowl. Stir to mix well.
3. Dredge the tilapia strips in the milk mixture first, then dunk the strips in the panko mixture to coat well. Shake the excess off.
4. Arrange the tilapia strips in the pan.
5. Put the air fryer basket on the baking pan and slide into Rack Position 2, select Air Fry, set temperature to 400ºF (205ºC) and set time to 5 minutes.
6. Flip the strips halfway through the cooking time.
7. When cooking is complete, the strips will be opaque on all sides and the panko will be golden brown.
8. Unfold the tortillas on a large plate, then divide the tilapia strips over the tortillas. Squeeze the lemon wedges on top before serving.

99. Amazing Strawberry Pancake

Servings:4
Cooking Time: 30 Minutes
Ingredients:
- 3 eggs, beaten
- 2 tbsp unsalted butter
- ½ cup flour
- 2 tbsp sugar, powdered
- ½ cup milk
- 1 ½ cups fresh strawberries, sliced

Directions:
1. Preheat to 330 F on Bake function. Add butter to a pan and melt over low heat. In a bowl, mix flour, milk, eggs, and vanilla. Add the mixture to the pan with melted butter.
2. Place the pan in the oven and press Start. Cook for 14-16 minutes until the pancake is fluffy and golden brown. Drizzle powdered sugar and toss sliced strawberries on top.

100. Easy Cheese Egg Casserole

Servings: 10
Cooking Time: 40 Minutes
Ingredients:
- 12 eggs
- 8 oz cheddar cheese, shredded
- 1/3 cup milk
- 1/4 tsp pepper
- 1 tsp salt

Directions:
1. Fit the oven with the rack in position
2. Spray 9*13-inch casserole dish with cooking spray and set aside.
3. In a bowl, whisk eggs with milk, pepper, and salt.
4. Add shredded cheese and stir well.
5. Pour egg mixture into the prepared casserole dish.
6. Set to bake at 350 F for 45 minutes. After 5 minutes place the casserole dish in the preheated oven.
7. Serve and enjoy.
- **Nutrition Info:** Calories 171 Fat 12.9 g Carbohydrates 1.1 g Sugar 0.9 g Protein 12.6 g Cholesterol 221 mg

101.Cheesy Potato Taquitos

Servings: 12 Taquitos
Cooking Time: 6 Minutes
Ingredients:
- 2 cups mashed potatoes
- ½ cup shredded Mexican cheese
- 12 corn tortillas
- Cooking spray

Directions:
1. Line the baking pan with parchment paper.
2. In a bowl, combine the potatoes and cheese until well mixed. Microwave the tortillas on high heat for 30 seconds, or until softened. Add some water to another bowl and set alongside.
3. On a clean work surface, lay the tortillas. Scoop 3 tablespoons of the potato mixture in the center of each tortilla. Roll up tightly and secure with toothpicks if necessary.
4. Arrange the filled tortillas, seam side down, in the prepared baking pan. Spritz the tortillas with cooking spray.
5. Put the air fryer basket on the baking pan and slide into Rack Position 2, select Air Fry, set temperature to 400ºF (205ºC) and set time to 6 minutes.
6. Flip the tortillas halfway through the cooking time.
7. When cooked, the tortillas should be crispy and golden brown.
8. Serve hot.

102.Glazed Strawberry Toast

Servings: 4 Toasts
Cooking Time: 8 Minutes
Ingredients:
- 4 slices bread, ½-inch thick
- 1 cup sliced strawberries
- 1 teaspoon sugar
- Cooking spray

Directions:
1. On a clean work surface, lay the bread slices and spritz one side of each slice of bread with cooking spray.
2. Place the bread slices in the air-fryer basket, sprayed side down. Top with the strawberries and a sprinkle of sugar.
3. Put the air fryer basket on the baking pan and slide into Rack Position 2, select Air Fry, set temperature to 375ºF (190ºC), and set time to 8 minutes.
4. When cooking is complete, the toast should be well browned on each side. Remove from the oven to a plate and serve.

103.Quick Cheddar Omelet

Servings:1
Cooking Time: 15 Minutes
Ingredients:
- 2 eggs, beaten
- 1 cup cheddar cheese, shredded
- 1 whole onion, chopped
- 2 tbsp soy sauce

Directions:
1. Preheat on AirFry function to 340 F. Drizzle soy sauce over the chopped onions. Sauté the onions ina greased pan over medium heat for 5 minutes; turn off the heat.
2. In a bowl, mix the eggs with salt and pepper. Pour the egg mixture over onions and cook in the for 6 minutes. Top with cheddar cheese and bake for 4 more minutes. Serve and enjoy!

104.Herby Parmesan Bagel

Servings: 1
Cooking Time: 10 Minutes
Ingredients:
- 2 tbsp butter, softened
- 1 tsp dried basil
- 1 tsp dried parsley
- 1 tsp garlic powder
- 1 tbsp Parmesan cheese
- Salt and black pepper to taste
- 1 bagel

Directions:
1. Preheat on Bake function to 370 degrees. Cut the bagel in half. Combine the butter, Parmesan cheese, garlic, basil, and parsley in a small bowl. Season with salt and pepper. Spread the mixture onto the bagel. Place the bagel in a baking pan and cook for 5 minutes. Serve.
2. Top each slice with 2 mozzarella slices. Return to the oven and cook for 1 minute more. Drizzle the caprese toasts with olive oil and top with chopped basil.

105.Cauliflower And Cod Mix

Servings: 4
Cooking Time: 20 Minutes
Ingredients:
- 2 cups cauliflower florets
- 1-pound cod fillets, boneless and cubed
- 1 cup baby spinach
- 1 cup baby arugula

- 1 tablespoon olive oil
- 1 teaspoon sweet paprika
- 1 teaspoon rosemary, dried
- A pinch of salt and black pepper

Directions:
1. Heat up your air fryer with the oil at 340 degrees F, add the cauliflower, cod and the other ingredients, toss gently and cook for 20 minutes.
2. Divide the mix into bowls and serve for breakfast.
- **Nutrition Info:** calories 240, fat 9, fiber 2, carbs 4, protein 8

106.Breakfast Tater Tot Casserole

Servings:4
Cooking Time: 17 To 18 Minutes
Ingredients:
- 4 eggs
- 1 cup milk
- Salt and pepper, to taste
- 12 ounces (340 g) ground chicken sausage
- 1 pound (454 g) frozen tater tots, thawed
- ¾ cup grated Cheddar cheese
- Cooking spray

Directions:
1. Whisk together the eggs and milk in a medium bowl. Season with salt and pepper to taste and stir until mixed. Set aside.
2. Place a skillet over medium-high heat and spritz with cooking spray. Place the ground sausage in the skillet and break it into smaller pieces with a spatula or spoon. Cook for 3 to 4 minutes until the sausage starts to brown, stirring occasionally. Remove from heat and set aside.
3. Coat the baking pan with cooking spray. Arrange the tater tots in the baking pan.
4. Slide the baking pan into Rack Position 1, select Convection Bake, set temperature to 400ºF (205ºC) and set time to 14 minutes.
5. After 6 minutes, remove the pan from the oven. Stir the tater tots and add the egg mixture and cooked sausage. Return the pan to the oven and continue cooking.
6. After 6 minutes, remove the pan from the oven. Scatter the cheese on top of the tater tots. Return the pan to the oven and continue to cook for another 2 minutes.
7. When done, the cheese should be bubbly and melted.
8. Let the mixture cool for 5 minutes and serve warm.

107.Spinach And Bacon Roll-ups

Servings:4
Cooking Time: 8 To 9 Minutes
Ingredients:
- 4 flour tortillas (6- or 7-inch size)
- 4 slices Swiss cheese
- 1 cup baby spinach leaves
- 4 slices turkey bacon
- Special Equipment:

- 4 toothpicks, soak in water for at least 30 minutes

Directions:
1. On a clean work surface, top each tortilla with one slice of cheese and ¼ cup of spinach, then tightly roll them up.
2. Wrap each tortilla with a strip of turkey bacon and secure with a toothpick.
3. Arrange the roll-ups in the air fryer basket, leaving space between each roll-up.
4. Put the air fryer basket on the baking pan and slide into Rack Position 2, select Air Fry, set temperature to 390ºF (199ºC), and set time to 8 minutes.
5. After 4 minutes, remove the pan from the oven. Flip the roll-ups with tongs and rearrange them for more even cooking. Return to the oven and continue cooking for another 4 minutes.
6. When cooking is complete, the bacon should be crisp. If necessary, continue cooking for 1 minute more. Remove the pan from the oven. Rest for 5 minutes and remove the toothpicks before serving.

108.Tasty Cheddar Omelet

Servings: 1
Cooking Time: 20 Minutes
Ingredients:
- 2 eggs
- 2 tbsp cheddar cheese, grated
- 1 tsp soy sauce
- ½ onion, sliced
- Salt and black pepper to taste
- 1 tbsp olive oil

Directions:
1. Preheat on Bake function to 350 F. Whisk the eggs with soy sauce, salt, and pepper. Stir in onion. Grease a baking dish with the olive oil and add in the egg mixture. Cook for 10-14 minutes. Top with the grated cheddar cheese and serve.

109.Fried Eggplant Parmesan With Mozzarella Cheese

Servings:x
Cooking Time:x
Ingredients:
- 1/3 cup (45g) all-purpose flour
- 2 eggs
- 1 (28-ounce/790g) can whole tomatoes
- 2 tablespoons olive oil
- 2 cloves garlic, minced
- 1 medium eggplant (about 1 pound/
- 450g)
- 1 cup (55g) panko breadcrumbs
- 1 cup (60g) finely grated Parmesan cheese
- 1 teaspoon dried oregano
- ½ teaspoon dried oregano
- Pinch red pepper flakes
- 1 cup (115g) shredded mozzarella cheese
- 1 cup (20g) finely grated Parmesan

- 1 teaspoon kosher salt
- ¼ teaspoon freshly ground black pepper
- 1 teaspoon kosher salt
- Cheese

Directions:
1. Slice eggplant crosswise into ½-inch (1cm) slices. Lay slices in single layer on a baking sheet and sprinkle with ½ teaspoon kosher salt. Flip slices and sprinkle with another ½ teaspoon salt. Let rest for 20 minutes while preparing breading.
2. Combine panko, Parmesan, oregano, salt and black pepper in bowl of food processor. Process until finely ground, about 15–20 seconds. Transfer to a shallow dish.
3. Place flour in a second shallow dish. Scramble eggs and 2 tablespoons water in a third shallow dish.
4. Use paper towels or a clean dish towel to dry the eggplant slices, pressing firmly on both sides to remove as much moisture as possible.
5. Working in batches, toss eggplant in flour and shake off any excess. Dip eggplant in egg and allow excess to drain off. Dredge eggplant in panko mixture, ensuring all sides are well crusted. If there are any extra breadcrumbs, reserve them to sprinkle on top of casserole.
6. Place half of eggplant on the air fry rack in a single layer. Reserve remaining eggplant on a dry baking pan.
7. Select AIRFRY/375°F (190°C)/SUPER CONVECTION/20 minutes and press START to preheat oven.
8. Cook in rack position 4 until brown and crispy, about 20 minutes. Repeat with remaining eggplant. 9. While eggplant is cooking, make the sauce.
9. Pour tomatoes and their juices into a large bowl and crush with your hands. Alternatively, blend with an immersion blender or food processor for a smoother sauce.
10. Heat olive oil in a medium saucepan over medium heat. Add minced garlic and cook, stirring constantly, until just golden, about 30 seconds. Add the crushed tomatoes, salt, oregano and red pepper flakes and stir to combine.
11. Simmer sauce for 10 minutes, stirring occasionally. Remove from heat and reserve.

110.Whole-wheat Blueberry Scones

Servings:14
Cooking Time: 20 Minutes
Ingredients:
- ½ cup low-fat buttermilk
- ¾ cup orange juice
- Zest of 1 orange
- 2¼ cups whole-wheat pastry flour
- $^1/_3$ cup agave nectar
- ¼ cup canola oil

- 1 teaspoon baking soda
- 1 teaspoon cream of tartar
- 1 cup fresh blueberries

Directions:
1. In a small bowl, stir together the buttermilk, orange juice and orange zest.
2. In a large bowl, whisk together the flour, agave nectar, canola oil, baking soda and cream of tartar.
3. Add the buttermilk mixture and blueberries to the bowl with the flour mixture. Mix gently by hand until well combined.
4. Transfer the batter onto a lightly floured baking pan. Pat into a circle about ¾ inch thick and 8 inches across. Use a knife to cut the circle into 14 wedges, cutting almost all the way through.
5. Slide the baking pan into Rack Position 1, select Convection Bake, set temperature to 375ºF (190ºC) and set time to 20 minutes.
6. When cooking is complete, remove the pan and check the scones. They should be lightly browned.
7. Let rest for 5 minutes and cut completely through the wedges before serving

111.Strawberries And Quinoa Salad

Servings: 4
Cooking Time: 15 Minutes
Ingredients:
- 1 cup strawberries
- 1 cup quinoa, cooked
- 1 cup coconut milk
- ½ cup heavy cream
- 2 tablespoons sugar
- Cooking spray

Directions:
1. Grease your air fryer with cooking spray, and combine the berries with the milk, quinoa, cream and sugar inside.
2. Toss, cook at 365 degrees F for 15 minutes, divide into bowls and serve for breakfast.
- **Nutrition Info:** calories 172, fat 6, fiber 8, carbs 11, protein 5

112.Montreal Steak And Seeds Burgers

Servings:4
Cooking Time: 10 Minutes
Ingredients:
- 1 teaspoon cumin seeds
- 1 teaspoon mustard seeds
- 1 teaspoon coriander seeds
- 1 teaspoon dried minced garlic
- 1 teaspoon dried red pepper flakes
- 1 teaspoon kosher salt
- 2 teaspoons ground black pepper
- 1 pound (454 g) 85% lean ground beef
- 2 tablespoons Worcestershire sauce
- 4 hamburger buns
- Mayonnaise, for serving
- Cooking spray

Directions:

1. Spritz the air fryer basket with cooking spray.
2. Put the seeds, garlic, red pepper flakes, salt, and ground black pepper in a food processor. Pulse to coarsely ground the mixture.
3. Put the ground beef in a large bowl. Pour in the seed mixture and drizzle with Worcestershire sauce. Stir to mix well.
4. Divide the mixture into four parts and shape each part into a ball, then bash each ball into a patty. Arrange the patties in the pan.
5. Put the air fryer basket on the baking pan and slide into Rack Position 2, select Air Fry, set temperature to 350ºF (180ºC) and set time to 10 minutes.
6. Flip the patties with tongs halfway through the cooking time.
7. When cooked, the patties will be well browned.
8. Assemble the buns with the patties, then drizzle the mayo over the patties to make the burgers. Serve immediately.

113. Vanilla Brownies With White Chocolate & Walnuts

Servings: 4
Cooking Time: 35 Minutes
Ingredients:
- 6 oz dark chocolate, chopped
- 6 oz butter
- ¾ cup white sugar
- 3 eggs, beaten
- 2 tsp vanilla extract
- ¾ cup flour
- ¼ cup cocoa powder
- 1 cup chopped walnuts
- 1 cup white chocolate chips

Directions:
1. Line a baking pan with parchment paper. In a saucepan, melt chocolate and butter over low heat. Do not stop stirring until you obtain a smooth mixture. Let cool slightly and whisk in eggs and vanilla. Sift flour and cocoa and stir to mix well.
2. Sprinkle the walnuts over and add the white chocolate into the batter. Pour the batter into the pan and cook for 20 minutes in the oven at 350 F on Bake function. Serve chilled with raspberry syrup and ice cream.

114. Prosciutto & Salami Egg Bake

Servings: 2
Cooking Time: 20 Minutes
Ingredients:
- 1 beef sausage, chopped
- 4 slices prosciutto, chopped
- 3 oz salami, chopped
- 1 cup grated mozzarella cheese
- 4 eggs, beaten
- ½ tsp onion powder

Directions:
1. Preheat on Bake function to 350 F. Whisk the eggs with the onion powder. Brown the sausage in a skillet over medium heat for 2 minutes. Remove to the egg mixture and add in mozzarella cheese, salami, and prosciutto and give it a stir. Pour the egg mixture in a greased baking pan and cook for 10-15 minutes until golden brown on top. Serve.

LUNCH RECIPES

115.Spanish Chicken Bake

Servings: 4
Cooking Time: 25 Minutes
Ingredients:
- ½ onion, quartered
- ½ red onion, quartered
- ½ lb. potatoes, quartered
- 4 garlic cloves
- 4 tomatoes, quartered
- 1/8 cup chorizo
- ¼ teaspoon paprika powder
- 4 chicken thighs, boneless
- ¼ teaspoon dried oregano
- ½ green bell pepper, julienned
- Salt
- Black pepper

Directions:
1. Toss chicken, veggies, and all the Ingredients: in a baking tray.
2. Press "Power Button" of Air Fry Oven and turn the dial to select the "Bake" mode.
3. Press the Time button and again turn the dial to set the cooking time to 25 minutes.
4. Now push the Temp button and rotate the dial to set the temperature at 425 degrees F.
5. Once preheated, place the baking pan inside and close its lid.
6. Serve warm.
- **Nutrition Info:** Calories 301 Total Fat 8.9 g Saturated Fat 4.5 g Cholesterol 57 mg Sodium 340 mg Total Carbs 24.7 g Fiber 1.2 g Sugar 1.3 g Protein 15.3 g

116.Chicken Caprese Sandwich

Servings: 2
Cooking Time: 3 Minutes
Ingredients:
- 2 leftover chicken breasts, or pre-cooked breaded chicken
- 1 large ripe tomato
- 4 ounces mozzarella cheese slices
- 4 slices of whole grain bread
- 1/4 cup olive oil
- 1/3 cup fresh basil leaves
- Salt and pepper to taste

Directions:
1. Start by slicing tomatoes into thin slices.
2. Layer tomatoes then cheese over two slices of bread and place on a greased baking sheet.
3. Toast in the toaster oven for about 2 minutes or until the cheese is melted.
4. Heat chicken while the cheese melts.
5. Remove from oven, sprinkle with basil, and add chicken.
6. Drizzle with oil and add salt and pepper.
7. Top with other slice of bread and serve.

- **Nutrition Info:** Calories: 808, Sodium: 847 mg, Dietary Fiber: 5.2 g, Total Fat: 43.6 g, Total Carbs: 30.7 g, Protein: 78.4 g.

117.Air Fried Steak Sandwich

Servings: 4
Cooking Time: 16 Minutes
Ingredients:
- Large hoagie bun, sliced in half
- 6 ounces of sirloin or flank steak, sliced into bite-sized pieces
- ½ tablespoon of mustard powder
- ½ tablespoon of soy sauce
- 1 tablespoon of fresh bleu cheese, crumbled
- 8 medium-sized cherry tomatoes, sliced in half
- 1 cup of fresh arugula, rinsed and patted dry

Directions:
1. Preparing the ingredients. In a small mixing bowl, combine the soy sauce and onion powder; stir with a fork until thoroughly combined.
2. Lay the raw steak strips in the soy-mustard mixture, and fully immerse each piece to marinate.
3. Set the instant crisp air fryer to 320 degrees for 10 minutes.
4. Arrange the soy-mustard marinated steak pieces on a piece of tin foil, flat and not overlapping, and set the tin foil on one side of the instant crisp air fryer basket. The foil should not take up more than half of the surface.
5. Lay the hoagie-bun halves, crusty-side up and soft-side down, on the other half of the air-fryer.
6. Air frying. Close air fryer lid.
7. After 10 minutes, the instant crisp air fryer will shut off; the hoagie buns should be starting to crisp and the steak will have begun to cook.
8. Carefully, flip the hoagie buns so they are now crusty-side down and soft-side up; crumble a layer of the bleu cheese on each hoagie half.
9. With a long spoon, gently stir the marinated steak in the foil to ensure even coverage.
10. Set the instant crisp air fryer to 360 degrees for 6 minutes.
11. After 6 minutes, when the fryer shuts off, the bleu cheese will be perfectly melted over the toasted bread, and the steak will be juicy on the inside and crispy on the outside.
12. Remove the cheesy hoagie halves first, using tongs, and set on a serving plate; then cover one side with the steak, and top with the cherry-tomato halves and the arugula.

Close with the other cheesy hoagie-half, slice into two pieces, and enjoy.

- **Nutrition Info:** Calories 284 Total fat 7.9 g Saturated fat 1.4 g Cholesterol 36 mg Sodium 704 mg Total carbs 46 g Fiber 3.6 g Sugar 5.5 g Protein 17.9 g

118.Zucchini And Cauliflower Stew

Servings: 4
Cooking Time: 12 Minutes
Ingredients:

- 1 cauliflower head, florets separated
- 1 ½ cups zucchinis; sliced
- 1 handful parsley leaves; chopped.
- ½ cup tomato puree
- 2 green onions; chopped.
- 1 tbsp. balsamic vinegar
- 1 tbsp. olive oil
- Salt and black pepper to taste.

Directions:

1. In a pan that fits your air fryer, mix the zucchinis with the rest of the ingredients except the parsley, toss, introduce the pan in the air fryer and cook at 380°F for 20 minutes
2. Divide into bowls and serve for lunch with parsley sprinkled on top.

- **Nutrition Info:** Calories: 193; Fat: 5g; Fiber: 2g; Carbs: 4g; Protein: 7g

119.Amazing Mac And Cheese

Servings:
Cooking Time: 12 Minutes
Ingredients:

- 1 cup cooked macaroni
- 1/2 cup warm milk
- 1 tablespoon parmesan cheese
- 1 cup grated cheddar cheese
- salt and pepper; to taste

Directions:

1. Preheat the Air Fryer to 350 - degrees Fahrenheit. Stir all of the ingredients; except Parmesan, in a baking dish.
2. Place the dish inside the Air Fryer and cook for 10 minutes. Top with the Parmesan cheese.

120.Balsamic Roasted Chicken

Servings: 4
Cooking Time: 1 Hour
Ingredients:

- 1/2 cup balsamic vinegar
- 1/4 cup Dijon mustard
- 1/3 cup olive oil
- Juice and zest from 1 lemon
- 3 minced garlic cloves
- 1 teaspoon salt
- 1 teaspoon pepper
- 4 bone-in, skin-on chicken thighs

- 4 bone-in, skin-on chicken drumsticks
- 1 tablespoon chopped parsley

Directions:

1. Mix vinegar, lemon juice, mustard, olive oil, garlic, salt, and pepper in a bowl, then pour into a sauce pan.
2. Roll chicken pieces in the pan, then cover and marinate for at least 2 hours, but up to 24 hours.
3. Preheat the toaster oven to 400°F and place the chicken on a fresh baking sheet, reserving the marinade for later.
4. Roast the chicken for 50 minutes.
5. Remove the chicken and cover it with foil to keep it warm. Place the marinade in the toaster oven for about 5 minutes until it simmers down and begins to thicken.
6. Pour marinade over chicken and sprinkle with parsley and lemon zest.

- **Nutrition Info:** Calories: 1537, Sodium: 1383 mg, Dietary Fiber: 0.8 g, Total Fat: 70.5 g, Total Carbs: 2.4 g, Protein: 210.4 g.

121.Vegetarian Philly Sandwich

Servings: 2
Cooking Time: 20 Minutes
Ingredients:

- 2 tablespoons olive oil
- 8 ounces sliced portabello mushrooms
- 1 vidalia onion, thinly sliced
- 1 green bell pepper, thinly sliced
- 1 red bell pepper, thinly sliced
- Salt and pepper
- 4 slices 2% provolone cheese
- 4 rolls

Directions:

1. Preheat toaster oven to 475°F.
2. Heat the oil in a medium sauce pan over medium heat.
3. Sauté mushrooms about 5 minutes, then add the onions and peppers and sauté another 10 minutes.
4. Slice rolls lengthwise and divide the vegetables into each roll.
5. Add the cheese and toast until the rolls start to brown and the cheese melts.

- **Nutrition Info:** Calories: 645, Sodium: 916 mg, Dietary Fiber: 7.2 g, Total Fat: 33.3 g, Total Carbs: 61.8 g, Protein: 27.1 g.

122.Ricotta Toasts With Salmon

Servings: 2
Cooking Time: 4 Minutes
Ingredients:

- 4 bread slices
- 1 garlic clove, minced
- 8 oz. ricotta cheese
- 1 teaspoon lemon zest
- Freshly ground black pepper, to taste

- 4 oz. smoked salmon

Directions:
1. In a food processor, add the garlic, ricotta, lemon zest and black pepper and pulse until smooth.
2. Spread ricotta mixture over each bread slices evenly.
3. Press "Power Button" of Air Fry Oven and turn the dial to select the "Air Fry" mode.
4. Press the Time button and again turn the dial to set the cooking time to 4 minutes.
5. Now push the Temp button and rotate the dial to set the temperature at 355 degrees F.
6. Press "Start/Pause" button to start.
7. When the unit beeps to show that it is preheated, open the lid and lightly, grease the sheet pan.
8. Arrange the bread slices into "Air Fry Basket" and insert in the oven.
9. Top with salmon and serve.
- **Nutrition Info:** Calories: 274 Cal Total Fat: 12 g Saturated Fat: 6.3 g Cholesterol: 48 mg Sodium: 1300 mg Total Carbs: 15.7 g Fiber: 0.5 g Sugar: 1.2 g Protein: 24.8 g

123.Chicken Wings With Prawn Paste

Servings: 6
Cooking Time: 8 Minutes
Ingredients:
- Corn flour, as required
- 2 pounds mid-joint chicken wings
- 2 tablespoons prawn paste
- 4 tablespoons olive oil
- 1½ teaspoons sugar
- 2 teaspoons sesame oil
- 1 teaspoon Shaoxing wine
- 2 teaspoons fresh ginger juice

Directions:
1. Preheat the Air fryer to 360 degree F and grease an Air fryer basket.
2. Mix all the ingredients in a bowl except wings and corn flour.
3. Rub the chicken wings generously with marinade and refrigerate overnight.
4. Coat the chicken wings evenly with corn flour and keep aside.
5. Set the Air fryer to 390 degree F and arrange the chicken wings in the Air fryer basket.
6. Cook for about 8 minutes and dish out to serve hot.
- **Nutrition Info:** Calories: 416, Fat: 31.5g, Carbohydrates: 11.2g, Sugar: 1.6g, Protein: 24.4g, Sodium: 661mg

124.Roasted Garlic(2)

Servings: 12 Cloves
Cooking Time: 12 Minutes
Ingredients:

- 1 medium head garlic
- 2 tsp. avocado oil

Directions:
1. Remove any hanging excess peel from the garlic but leave the cloves covered. Cut off ¼ of the head of garlic, exposing the tips of the cloves
2. Drizzle with avocado oil. Place the garlic head into a small sheet of aluminum foil, completely enclosing it. Place it into the air fryer basket. Adjust the temperature to 400 Degrees F and set the timer for 20 minutes. If your garlic head is a bit smaller, check it after 15 minutes
3. When done, garlic should be golden brown and very soft
4. To serve, cloves should pop out and easily be spread or sliced. Store in an airtight container in the refrigerator up to 5 days.
5. You may also freeze individual cloves on a baking sheet, then store together in a freezer-safe storage bag once frozen.
- **Nutrition Info:** Calories: 11; Protein: 2g; Fiber: 1g; Fat: 7g; Carbs: 0g

125.Baked Shrimp Scampi

Servings: 4
Cooking Time: 10 Minutes
Ingredients:
- 1 lb large shrimp
- 8 tbsp butter
- 1 tbsp minced garlic (use 2 for extra garlic flavor)
- 1/4 cup white wine or cooking sherry
- 1/2 tsp salt
- 1/4 tsp cayenne pepper
- 1/4 tsp paprika
- 1/2 tsp onion powder
- 3/4 cup bread crumbs

Directions:
1. Take a bowl and mix the bread crumbs with dry seasonings.
2. On the stovetop (or in the Instant Pot on saute), melt the butter with the garlic and the white wine.
3. Remove from heat and add the shrimp and the bread crumb mix.
4. Transfer the mix to a casserole dish.
5. Choose the Bake operation and add food to the Instant Pot Duo Crisp Air Fryer. Close the lid and Bake at 350°F for 10 minutes or until they are browned.
6. Serve and enjoy.
- **Nutrition Info:** Calories 422, Total Fat 26g, Total Carbs 18g, Protein 29 g

126.Perfect Size French Fries

Servings: 1
Cooking Time: 30 Minutes

Ingredients:

- 1 medium potato
- 1 tablespoon olive oil
- Salt and pepper to taste

Directions:

1. Start by preheating your oven to 425°F.
2. Clean the potato and cut it into fries or wedges.
3. Place fries in a bowl of cold water to rinse.
4. Lay the fries on a thick sheet of paper towels and pat dry.
5. Toss in a bowl with oil, salt, and pepper.
6. Bake for 30 minutes.
- **Nutrition Info:** Calories: 284, Sodium: 13 mg, Dietary Fiber: 4.7 g, Total Fat: 14.2 g, Total Carbs: 37.3 g, Protein: 4.3 g.

127.Carrot And Beef Cocktail Balls

Servings: 10
Cooking Time: 20 Minutes
Ingredients:

- 1-pound ground beef
- 2 carrots
- 1 red onion, peeled and chopped
- 2 cloves garlic
- 1/2 teaspoon dried rosemary, crushed
- 1/2 teaspoon dried basil
- 1 teaspoon dried oregano
- 1 egg
- 3/4 cup breadcrumbs
- 1/2 teaspoon salt
- 1/2 teaspoon black pepper, or to taste
- 1 cup plain flour

Directions:

1. Preparing the ingredients. Place ground beef in a large bowl.
2. In a food processor, pulse the carrot, onion and garlic; transfer the vegetable mixture to a large-sized bowl.
3. Then, add the rosemary, basil, oregano, egg, breadcrumbs, salt, and black pepper.
4. Shape the mixture into even balls; refrigerate for about 30 minutes.
5. Roll the balls into the flour.
6. Air frying. Close air fryer lid.
7. Then, air-fry the balls at 350 degrees f for about 20 minutes, turning occasionally; work with batches. Serve with toothpicks.
- **Nutrition Info:** Calories 284 Total fat 7.9 g Saturated fat 1.4 g Cholesterol 36 mg Sodium 704 mg Total carbs 46 g Fiber 3.6 g Sugar 5.5 g Protein 17.9 g

128.Persimmon Toast With Sour Cream & Cinnamon

Servings: 1
Cooking Time: 5 Minutes
Ingredients:

- 1 slice of wheat bread
- 1/2 persimmon
- Sour cream to taste
- Sugar to taste
- Cinnamon to taste

Directions:

1. Spread a thin layer of sour cream across the bread.
2. Slice the persimmon into 1/4 inch pieces and lay them across the bread.
3. Sprinkle cinnamon and sugar over persimmon.
4. Toast in toaster oven until bread and persimmon begin to brown.
- **Nutrition Info:** Calories: 89, Sodium: 133 mg, Dietary Fiber: 2.0 g, Total Fat: 1.1 g, Total Carbs: 16.5 g, Protein: 3.8 g.

129.Lemon Chicken Breasts

Servings: 4
Cooking Time: 30 Minutes
Ingredients:

- 1/4 cup olive oil
- 3 tablespoons garlic, minced
- 1/3 cup dry white wine
- 1 tablespoon lemon zest, grated
- 2 tablespoons lemon juice
- 1 1/2 teaspoons dried oregano, crushed
- 1 teaspoon thyme leaves, minced
- Salt and black pepper
- 4 skin-on boneless chicken breasts
- 1 lemon, sliced

Directions:

1. Whisk everything in a baking pan to coat the chicken breasts well.
2. Place the lemon slices on top of the chicken breasts.
3. Spread the mustard mixture over the toasted bread slices.
4. Press "Power Button" of Air Fry Oven and turn the dial to select the "Bake" mode.
5. Press the Time button and again turn the dial to set the cooking time to 30 minutes.
6. Now push the Temp button and rotate the dial to set the temperature at 370 degrees F.
7. Once preheated, place the baking pan inside and close its lid.
8. Serve warm.
- **Nutrition Info:** Calories 388 Total Fat 8 g Saturated Fat 1 g Cholesterol 153mg sodium 339 mg Total Carbs 8 g Fiber 1 g Sugar 2 g Protein 13 g

130.Roasted Stuffed Peppers

Servings: 4
Cooking Time: 20 Minutes
Ingredients:

- 4 ounces shredded cheddar cheese
- ½ tsp. Pepper
- ½ tsp. Salt

- 1 tsp. Worcestershire sauce
- ½ c. Tomato sauce
- 8 ounces lean ground beef
- 1 tsp. Olive oil
- 1 minced garlic clove
- ½ chopped onion
- 2 green peppers

Directions:

1. Preparing the ingredients. Ensure your instant crisp air fryer is preheated to 390 degrees. Spray with olive oil.
2. Cut stems off bell peppers and remove seeds. Cook in boiling salted water for 3 minutes.
3. Sauté garlic and onion together in a skillet until golden in color.
4. Take skillet off the heat. Mix pepper, salt, Worcestershire sauce, ¼ cup of tomato sauce, half of cheese and beef together.
5. Divide meat mixture into pepper halves. Top filled peppers with remaining cheese and tomato sauce.
6. Place filled peppers in the instant crisp air fryer.
7. Air frying. Close air fryer lid. Set temperature to 390°f, and set time to 20 minutes, bake 15-20 minutes.
- **Nutrition Info:** Calories: 295; Fat: 8g; Protein:23g; Sugar:2g

131.Turkey And Mushroom Stew

Servings: 4
Cooking Time: 12 Minutes
Ingredients:

- ½ lb. brown mushrooms; sliced
- 1 turkey breast, skinless, boneless; cubed and browned
- ¼ cup tomato sauce
- 1 tbsp. parsley; chopped.
- Salt and black pepper to taste.

Directions:

1. In a pan that fits your air fryer, mix the turkey with the mushrooms, salt, pepper and tomato sauce, toss, introduce in the fryer and cook at 350°F for 25 minutes
2. Divide into bowls and serve for lunch with parsley sprinkled on top.
- **Nutrition Info:** Calories: 220; Fat: 12g; Fiber: 2g; Carbs: 5g; Protein: 12g

132.Easy Turkey Breasts With Basil

Servings: 4
Cooking Time: 10 Minutes
Ingredients:

- 2 tablespoons olive oil
- 2 pounds turkey breasts, bone-in skin-on
- Coarse sea salt and ground black pepper, to taste
- 1 teaspoon fresh basil leaves, chopped
- 2 tablespoons lemon zest, grated

Directions:

1. Rub olive oil on all sides of the turkey breasts; sprinkle with salt, pepper, basil, and lemon zest.
2. Place the turkey breasts skin side up on a parchment-lined cooking basket.
3. Cook in the preheated Air Fryer at 330 degrees F for 30 minutes. Now, turn them over and cook an additional 28 minutes.
4. Serve with lemon wedges, if desired.
- **Nutrition Info:** 416 Calories; 26g Fat; 0g Carbs; 49g Protein; 0g Sugars; 2g Fiber

133.Greek Lamb Meatballs

Servings: 12
Cooking Time: 12 Minutes
Ingredients:

- 1 pound ground lamb
- ½ cup breadcrumbs
- ¼ cup milk
- 2 egg yolks
- 1 teaspoon ground coriander
- 1 teaspoon ground cumin
- 3 garlic cloves, minced
- 1 teaspoon dried oregano
- ½ teaspoon salt
- ½ teaspoon black pepper
- 1 lemon, juiced and zested
- ¼ cup fresh parsley, chopped
- ½ cup crumbled feta cheese
- Olive oil, for shaping
- Tzatziki, for dipping

Directions:

1. Combine all ingredients except olive oil in a large mixing bowl and mix until fully incorporated.
2. Form 12 meatballs, about 2 ounces each. Use olive oil on your hands so they don't stick to the meatballs. Set aside.
3. Select the Broil function on the COSORI Air Fryer Toaster Oven, set time to 12 minutes, then press Start/Cancel to preheat.
4. Place the meatballs on the food tray, then insert the tray at top position in the preheated air fryer toaster oven. Press Start/Cancel.
5. Take out the meatballs when done and serve with a side of tzatziki.
- **Nutrition Info:** Calories: 129 kcal Total Fat: 6.4 g Saturated Fat: 0 g Cholesterol: 0 mg Sodium: 0 mg Total Carbs: 4.9 g Fiber: 0 g Sugar: 0 g Protein: 12.9 g

134.Buttermilk Brined Turkey Breast

Servings: 8
Cooking Time: 20 Minutes
Ingredients:

- ¾ cup brine from a can of olives

- 3½ pounds boneless, skinless turkey breast
- 2 fresh thyme sprigs
- 1 fresh rosemary sprig
- ½ cup buttermilk

Directions:
1. Preheat the Air fryer to 350 degree F and grease an Air fryer basket.
2. Mix olive brine and buttermilk in a bowl until well combined.
3. Place the turkey breast, buttermilk mixture and herb sprigs in a resealable plastic bag.
4. Seal the bag and refrigerate for about 12 hours.
5. Remove the turkey breast from bag and arrange the turkey breast into the Air fryer basket.
6. Cook for about 20 minutes, flipping once in between.
7. Dish out the turkey breast onto a cutting board and cut into desired size slices to serve.
- **Nutrition Info:** Calories: 215, Fat: 3.5g, Carbohydrates: 9.4g, Sugar: 7.7g, Protein: 34.4g, Sodium: 2000mg

135.Kale And Pine Nuts

Servings: 4
Cooking Time: 12 Minutes
Ingredients:
- 10 cups kale; torn
- 1/3 cup pine nuts
- 2 tbsp. lemon zest; grated
- 1 tbsp. lemon juice
- 2 tbsp. olive oil
- Salt and black pepper to taste.

Directions:
1. In a pan that fits the air fryer, combine all the ingredients, toss, introduce the pan in the machine and cook at 380°F for 15 minutes
2. Divide between plates and serve as a side dish.
- **Nutrition Info:** Calories: 121; Fat: 9g; Fiber: 2g; Carbs: 4g; Protein: 5g

136.Lime And Mustard Marinated Chicken

Servings: 4
Cooking Time: 10 Minutes
Ingredients:
- 1/2 teaspoon stone-ground mustard
- 1/2 teaspoon minced fresh oregano
- 1/3 cup freshly squeezed lime juice
- 2 small-sized chicken breasts, skin-on
- 1 teaspoon kosher salt
- 1teaspoon freshly cracked mixed peppercorns

Directions:
1. Preheat your Air Fryer to 345 degrees F.

2. Toss all of the above ingredients in a medium-sized mixing dish; allow it to marinate overnight.
3. Cook in the preheated Air Fryer for 26 minutes.
- **Nutrition Info:** 255 Calories; 15g Fat; 7g Carbs; 33g Protein; 8g Sugars; 3g Fiber

137.Skinny Black Bean Flautas

Servings: 10
Cooking Time: 25 Minutes
Ingredients:
- 2 (15-ounce) cans black beans
- 1 cup shredded cheddar
- 1 (4-ounce) can diced green chilies
- 2 teaspoons taco seasoning
- 10 (8-inch) whole wheat flour tortillas
- Olive oil

Directions:
1. Start by preheating toaster oven to 350°F.
2. Drain black beans and mash in a medium bowl with a fork.
3. Mix in cheese, chilies, and taco seasoning until all ingredients are thoroughly combined.
4. Evenly spread the mixture over each tortilla and wrap tightly.
5. Brush each side lightly with olive oil and place on a baking sheet.
6. Bake for 12 minutes, turn, and bake for another 13 minutes.
- **Nutrition Info:** Calories: 367, Sodium: 136 mg, Dietary Fiber: 14.4 g, Total Fat: 2.8 g, Total Carbs: 64.8 g, Protein: 22.6 g.

138.Nutmeg Chicken Thighs

Servings: 4
Cooking Time: 10 Minutes
Ingredients:
- 2 lb. chicken thighs
- 2 tbsp. olive oil
- ½ tsp. nutmeg, ground
- A pinch of salt and black pepper

Directions:
1. Season the chicken thighs with salt and pepper and rub with the rest of the ingredients
2. Put the chicken thighs in air fryer's basket, cook at 360°F for 15 minutes on each side, divide between plates and serve.
- **Nutrition Info:** Calories: 271; Fat: 12g; Fiber: 4g; Carbs: 6g; Protein: 13g

139.Basic Roasted Tofu

Servings: 4
Cooking Time: 45 Minutes
Ingredients:
- 1 or more (16-ounce) containers extra-firm tofu

- 1 tablespoon sesame oil
- 1 tablespoon soy sauce
- 1 tablespoon rice vinegar
- 1 tablespoon water

Directions:
1. Start by drying the tofu: first pat dry with paper towels, then lay on another set of paper towels or a dish towel.
2. Put a plate on top of the tofu then put something heavy on the plate (like a large can of vegetables). Leave it there for at least 20 minutes.
3. While tofu is being pressed, whip up marinade by combining oil, soy sauce, vinegar, and water in a bowl and set aside.
4. Cut the tofu into squares or sticks. Place the tofu in the marinade for at least 30 minutes.
5. Preheat toaster oven to 350°F. Line a pan with parchment paper and add as many pieces of tofu as you can, giving each piece adequate space.
6. Bake 20–45 minutes; tofu is done when the outside edges look golden brown. Time will vary depending on tofu size and shape.
- **Nutrition Info:** Calories: 114, Sodium: 239 mg, Dietary Fiber: 1.1 g, Total Fat: 8.1 g, Total Carbs: 2.2 g, Protein: 9.5 g.

140.Chives Radishes

Servings: 4
Cooking Time: 12 Minutes
Ingredients:
- 20 radishes; halved
- 2 tbsp. olive oil
- 1 tbsp. garlic; minced
- 1 tsp. chives; chopped.
- Salt and black pepper to taste.

Directions:
1. In your air fryer's pan, combine all the ingredients and toss.
2. Introduce the pan in the machine and cook at 370°F for 15 minutes
3. Divide between plates and serve as a side dish.
- **Nutrition Info:** Calories: 160; Fat: 2g; Fiber: 3g; Carbs: 4g; Protein: 6g

141.Parmesan-crusted Pork Loin

Servings: 4
Cooking Time: 20 Minutes
Ingredients:
- 1 pound pork loin
- 1 teaspoon salt
- 1/2 tablespoon garlic powder
- 1/2 tablespoon onion powder
- 2 tablespoons parmesan cheese
- 1 tablespoon olive oil

Directions:
1. Start by preheating toaster oven to 475°F.
2. Place pan in the oven and let it heat while the oven preheats.

3. Mix all ingredients in a shallow dish and roll the pork loin until it is fully coated.
4. Remove pan and sear the pork in the pan on each side.
5. Once seared, bake pork in the pan for 20 minutes.
- **Nutrition Info:** Calories: 334, Sodium: 718 mg, Dietary Fiber: 0 g, Total Fat: 20.8 g, Total Carbs: 1.7 g, Protein: 33.5 g.

142.Herbed Radish Sauté(3)

Servings: 4
Cooking Time: 12 Minutes
Ingredients:
- 2 bunches red radishes; halved
- 2 tbsp. parsley; chopped.
- 2 tbsp. balsamic vinegar
- 1 tbsp. olive oil
- Salt and black pepper to taste.

Directions:
1. Take a bowl and mix the radishes with the remaining ingredients except the parsley, toss and put them in your air fryer's basket.
2. Cook at 400°F for 15 minutes, divide between plates, sprinkle the parsley on top and serve as a side dish
- **Nutrition Info:** Calories: 180; Fat: 4g; Fiber: 2g; Carbs: 3g; Protein: 5g

143.Chicken Breast With Rosemary

Servings: 4
Cooking Time: 60 Minutes
Ingredients:
- 4 bone-in chicken breast halves
- 3 tablespoons softened butter
- 1/2 teaspoon salt
- 1/4 teaspoon pepper
- 1 tablespoon rosemary
- 1 tablespoon extra-virgin olive oil

Directions:
1. Start by preheating toaster oven to 400°F.
2. Mix butter, salt, pepper, and rosemary in a bowl.
3. Coat chicken with the butter mixture and place in a shallow pan.
4. Drizzle oil over chicken and roast for 25 minutes.
5. Flip chicken and roast for another 20 minutes.
6. Flip chicken one more time and roast for a final 15 minutes.
- **Nutrition Info:** Calories: 392, Sodium: 551 mg, Dietary Fiber: 0 g, Total Fat: 18.4 g, Total Carbs: 0.6 g, Protein: 55.4 g.

144.Beer Coated Duck Breast

Servings: 2
Cooking Time: 20 Minutes
Ingredients:
- 1 tablespoon fresh thyme, chopped
- 1 cup beer
- 1: 10½-ouncesduck breast

- 6 cherry tomatoes
- 1 tablespoon olive oil
- 1 teaspoon mustard
- Salt and ground black pepper, as required
- 1 tablespoon balsamic vinegar

Directions:
1. Preheat the Air fryer to 390 degree F and grease an Air fryer basket.
2. Mix the olive oil, mustard, thyme, beer, salt, and black pepper in a bowl.
3. Coat the duck breasts generously with marinade and refrigerate, covered for about 4 hours.
4. Cover the duck breasts and arrange into the Air fryer basket.
5. Cook for about 15 minutes and remove the foil from breast.
6. Set the Air fryer to 355 degree F and place the duck breast and tomatoes into the Air Fryer basket.
7. Cook for about 5 minutes and dish out the duck breasts and cherry tomatoes.
8. Drizzle with vinegar and serve immediately.
- **Nutrition Info:** Calories: 332, Fat: 13.7g, Carbohydrates: 9.2g, Sugar: 2.5g, Protein: 34.6g, Sodium: 88mg

145.Okra Casserole

Servings: 4
Cooking Time: 12 Minutes
Ingredients:
- 2 red bell peppers; cubed
- 2 tomatoes; chopped.
- 3 garlic cloves; minced
- 3 cups okra
- ½ cup cheddar; shredded
- ¼ cup tomato puree
- 1 tbsp. cilantro; chopped.
- 1 tsp. olive oil
- 2 tsp. coriander, ground
- Salt and black pepper to taste.

Directions:
1. Grease a heat proof dish that fits your air fryer with the oil, add all the ingredients except the cilantro and the cheese and toss them really gently
2. Sprinkle the cheese and the cilantro on top, introduce the dish in the fryer and cook at 390°F for 20 minutes.
3. Divide between plates and serve for lunch.
- **Nutrition Info:** Calories: 221; Fat: 7g; Fiber: 2g; Carbs: 4g; Protein: 9g

146.Simple Lamb Bbq With Herbed Salt

Servings: 8
Cooking Time: 1 Hour 20 Minutes
Ingredients:
- 2 ½ tablespoons herb salt
- 2 tablespoons olive oil
- 4 pounds boneless leg of lamb, cut into 2-inch chunks

Directions:

1. Preheat the air fryer to 390 ºF.
2. Place the grill pan accessory in the air fryer.
3. Season the meat with the herb salt and brush with olive oil.
4. Grill the meat for 20 minutes per batch.
5. Make sure to flip the meat every 10 minutes for even cooking.
- **Nutrition Info:** Calories: 347 kcal Total Fat: 17.8 g Saturated Fat: 0 g Cholesterol: 0 mg Sodium: 0 mg Total Carbs: 0 g Fiber: 0 g Sugar: 0 g Protein: 46.6 g

147.Marinated Chicken Parmesan

Servings: 4
Cooking Time: 20 Minutes
Ingredients:
- 2 cups breadcrumbs
- 1 teaspoon dried oregano
- 1/2 teaspoon garlic powder
- 4 teaspoons paprika
- 1/2 teaspoon salt
- 1/2 teaspoon black pepper
- 2 egg whites
- 1/2 cup skim milk
- 1/2 cup flour
- 4 (6 oz.) chicken breast halves, lb.ed
- Cooking spray
- 1 jar marinara sauce
- 3/4 cup mozzarella cheese, shredded
- 2 tablespoons Parmesan, shredded

Directions:
1. Whisk the flour with all the spices in a bowl and beat the eggs in another.
2. Coat the pounded chicken with flour then dip in the egg whites.
3. Dredge the chicken breast through the crumbs well.
4. Spread marinara sauce in a baking dish and place the crusted chicken on it.
5. Drizzle cheese on top of the chicken.
6. Press "Power Button" of Air Fry Oven and turn the dial to select the "Bake" mode.
7. Press the Time button and again turn the dial to set the cooking time to 20 minutes.
8. Now push the Temp button and rotate the dial to set the temperature at 400 degrees F.
9. Once preheated, place the baking pan inside and close its lid.
10. Serve warm.
- **Nutrition Info:** Calories 361 Total Fat 16.3 g Saturated Fat 4.9 g Cholesterol 114 mg Sodium 515 mg Total Carbs 19.3 g Fiber 0.1 g Sugar 18.2 g Protein 33.3 g

148.Country Comfort Corn Bread

Servings: 12
Cooking Time: 20 Minutes
Ingredients:
- 1 cup yellow cornmeal
- 1-1/2 cups oatmeal
- 1/4 teaspoon salt
- 1/4 cup granulated sugar

- 2 teaspoons baking powder
- 1 cup milk
- 1 large egg
- 1/2 cup applesauce

Directions:
1. Start by blending oatmeal into a fine powder.
2. Preheat toaster oven to 400°F.
3. Mix oatmeal, cornmeal, salt, sugar, and baking powder, and stir to blend.
4. Add milk, egg, and applesauce, and mix well.
5. Pour into a pan and bake for 20 minutes.
- **Nutrition Info:** Calories: 113, Sodium: 71 mg, Dietary Fiber: 1.9 g, Total Fat: 1.9 g, Total Carbs: 21.5 g, Protein: 3.4 g.

149.Cheddar & Cream Omelet

Servings: 2
Cooking Time: 8 Minutes
Ingredients:
- 4 eggs
- ¼ cup cream
- Salt and ground black pepper, as required
- ¼ cup Cheddar cheese, grated

Directions:
1. In a bowl, add the eggs, cream, salt, and black pepper and beat well.
2. Place the egg mixture into a small baking pan.
3. Press "Power Button" of Air Fry Oven and turn the dial to select the "Air Fry" mode.
4. Press the Time button and again turn the dial to set the cooking time to 8 minutes.
5. Now push the Temp button and rotate the dial to set the temperature at 350 degrees F.
6. Press "Start/Pause" button to start.
7. When the unit beeps to show that it is preheated, open the lid.
8. Arrange pan over the "Wire Rack" and insert in the oven.
9. After 4 minutes, sprinkle the omelet with cheese evenly.
10. Cut the omelet into 2 portions and serve hot.
11. Cut into equal-sized wedges and serve hot.
- **Nutrition Info:** Calories: 202 Cal Total Fat: 15.1 g Saturated Fat: 6.8 g Cholesterol: 348 mg Sodium: 298 mg Total Carbs: 1.8 g Fiber: 0 g Sugar: 1.4 g Protein: 14.8 g

150.Chicken Breasts With Chimichurri

Servings: 1
Cooking Time: 35 Minutes
Ingredients:
- 1 chicken breast, bone-in, skin-on
- Chimichurri
- ½ bunch fresh cilantro
- 1/4 bunch fresh parsley
- ½ shallot, peeled, cut in quarters
- ½ tablespoon paprika ground
- ½ tablespoon chili powder
- ½ tablespoon fennel ground
- ½ teaspoon black pepper, ground

- ½ teaspoon onion powder
- 1 teaspoon salt
- ½ teaspoon garlic powder
- ½ teaspoon cumin ground
- ½ tablespoon canola oil
- Chimichurri
- 2 tablespoons olive oil
- 4 garlic cloves, peeled
- Zest and juice of 1 lemon
- 1 teaspoon kosher salt

Directions:
1. Preheat the Air fryer to 300 degree F and grease an Air fryer basket.
2. Combine all the spices in a suitable bowl and season the chicken with it.
3. Sprinkle with canola oil and arrange the chicken in the Air fryer basket.
4. Cook for about 35 minutes and dish out in a platter.
5. Put all the ingredients in the blender and blend until smooth.
6. Serve the chicken with chimichurri sauce.
- **Nutrition Info:** Calories: 140, Fats: 7.9g, Carbohydrates: 1.8g, Sugar: 7.1g, Proteins: 7.2g, Sodium: 581mg

151.Roasted Beet Salad With Oranges & Beet Greens

Servings: 6
Cooking Time: 1-1/2 Hours
Ingredients:
- 6 medium beets with beet greens attached
- 2 large oranges
- 1 small sweet onion, cut into wedges
- 1/3 cup red wine vinegar
- 1/4 cup extra-virgin olive oil
- 2 garlic cloves, minced
- 1/2 teaspoon grated orange peel

Directions:
1. Start by preheating toaster oven to 400°F.
2. Trim leaves from beets and chop, then set aside.
3. Pierce beets with a fork and place in a roasting pan.
4. Roast beets for 1-1/2 hours.
5. Allow beets to cool, peel, then cut into 8 wedges and put into a bowl.
6. Place beet greens in a sauce pan and cover with just enough water to cover. Heat until water boils, then immediately remove from heat.
7. Drain greens and press to remove liquid from greens, then add to beet bowl.
8. Remove peel and pith from orange and segment, adding each segment to the bowl.
9. Add onion to beet mixture. In a separate bowl mix together vinegar, oil, garlic and orange peel.
10. Combine both bowls and toss, sprinkle with salt and pepper.
11. Let stand for an hour before serving.

- **Nutrition Info:** Calories: 214, Sodium: 183 mg, Dietary Fiber: 6.5 g, Total Fat: 8.9 g, Total Carbs: 32.4 g, Protein: 4.7 g.

152.Buttered Duck Breasts

Servings: 4
Cooking Time: 22 Minutes
Ingredients:
- 2: 12-ouncesduck breasts
- 3 tablespoons unsalted butter, melted
- Salt and ground black pepper, as required
- ½ teaspoon dried thyme, crushed
- ¼ teaspoon star anise powder

Directions:
1. Preheat the Air fryer to 390 degree F and grease an Air fryer basket.
2. Season the duck breasts generously with salt and black pepper.
3. Arrange the duck breasts into the prepared Air fryer basket and cook for about 10 minutes.
4. Dish out the duck breasts and drizzle with melted butter.
5. Season with thyme and star anise powder and place the duck breasts again into the Air fryer basket.
6. Cook for about 12 more minutes and dish out to serve warm.
- **Nutrition Info:** Calories: 296, Fat: 15.5g, Carbohydrates: 0.1g, Sugar: 0g, Protein: 37.5g, Sodium: 100mg

153.Squash And Zucchini Mini Pizza

Servings: 4
Cooking Time: 15 Minutes
Ingredients:
- 1 pizza crust
- 1/2 cup parmesan cheese
- 4 tablespoons oregano
- 1 zucchini
- 1 yellow summer squash
- Olive oil
- Salt and pepper

Directions:
1. Start by preheating toaster oven to 350°F.
2. If you are using homemade crust, roll out 8 mini portions; if crust is store-bought, use a cookie cutter to cut out the portions.
3. Sprinkle parmesan and oregano equally on each piece. Layer the zucchini and squash in a circle – one on top of the other – around the entire circle.
4. Brush with olive oil and sprinkle salt and pepper to taste.
5. Bake for 15 minutes and serve.
- **Nutrition Info:** Calories: 151, Sodium: 327 mg, Dietary Fiber: 3.1 g, Total Fat: 8.6 g, Total Carbs: 10.3 g, Protein: 11.4 g.

154.Boneless Air Fryer Turkey Breasts

Servings: 4
Cooking Time: 50 Minutes
Ingredients:
- 3 lb boneless breast
- ¼ cup mayonnaise
- 2 tsp poultry seasoning
- 1 tsp salt
- ½ tsp garlic powder
- ¼ tsp black pepper

Directions:
1. Choose the Air Fry option on the Instant Pot Duo Crisp Air fryer. Set the temperature to 360°F and push start. The preheating will start.
2. Season your boneless turkey breast with mayonnaise, poultry seasoning, salt, garlic powder, and black pepper.
3. Once preheated, Air Fry the turkey breasts on 360°F for 1 hour, turning every 15 minutes or until internal temperature has reached a temperature of 165°F.
- **Nutrition Info:** Calories 558, Total Fat 18g, Total Carbs 1g, Protein 98g

155.Lobster Tails

Servings: 2
Cooking Time: 8 Minutes
Ingredients:
- 2 6oz lobster tails
- 1 tsp salt
- 1 tsp chopped chives
- 2 Tbsp unsalted butter melted
- 1 Tbsp minced garlic
- 1 tsp lemon juice

Directions:
1. Combine butter, garlic, salt, chives, and lemon juice to prepare butter mixture.
2. Butterfly lobster tails by cutting through shell followed by removing the meat and resting it on top of the shell.
3. Place them on the tray in the Instant Pot Duo Crisp Air Fryer basket and spread butter over the top of lobster meat. Close the Air Fryer lid, select the Air Fry option and cook on 380°F for 4 minutes.
4. Open the Air Fryer lid and spread more butter on top, cook for extra 2-4 minutes until done.
- **Nutrition Info:** Calories 120, Total Fat 12g, Total Carbs 2g, Protein 1g

156.Beef Steaks With Beans

Servings: 4
Cooking Time: 10 Minutes
Ingredients:
- 4 beef steaks, trim the fat and cut into strips
- 1 cup green onions, chopped
- 2 cloves garlic, minced
- 1 red bell pepper, seeded and thinly sliced
- 1 can tomatoes, crushed
- 1 can cannellini beans
- 3/4 cup beef broth
- 1/4 teaspoon dried basil
- 1/2 teaspoon cayenne pepper
- 1/2 teaspoon sea salt

- 1/4 teaspoon ground black pepper, or to taste

Directions:
1. Preparing the ingredients. Add the steaks, green onions and garlic to the instant crisp air fryer basket.
2. Air frying. Close air fryer lid. Cook at 390 degrees f for 10 minutes, working in batches.
3. Stir in the remaining ingredients and cook for an additional 5 minutes.
- **Nutrition Info:** Calories 284 Total fat 7.9 g Saturated fat 1.4 g Cholesterol 36 mg Sodium 704 mg Total carbs 46 g Fiber 3.6 g Sugar 5.5 g Protein 17.9 g

157.Tomato Avocado Melt

Servings: 2
Cooking Time: 4 Minutes
Ingredients:
- 4 slices of bread
- 1-2 tablespoons mayonnaise
- Cayenne pepper
- 1 small Roma tomato
- 1/2 avocado
- 8 slices of cheese of your choice

Directions:
1. Start by slicing avocado and tomato and set aside.
2. Spread mayonnaise on the bread.
3. Sprinkle cayenne pepper over the mayo to taste.
4. Layer tomato and avocado on top of cayenne pepper.
5. Top with cheese and put on greased baking sheet.
6. Broil on high for 2–4 minutes, until the cheese is melted and bread is toasted.
- **Nutrition Info:** Calories: 635, Sodium: 874 mg, Dietary Fiber: 4.1 g, Total Fat: 50.1 g, Total Carbs: 17.4 g, Protein: 30.5 g.

158.Chicken Legs With Dilled Brussels Sprouts

Servings: 2
Cooking Time: 10 Minutes
Ingredients:
- 2 chicken legs
- 1/2 teaspoon paprika
- 1/2 teaspoon kosher salt
- 1/2 teaspoon black pepper
- 1/2 pound Brussels sprouts
- 1 teaspoon dill, fresh or dried

Directions:
1. Start by preheating your Air Fryer to 370 degrees F.
2. Now, season your chicken with paprika, salt, and pepper. Transfer the chicken legs to the cooking basket. Cook for 10 minutes.
3. Flip the chicken legs and cook an additional 10 minutes. Reserve.
4. Add the Brussels sprouts to the cooking basket; sprinkle with dill. Cook at 380 degrees F for 15 minutes, shaking the basket halfway through.
5. Serve with the reserved chicken legs.
- **Nutrition Info:** 365 Calories; 21g Fat; 3g Carbs; 36g Protein; 2g Sugars; 3g Fiber

159.Eggplant And Leeks Stew

Servings: 4
Cooking Time: 12 Minutes
Ingredients:
- 2 big eggplants, roughly cubed
- ½ bunch cilantro; chopped.
- 1 cup veggie stock
- 2 garlic cloves; minced
- 3 leeks; sliced
- 2 tbsp. olive oil
- 1 tbsp. hot sauce
- 1 tbsp. sweet paprika
- 1 tbsp. tomato puree
- Salt and black pepper to taste.

Directions:
1. In a pan that fits the air fryer, mix all the ingredients, toss, introduce in the fryer and cook at 380°F for 20 minutes
2. Divide the stew into bowls and serve for lunch.
- **Nutrition Info:** Calories: 183; Fat: 4g; Fiber: 2g; Carbs: 4g; Protein: 12g

160.Maple Chicken Thighs

Servings: 4
Cooking Time: 30 Minutes
Ingredients:
- 4 large chicken thighs, bone-in
- 2 tablespoons French mustard
- 2 tablespoons Dijon mustard
- 1 clove minced garlic
- 1/2 teaspoon dried marjoram
- 2 tablespoons maple syrup

Directions:
1. Mix chicken with everything in a bowl and coat it well.
2. Place the chicken along with its marinade in the baking pan.
3. Press "Power Button" of Air Fry Oven and turn the dial to select the "Bake" mode.
4. Press the Time button and again turn the dial to set the cooking time to 30 minutes.
5. Now push the Temp button and rotate the dial to set the temperature at 370 degrees F.
6. Once preheated, place the baking pan inside and close its lid.
7. Serve warm.
- **Nutrition Info:** Calories 301 Total Fat 15.8 g Saturated Fat 2.7 g Cholesterol 75 mg Sodium 189 mg Total Carbs 31.7 g Fiber 0.3 g Sugar 0.1 g Protein 28.2 g

161.Pecan Crunch Catfish And Asparagus

Servings: 4

Cooking Time: 12 Minutes
Ingredients:
- 1 cup whole wheat panko breadcrumbs
- 1/4 cup chopped pecans
- 3 teaspoons chopped fresh thyme
- 1-1/2 tablespoons extra-virgin olive oil, plus more for the pan
- Salt and pepper to taste
- 1-1/4 pounds asparagus
- 1 tablespoon honey
- 4 (5- to 6-ounce each) catfish filets

Directions:
1. Start by preheating toaster oven to 425°F.
2. Combine breadcrumbs, pecans, 2 teaspoons thyme, 1 tablespoon oil, salt, pepper and 2 tablespoons water.
3. In another bowl combine asparagus, the rest of the thyme, honey, salt, and pepper.
4. Spread the asparagus in a flat layer on a baking sheet. Sprinkle a quarter of the breadcrumb mixture over the asparagus.
5. Lay the catfish over the asparagus and press the rest of the breadcrumb mixture into each piece. Roast for 12 minutes.
- **Nutrition Info:** Calories: 531, Sodium: 291 mg, Dietary Fiber: 6.1 g, Total Fat: 30.4 g, Total Carbs: 31.9 g, Protein: 34.8 g.

162.Okra And Green Beans Stew

Servings: 4
Cooking Time: 12 Minutes
Ingredients:
- 1 lb. green beans; halved
- 4 garlic cloves; minced
- 1 cup okra
- 3 tbsp. tomato sauce
- 1 tbsp. thyme; chopped.
- Salt and black pepper to taste.

Directions:
1. In a pan that fits your air fryer, mix all the ingredients, toss, introduce the pan in the air fryer and cook at 370°F for 15 minutes
2. Divide the stew into bowls and serve.
- **Nutrition Info:** Calories: 183; Fat: 5g; Fiber: 2g; Carbs: 4g; Protein: 8g

163.Chicken Parmesan

Servings: 4
Cooking Time: 10 Minutes
Ingredients:
- 2 (6-oz.boneless, skinless chicken breasts
- 1 oz. pork rinds, crushed
- ½ cup grated Parmesan cheese, divided.
- 1 cup low-carb, no-sugar-added pasta sauce.
- 1 cup shredded mozzarella cheese, divided.
- 4 tbsp. full-fat mayonnaise, divided.
- ½ tsp. garlic powder.
- ¼ tsp. dried oregano.
- ½ tsp. dried parsley.

Directions:
1. Slice each chicken breast in half lengthwise and lb. out to 3/4-inch thickness. Sprinkle with garlic powder, oregano and parsley
2. Spread 1 tbsp. mayonnaise on top of each piece of chicken, then sprinkle ¼ cup mozzarella on each piece.
3. In a small bowl, mix the crushed pork rinds and Parmesan. Sprinkle the mixture on top of mozzarella
4. Pour sauce into 6-inch round baking pan and place chicken on top. Place pan into the air fryer basket. Adjust the temperature to 320 Degrees F and set the timer for 25 minutes
5. Cheese will be browned and internal temperature of the chicken will be at least 165 Degrees F when fully cooked. Serve warm.
- **Nutrition Info:** Calories: 393; Protein: 32g; Fiber: 1g; Fat: 28g; Carbs: 8g

164.Kalamta Mozarella Pita Melts

Servings: 2
Cooking Time: 5 Minutes
Ingredients:
- 2 (6-inch) whole wheat pitas
- 1 teaspoon extra-virgin olive oil
- 1 cup grated part-skim mozzarella cheese
- 1/4 small red onion
- 1/4 cup pitted Kalamata olives
- 2 tablespoons chopped fresh herbs such as parsley, basil, or oregano

Directions:
1. Start by preheating toaster oven to 425°F.
2. Brush the pita on both sides with oil and warm in the oven for one minute.
3. Dice onions and halve olives.
4. Sprinkle mozzarella over each pita and top with onion and olive.
5. Return to the oven for another 5 minutes or until the cheese is melted.
6. Sprinkle herbs over the pita and serve.
- **Nutrition Info:** Calories: 387, Sodium: 828 mg, Dietary Fiber: 7.4 g, Total Fat: 16.2 g, Total Carbs: 42.0 g, Protein: 23.0 g.

165.Creamy Chicken Tenders

Servings: 8
Cooking Time: 20 Minutes
Ingredients:
- 2 pounds chicken tenders
- 1 cup feta cheese
- 4 tablespoons olive oil
- 1 cup cream
- Salt and black pepper, to taste

Directions:
1. Preheat the Air fryer to 340 degree F and grease an Air fryer basket.
2. Season the chicken tenders with salt and black pepper.
3. Arrange the chicken tenderloins in the Air fryer basket and drizzle with olive oil.\

4. Cook for about 15 minutes and set the Air fryer to 390 degree F.
5. Cook for about 5 more minutes and dish out to serve warm.
6. Repeat with the remaining mixture and dish out to serve hot.
- **Nutrition Info:** Calories: 344, Fat: 21.1g, Carbohydrates: 1.7g, Sugar: 1.4g, Protein: 35.7g, Sodium: 317mg

166.Simple Turkey Breast

Servings: 10
Cooking Time: 40 Minutes
Ingredients:
- 1: 8-poundsbone-in turkey breast
- Salt and black pepper, as required
- 2 tablespoons olive oil

Directions:
1. Preheat the Air fryer to 360 degree F and grease an Air fryer basket.
2. Season the turkey breast with salt and black pepper and drizzle with oil.
3. Arrange the turkey breast into the Air Fryer basket, skin side down and cook for about 20 minutes.
4. Flip the side and cook for another 20 minutes.
5. Dish out in a platter and cut into desired size slices to serve.
- **Nutrition Info:** Calories: 719, Fat: 35.9g, Carbohydrates: 0g, Sugar: 0g, Protein: 97.2g, Sodium: 386mg

167.Ranch Chicken Wings

Servings: 3
Cooking Time: 10 Minutes
Ingredients:
- 1/4 cup almond meal
- 1/4 cup flaxseed meal
- 2 tablespoons butter, melted
- 6 tablespoons parmesan cheese, preferably freshly grated
- 1 tablespoon Ranch seasoning mix
- 2 tablespoons oyster sauce
- 6 chicken wings, bone-in

Directions:
1. Start by preheating your Air Fryer to 370 degrees F.
2. In a resealable bag, place the almond meal, flaxseed meal, butter, parmesan, Ranch seasoning mix, andoyster sauce. Add the chicken wings and shake to coat on all sides.
3. Arrange the chicken wings in the Air Fryer basket. Spritz the chicken wings with a nonstick cooking spray.
4. Cook for 11 minutes. Turn them over and cook an additional 11 minutes. Serve warm with your favorite dipping sauce, if desired. Enjoy!
- **Nutrition Info:** 285 Calories; 22g Fat; 3g Carbs; 12g Protein; 5g Sugars; 6g Fiber

168.Philly Cheesesteak Egg Rolls

Servings: 4-5
Cooking Time: 20 Minutes
Ingredients:
- 1 egg
- 1 tablespoon milk
- 2 tablespoons olive oil
- 1 small red onion
- 1 small red bell pepper
- 1 small green bell pepper
- 1 pound thinly slice roast beef
- 8 ounces shredded pepper jack cheese
- 8 ounces shredded provolone cheese
- 8-10 egg roll skins
- Salt and pepper

Directions:
1. Start by preheating toaster oven to 425°F.
2. Mix together egg and milk in a shallow bowl and set aside for later use.
3. Chop onions and bell peppers into small pieces.
4. Heat the oil in a medium sauce pan and add the onions and peppers.
5. Cook onions and peppers for 2–3 minutes until softened.
6. Add roast beef to the pan and sauté for another 5 minutes.
7. Add salt and pepper to taste.
8. Add cheese and mix together until melted.
9. Remove from heat and drain liquid from pan.
10. Roll the egg roll skins flat.
11. Add equal parts of the mix to each egg roll and roll them up per the instructions on the package.
12. Brush each egg roll with the egg mixture.
13. Line a pan with parchment paper and lay egg rolls seam-side down with a gap between each roll.
14. Bake for 20–25 minutes, depending on your preference of egg roll crispness.
- **Nutrition Info:** Calories: 769, Sodium: 1114 mg, Dietary Fiber: 2.1 g, Total Fat: 39.9 g, Total Carbs: 41.4 g, Protein: 58.4 g.

169.Moroccan Pork Kebabs

Servings: 4
Cooking Time: 45 Minutes
Ingredients:
- 1/4 cup orange juice
- 1 tablespoon tomato paste
- 1 clove chopped garlic
- 1 tablespoon ground cumin
- 1/8 teaspoon ground cinnamon
- 4 tablespoons olive oil
- 1-1/2 teaspoons salt
- 3/4 teaspoon black pepper
- 1-1/2 pounds boneless pork loin
- 1 small eggplant
- 1 small red onion
- Pita bread (optional)
- 1/2 small cucumber

- 2 tablespoons chopped fresh mint
- Wooden skewers

Directions:

1. Start by placing wooden skewers in water to soak.
2. Cut pork loin and eggplant into 1- to 1-1/2-inch chunks.
3. Preheat toaster oven to 425°F.
4. Cut cucumber and onions into pieces and chop the mint.
5. In a large bowl, combine the orange juice, tomato paste, garlic, cumin, cinnamon, 2 tablespoons of oil, 1 teaspoon of salt, and 1/2 teaspoon of pepper.
6. Add the pork to this mixture and refrigerate for at least 30 minutes, but up to 8 hours.
7. Mix together vegetables, remaining oil, and salt and pepper.
8. Skewer the vegetables and bake for 20 minutes.
9. Add the pork to the skewers and bake for an additional 25 minutes.
10. Remove ingredients from skewers and sprinkle with mint; serve with flatbread if using.
- **Nutrition Info:** Calories: 465, Sodium: 1061 mg, Dietary Fiber: 5.6 g, Total Fat: 20.8 g, Total Carbs: 21.9 g, Protein: 48.2 g.

170.Creamy Green Beans And Tomatoes

Servings: 4
Cooking Time: 20 Minutes
Ingredients:

- 1 pound green beans, trimmed and halved
- ½ pound cherry tomatoes, halved
- 2 tablespoons olive oil
- 1 teaspoon oregano, dried
- 1 teaspoon basil, dried
- Salt and black pepper to the taste
- 1 cup heavy cream
- ½ tablespoon cilantro, chopped

Directions:

1. In your air fryer's pan, combine the green beans with the tomatoes and the other Ingredients:, toss and cook at 360 degrees F for 20 minutes.
2. Divide the mix between plates and serve.
- **Nutrition Info:** Calories 174, fat 5, fiber 7, carbs 11, protein 4

171.Duck Breast With Figs

Servings: 2
Cooking Time: 45 Minutes
Ingredients:

- 1 pound boneless duck breast
- 6 fresh figs, halved
- 1 tablespoon fresh thyme, chopped
- 2 cups fresh pomegranate juice
- 2 tablespoons lemon juice
- 3 tablespoons brown sugar
- 1 teaspoon olive oil
- Salt and black pepper, as required

Directions:

1. Preheat the Air fryer to 400 degree F and grease an Air fryer basket.
2. Put the pomegranate juice, lemon juice, and brown sugar in a medium saucepan over medium heat.
3. Bring to a boil and simmer on low heat for about 25 minutes.
4. Season the duck breasts generously with salt and black pepper.
5. Arrange the duck breasts into the Air fryer basket, skin side up and cook for about 14 minutes, flipping once in between.
6. Dish out the duck breasts onto a cutting board for about 10 minutes.
7. Meanwhile, put the figs, olive oil, salt, and black pepper in a bowl until well mixed.
8. Set the Air fryer to 400 degree F and arrange the figs into the Air fryer basket.
9. Cook for about 5 more minutes and dish out in a platter.
10. Put the duck breast with the roasted figs and drizzle with warm pomegranate juice mixture.
11. Garnish with fresh thyme and serve warm.
- **Nutrition Info:** Calories: 699, Fat: 12.1g, Carbohydrates: 90g, Sugar: 74g, Protein: 519g, Sodium: 110mg

DINNER RECIPES

172.Broccoli And Avocado Tacos

Servings: 3
Cooking Time: 5 Minutes
Ingredients:
- 6-10 authentic Mexican corn tortillas
- 1 large ripe avocado
- 1 large head broccoli
- 6-8 white mushrooms, sliced
- 1/2 bunch cilantro
- 1/2 teaspoon garlic powder
- Sea salt and pepper
- Olive oil

Directions:
1. Start by preheating toaster oven to 400°F.
2. Slice avocado into thin slices and chop the broccoli into bite-sized florets.
3. Arrange the broccoli and mushrooms on a baking sheet; drizzle oil and sprinkle salt, pepper, and garlic powder over the veggies.
4. Bake for 20 minutes. Warm the tortillas, then fill with mushrooms and broccoli, and top with avocado.
5. Sprinkle cilantro over tacos and serve.
- **Nutrition Info:** Calories: 313, Sodium: 99 mg, Dietary Fiber: 12.6 g, Total Fat: 15.3 g, Total Carbs: 40.5 g, Protein: 10.4 g.

173.Shrimp Kebabs

Servings: 2
Cooking Time: 10 Minutes
Ingredients:
- ¾ pound shrimp, peeled and deveined
- 1 tablespoon fresh cilantro, chopped
- Wooden skewers, presoaked
- 2 tablespoons fresh lemon juice
- 1 teaspoon garlic, minced
- ½ teaspoon paprika
- ½ teaspoon ground cumin
- Salt and ground black pepper, as required

Directions:
1. Preheat the Air fryer to 350 degree F and grease an Air fryer basket.
2. Mix lemon juice, garlic, and spices in a bowl.
3. Stir in the shrimp and mix to coat well.
4. Thread the shrimp onto presoaked wooden skewers and transfer to the Air fryer basket.
5. Cook for about 10 minutes, flipping once in between.
6. Dish out the mixture onto serving plates and serve garnished with fresh cilantro.
- **Nutrition Info:** Calories: 212, Fat: 3.2g, Carbohydrates: 3.9g, Sugar: 0.4g, Protein: 39.1g, Sodium: 497mg

174.Effortless Beef Schnitzel

Servings: 2
Cooking Time: 25 Minutes

Ingredients:
- 2 tbsp vegetable oil
- 2 oz breadcrumbs
- 1 whole egg, whisked
- 1 thin beef schnitzel, cut into strips
- 1 whole lemon

Directions:
1. Preheat your fryer to 356 F. In a bowl, add breadcrumbs and oil and stir well to get a loose mixture. Dip schnitzel in egg, then dip in breadcrumbs coat well. Place the prepared schnitzel your Air Fryer's cooking basket and cook for 12 minutes. Serve with a drizzle of lemon juice.
- **Nutrition Info:** 346 Calories; 11g Fat; 4g Carbs; 32g Protein; 1g Sugars; 1g Fiber

175.Hasselback Potatoes

Servings: 4
Cooking Time: 30 Minutes
Ingredients:
- 4 potatoes
- 2 tablespoons Parmesan cheese, shredded
- 1 tablespoon fresh chives, chopped
- 2 tablespoons olive oil

Directions:
1. Preheat the Air fryer to 355 ºF and grease an Air fryer basket.
2. Cut slits along each potato about ¼-inch apart with a sharp knife, making sure slices should stay connected at the bottom.
3. Coat the potatoes with olive oil and arrange into the Air fryer basket.
4. Cook for about 30 minutes and dish out in a platter.
5. Top with chives and Parmesan cheese to serve.
- **Nutrition Info:** Calories: 218, Fat: 7.9g, Carbohydrates: 33.6g, Sugar: 2.5g, Protein: 4.6g, Sodium: 55mg

176.Filet Mignon With Chili Peanut Sauce

Servings: 4
Cooking Time: 20 Minutes
Ingredients:
- 2 pounds filet mignon, sliced into bite-sized strips
- 1 tablespoon oyster sauce
- 2 tablespoons sesame oil
- 2 tablespoons tamari sauce
- 1 tablespoon ginger-garlic paste
- 1 tablespoon mustard
- 1 teaspoon chili powder
- 1/4 cup peanut butter
- 2 tablespoons lime juice
- 1 teaspoon red pepper flakes
- 2 tablespoons water

Directions:

1. Place the beef strips, oyster sauce, sesame oil, tamari sauce, ginger-garlic paste, mustard, and chili powder in a large ceramic dish.
2. Cover and allow it to marinate for 2 hours in your refrigerator.
3. Cook in the preheated Air Fryer at 400 degrees F for 18 minutes, shaking the basket occasionally.
4. Mix the peanut butter with lime juice, red pepper flakes, and water. Spoon the sauce onto the air fried beef strips and serve warm.
- **Nutrition Info:** 420 Calories; 21g Fat; 5g Carbs; 50g Protein; 7g Sugars; 1g Fiber

177.Cinnamon Pork Rinds

Servings: 2
Cooking Time: 20 Minutes
Ingredients:
- 2 oz. pork rinds
- ¼ cup powdered erythritol
- 2 tbsp. unsalted butter; melted.
- ½ tsp. ground cinnamon.

Directions:
1. Take a large bowl, toss pork rinds and butter. Sprinkle with cinnamon and erythritol, then toss to evenly coat.
2. Place pork rinds into the air fryer basket. Adjust the temperature to 400 Degrees F and set the timer for 5 minutes. Serve immediately.
- **Nutrition Info:** Calories: 264; Protein: 13g; Fiber: 4g; Fat: 28g; Carbs: 15g

178.Cheddar Pork Meatballs

Servings: 4 To 6
Cooking Time: 25 Minutes
Ingredients:
- 1 lb ground pork
- 1 large onion, chopped
- ½ tsp maple syrup
- 2 tsp mustard
- ½ cup chopped basil leaves
- Salt and black pepper to taste
- 2 tbsp. grated cheddar cheese

Directions:
1. In a mixing bowl, add the ground pork, onion, maple syrup, mustard, basil leaves, salt, pepper, and cheddar cheese; mix well. Use your hands to form bite-size balls. Place in the fryer basket and cook at 400 f for 10 minutes.
2. Slide out the fryer basket and shake it to toss the meatballs. Cook further for 5 minutes. Remove them onto a wire rack and serve with zoodles and marinara sauce.
- **Nutrition Info:** Calories: 300 Cal Total Fat: 24 g Saturated Fat: 9 g Cholesterol: 70 mg

Sodium: 860 mg Total Carbs: 3 g Fiber: 0 g Sugar: 0 g Protein: 16 g

179.Garlic Butter Pork Chops

Servings: 4
Cooking Time: 8 Minutes
Ingredients:
- 4 pork chops
- 1 tablespoon coconut butter
- 2 teaspoons parsley
- 1 tablespoon coconut oil
- 2 teaspoons garlic, grated
- Salt and black pepper, to taste

Directions:
1. Preheat the Air fryer to 350 degree F and grease an Air fryer basket.
2. Mix all the seasonings, coconut oil, garlic, butter, and parsley in a bowl and coat the pork chops with it.
3. Cover the chops with foil and refrigerate to marinate for about 1 hour.
4. Remove the foil and arrange the chops in the Air fryer basket.
5. Cook for about 8 minutes and dish out in a bowl to serve warm.
- **Nutrition Info:** Calories: 311, Fat: 25.5g, Carbohydrates: 1.4g, Sugar: 0.3g, Protein: 18.4g, Sodium: 58mg

180.Broccoli With Olives

Servings: 4
Cooking Time: 19 Minutes
Ingredients:
- 2 pounds broccoli, stemmed and cut into 1-inch florets
- 1/3 cup Kalamata olives, halved and pitted
- ¼ cup Parmesan cheese, grated
- 2 tablespoons olive oil
- Salt and ground black pepper, as required
- 2 teaspoons fresh lemon zest, grated

Directions:
1. Preheat the Air fryer to 400 ºF and grease an Air fryer basket.
2. Boil the broccoli for about 4 minutes and drain well.
3. Mix broccoli, oil, salt, and black pepper in a bowl and toss to coat well.
4. Arrange broccoli into the Air fryer basket and cook for about 15 minutes.
5. Stir in the olives, lemon zest and cheese and dish out to serve.
- **Nutrition Info:** Calories: 169, Fat: 10.2g, Carbohydrates: 16g, Sugar: 3.9g, Protein: 8.5g, Sodium: 254mg

181.Prawn Burgers

Servings: 2
Cooking Time: 6 Minutes
Ingredients:

- ½ cup prawns, peeled, deveined and finely chopped
- ½ cup breadcrumbs
- 2-3 tablespoons onion, finely chopped
- 3 cups fresh baby greens
- ½ teaspoon ginger, minced
- ½ teaspoon garlic, minced
- ½ teaspoon red chili powder
- ½ teaspoon ground cumin
- ¼ teaspoon ground turmeric
- Salt and ground black pepper, as required

Directions:
1. Preheat the Air fryer to 390 degree F and grease an Air fryer basket.
2. Mix the prawns, breadcrumbs, onion, ginger, garlic, and spices in a bowl.
3. Make small-sized patties from the mixture and transfer to the Air fryer basket.
4. Cook for about 6 minutes and dish out in a platter.
5. Serve immediately warm alongside the baby greens.
- **Nutrition Info:** Calories: 240, Fat: 2.7g, Carbohydrates: 37.4g, Sugar: 4g, Protein: 18g, Sodium: 371mg

182.Red Wine Infused Mushrooms

Servings: 6
Cooking Time: 30 Minutes
Ingredients:
- 1 tablespoon butter
- 2 pounds fresh mushrooms, quartered
- 2 teaspoons Herbs de Provence
- ½ teaspoon garlic powder
- 2 tablespoons red wine

Directions:
1. Preheat the Air fryer to 325 ºF and grease an Air fryer pan.
2. Mix the butter, Herbs de Provence, and garlic powder in the Air fryer pan and toss to coat well.
3. Cook for about 2 minutes and stir in the mushrooms and red wine.
4. Cook for about 28 minutes and dish out in a platter to serve hot.
- **Nutrition Info:** Calories: 54, Fat: 2.4g, Carbohydrates: 5.3g, Sugar: 2.7g, Protein: 4.8g, Sodium: 23mg

183.Air Fryer Buffalo Mushroom Poppers

Servings: 8
Cooking Time: 50 Minutes
Ingredients:
- 1 pound fresh whole button mushrooms
- 1/2 teaspoon kosher salt
- 3 tablespoons 1/3-less-fat cream cheese,
- 1/4 cup all-purpose flour
- Softened 1 jalapeño chile, seeded and minced
- Cooking spray
- 1/4 teaspoon black pepper
- 1 cup panko breadcrumbs
- 2 large eggs, lightly beaten
- 1/4 cup buffalo-style hot sauce
- 2 tablespoons chopped fresh chives
- 1/2 cup low-fat buttermilk
- 1/2 cup plain fat-free yogurt
- 2 ounces blue cheese, crumbled (about 1/2 cup)
- 3 tablespoons apple cider vinegar

Directions:
1. Remove stems from mushroom caps, chop stems and set caps aside. Stir together chopped mushroom stems, cream cheese, jalapeño, salt, and pepper. Stuff about 1 teaspoon of the mixture into each mushroom cap, rounding the filling to form a smooth ball.
2. Place panko in a bowl, place flour in a second bowl, and eggs in a third Coat mushrooms in flour, dip in egg mixture, and dredge in panko, pressing to adhere. Spray mushrooms well with cooking spray.
3. Place half of the mushrooms in air fryer basket, and cook for 20 minutes at 350°F. Transfer cooked mushrooms to a large bowl. Drizzle buffalo sauce over mushrooms; toss to coat then sprinkle with chives.
4. Stir buttermilk, yogurt, blue cheese, and cider vinegar in a small bowl. Serve mushroom poppers with blue cheese sauce.
- **Nutrition Info:** Calories 133 Fat 4g Saturated fat 2g Unsaturated fat 2g Protein 7g Carbohydrate 16g Fiber 1g Sugars 3g Sodium 485mg Calcium 10% DV Potassium 7% DV

184.Okra With Green Beans

Servings: 2
Cooking Time: 20 Minutes
Ingredients:
- ½, 10-ouncesbag frozen cut okra
- ½, 10-ouncesbag frozen cut green beans
- ¼ cup nutritional yeast
- 3 tablespoons balsamic vinegar
- Salt and black pepper, to taste

Directions:
1. Preheat the Air fryer to 400 ºF and grease an Air fryer basket.
2. Mix the okra, green beans, nutritional yeast, vinegar, salt, and black pepper in a bowl and toss to coat well.
3. Arrange the okra mixture into the Air fryer basket and cook for about 20 minutes.
4. Dish out in a serving dish and serve hot.
- **Nutrition Info:** Calories: 126, Fat: 1.3g, Carbohydrates: 19.7g, Sugar: 2.1g, Protein: 11.9g, Sodium: 100mg

185.Salsa Stuffed Eggplants

Servings: 2
Cooking Time: 25 Minutes
Ingredients:
- 1 large eggplant
- 8 cherry tomatoes, quartered
- ½ tablespoon fresh parsley
- 2 teaspoons olive oil, divided
- 2 teaspoons fresh lemon juice, divided
- 2 tablespoons tomato salsa
- Salt and black pepper, as required

Directions:
1. Preheat the Air fryer to 390 degree F and grease an Air fryer basket.
2. Arrange the eggplant into the Air fryer basket and cook for about 15 minutes.
3. Cut the eggplant in half lengthwise and drizzle evenly with one teaspoon of oil.
4. Set the Air fryer to 355 degree F and arrange the eggplant into the Air fryer basket, cut-side up.
5. Cook for another 10 minutes and dish out in a bowl.
6. Scoop out the flesh from the eggplant and transfer into a bowl.
7. Stir in the tomatoes, salsa, parsley, salt, black pepper, remaining oil, and lemon juice.
8. Squeeze lemon juice on the eggplant halves and stuff with the salsa mixture to serve.
- **Nutrition Info:** Calories: 192, Fat: 6.1g, Carbohydrates: 33.8g, Sugar: 20.4g, Protein: 6.9g, Sodium: 204mg

186.Spicy Paprika Steak

Servings: 2
Cooking Time: 20 Minutes
Ingredients:
- 1/2 Ancho chili pepper, soaked in hot water before using
- 1 tablespoon brandy
- 2 teaspoons smoked paprika
- 1 1/2 tablespoons olive oil
- 2 beef steaks
- Kosher salt, to taste
- 1 teaspoon ground allspice
- 3 cloves garlic, sliced

Directions:
1. Sprinkle the beef steaks with salt, paprika, and allspice. Add the steak to a baking dish that fits your fryer. Scatter the sliced garlic over the top.
2. Now, drizzle it with brandy and olive oil; spread minced Ancho chili pepper over the top.
3. Bake at 385 degrees F for 14 minutes, turning halfway through. Serve warm.
- **Nutrition Info:** 450 Calories; 26g Fat; 4g Carbs; 58g Protein; 3g Sugars; 3g Fiber

187.Garlic Parmesan Shrimp

Servings: 2
Cooking Time: 10 Minutes
Ingredients:
- 1 pound shrimp, deveined and peeled
- ½ cup parmesan cheese, grated
- ¼ cup cilantro, diced
- 1 tablespoon olive oil
- 1 teaspoon salt
- 1 teaspoon fresh cracked pepper
- 1 tablespoon lemon juice
- 6 garlic cloves, diced

Directions:
1. Preheat the Air fryer to 350 degree F and grease an Air fryer basket.
2. Drizzle shrimp with olive oil and lemon juice and season with garlic, salt and cracked pepper.
3. Cover the bowl with plastic wrap and refrigerate for about 3 hours.
4. Stir in the parmesan cheese and cilantro to the bowl and transfer to the Air fryer basket.
5. Cook for about 10 minutes and serve immediately.
- **Nutrition Info:** Calories: 602, Fat: 23.9g, Carbohydrates: 46.5g, Sugar: 2.9g, Protein: 11.3g, Sodium: 886mg

188.Veggie Stuffed Bell Peppers

Servings: 6
Cooking Time: 25 Minutes
Ingredients:
- 6 large bell peppers, tops and seeds removed
- 1 carrot, peeled and finely chopped
- 1 potato, peeled and finely chopped
- ½ cup fresh peas, shelled
- 1/3 cup cheddar cheese, grated
- 2 garlic cloves, minced
- Salt and black pepper, to taste

Directions:
1. Preheat the Air fryer to 350 ºF and grease an Air fryer basket.
2. Mix vegetables, garlic, salt and black pepper in a bowl.
3. Stuff the vegetable mixture in each bell pepper and arrange in the Air fryer pan.
4. Cook for about 20 minutes and top with cheddar cheese.
5. Cook for about 5 more minutes and dish out to serve warm.
- **Nutrition Info:** Calories: 101, Fat: 2.5g, Carbohydrates: 17.1g, Sugar: 7.4g, Protein: 4.1g, Sodium: 51mg

189.Roasted Butternut Squash With Brussels Sprouts & Sweet Potato Noodles

Servings: 2
Cooking Time: 15 Minutes
Ingredients:
- Squash:
- 3 cups chopped butternut squash
- 2 teaspoons extra light olive oil
- 1/8 teaspoon sea salt
- Veggies:
- 5-6 Brussels sprouts
- 5 fresh shiitake mushrooms
- 2 cloves garlic
- 1/2 teaspoon black sesame seeds
- 1/2 teaspoon white sesame seeds
- A few sprinkles ground pepper
- A small pinch red pepper flakes
- 1 tablespoon extra light olive oil
- 1 teaspoon sesame oil
- 1 teaspoon onion powder
- 1 teaspoon garlic powder
- 1/4 teaspoon sea salt
- Noodles:
- 1 bundle sweet potato vermicelli
- 2-3 teaspoons low-sodium soy sauce

Directions:
1. Start by soaking potato vermicelli in water for at least 2 hours.
2. Preheat toaster oven to 375°F.
3. Place squash on a baking sheet with edges, then drizzle with olive oil and sprinkle with salt and pepper. Mix together well on pan.
4. Bake the squash for 30 minutes, mixing and flipping half way through.
5. Remove the stems from the mushrooms and chop the Brussels sprouts.
6. Chop garlic and mix the veggies.
7. Drizzle sesame and olive oil over the mixture, then add garlic powder, onion powder, sesame seeds, red pepper flakes, salt, and pepper.
8. Bake veggie mix for 15 minutes.
9. While the veggies bake, put noodles in a small sauce pan and add just enough water to cover.
10. Bring water to a rolling boil and boil noodles for about 8 minutes.
11. Drain noodles and combine with squash and veggies in a large bowl.
12. Drizzle with soy sauce, sprinkle with sesame seeds, and serve.
- **Nutrition Info:** Calories: 409, Sodium: 1124 mg, Dietary Fiber: 12.2 g, Total Fat: 15.6 g, Total Carbs: 69.3 g, Protein: 8.8 g.

190.Basil Tomatoes

Servings: 2
Cooking Time: 10 Minutes
Ingredients:
- 2 tomatoes, halved
- 1 tablespoon fresh basil, chopped
- Olive oil cooking spray
- Salt and black pepper, as required

Directions:
1. Preheat the Air fryer to 320 degree F and grease an Air fryer basket.
2. Spray the tomato halves evenly with olive oil cooking spray and season with salt, black pepper and basil.
3. Arrange the tomato halves into the Air fryer basket, cut sides up.
4. Cook for about 10 minutes and dish out onto serving plates.
- **Nutrition Info:** Calories: 22, Fat: 4.8g, Carbohydrates: 4.8g, Sugar: 3.2g, Protein: 1.1g, Sodium: 84mg

191.Corned Beef With Carrots

Servings: 3
Cooking Time: 35 Minutes
Ingredients:
- 1 tbsp beef spice
- 1 whole onion, chopped
- 4 carrots, chopped
- 12 oz bottle beer
- 1½ cups chicken broth
- 4 pounds corned beef

Directions:
1. Preheat your air fryer to 380 f. Cover beef with beer and set aside for 20 minutes. Place carrots, onion and beef in a pot and heat over high heat. Add in broth and bring to a boil. Drain boiled meat and veggies; set aside.
2. Top with beef spice. Place the meat and veggies in your air fryer's cooking basket and cook for 30 minutes.
- **Nutrition Info:** Calories: 464 Cal Total Fat: 17 g Saturated Fat: 6.8 g Cholesterol: 91.7 mg Sodium: 1904.2 mg Total Carbs: 48.9 g Fiber: 7.2 g Sugar: 5.8 g Protein: 30.6 g

192.Smoked Sausage And Bacon Shashlik

Servings: 4
Cooking Time: 20 Minutes
Ingredients:
- 1 pound smoked Polish beef sausage, sliced
- 1 tablespoon mustard
- 1 tablespoon olive oil
- 2 tablespoons Worcestershire sauce
- 2 bell peppers, sliced
- Salt and ground black pepper, to taste

Directions:
1. Toss the sausage with the mustard, olive, and Worcestershire sauce. Thread sausage and peppers onto skewers.

2. Sprinkle with salt and black pepper.
3. Cook in the preheated Air Fryer at 360 degrees Ffor 11 minutes. Brush the skewers with the reserved marinade.
- **Nutrition Info:** 422 Calories; 36g Fat; 9g Carbs; 18g Protein; 6g Sugars; 7g Fiber

193.Keto Lamb Kleftiko

Servings: 6
Cooking Time: 30 Minutes
Ingredients:
- 2 oz. garlic clove, peeled
- 1 tablespoon dried oregano
- ½ lemon
- ¼ tablespoon ground cinnamon
- 3 tablespoon butter, frozen
- 18 oz. leg of lamb
- 1 cup heavy cream
- 1 teaspoon bay leaf
- 1 teaspoon dried mint
- 1 tablespoon olive oil

Directions:
1. Crush the garlic cloves and combine them with the dried oregano, and ground cinnamon. Mix it.
2. Then chop the lemon.
3. Sprinkle the leg of lamb with the crushed garlic mixture.
4. Then rub it with the chopped lemon.
5. Combine the heavy cream, bay leaf, and dried mint together.
6. Whisk the mixture well.
7. After this, add the olive oil and whisk it one more time more.
8. Then pour the cream mixture on the leg of lamb and stir it carefully.
9. Leave the leg of lamb for 10 minutes to marinate.
10. Preheat the air fryer to 380 F.
11. Chop the butter and sprinkle the marinated lamb.
12. Then place the leg of lamb in the air fryer basket tray and sprinkle it with the remaining cream mixture.
13. Then sprinkle the meat with the chopped butter.
14. Cook the meat for 30 minutes.
15. When the time is over – remove the meat from the air fryer and sprinkle it gently with the remaining cream mixture.
16. Serve it!
- **Nutrition Info:** calories 318, fat 21.9, fiber 0.9, carbs 4.9, protein 25.1

194.Sweet Chicken Breast

Servings: 4
Cooking Time: 12 Minutes
Ingredients:
- 1-pound chicken breast, boneless, skinless
- 3 tablespoon Stevia extract
- 1 teaspoon ground white pepper
- ½ teaspoon paprika
- 1 teaspoon cayenne pepper
- 1 teaspoon lemongrass
- 1 teaspoon lemon zest
- 1 tablespoon apple cider vinegar
- 1 tablespoon butter

Directions:
1. Sprinkle the chicken breast with the apple cider vinegar.
2. After this, rub the chicken breast with the ground white pepper, paprika, cayenne pepper, lemongrass, and lemon zest.
3. Leave the chicken breast for 5 minutes to marinate.
4. After this, rub the chicken breast with the stevia extract and leave it for 5 minutes more.
5. Preheat the air fryer to 380 F.
6. Rub the prepared chicken breast with the butter and place it in the air fryer basket tray.
7. Cook the chicken breast for 12 minutes.
8. Turn the chicken breast into another side after 6 minutes of cooking.
9. Serve the dish hot!
10. Enjoy!
- **Nutrition Info:** calories 160, fat 5.9, fiber 0.4, carbs 1, protein 24.2

195.Creamy Lemon Turkey

Servings: 4
Cooking Time: 20 Minutes
Ingredients:
- 1/3 cup sour cream
- 2 cloves garlic, finely minced 1/3 tsp. lemon zest
- 2 small-sized turkey breasts, skinless and cubed 1/3 cup thickened cream
- 2 tablespoons lemon juice
- 1 tsp. fresh marjoram, chopped
- Salt and freshly cracked mixed peppercorns, to taste 1/2 cup scallion, chopped
- 1/2 can tomatoes, diced
- 1½ tablespoons canola oil

Directions:
1. Firstly, pat dry the turkey breast. Mix the remaining items; marinate the turkey for 2 hours.
2. Set the air fryer to cook at 355 °F. Brush the turkey with a nonstick spray; cook for 23 minutes, turning once. Serve with naan and enjoy!
- **Nutrition Info:** 260 Calories; 15.3g Fat; 8.9g Carbs; 28.6g Protein; 1.9g Sugars

196.Almond Pork Bites

Servings: 10

Cooking Time: 40 Minutes
Ingredients:

- 16 oz sausage meat
- 1 whole egg, beaten
- 3 ½ oz onion, chopped
- 2 tbsp dried sage
- 2 tbsp almonds, chopped
- ½ tsp pepper
- 3 ½ oz apple, sliced
- ½ tsp salt

Directions:

1. Preheat your air fryer to 350 f. In a bowl, mix onion, almonds, sliced apples, egg, pepper and salt. Add the almond mixture and sausage in a ziploc bag. Mix to coat well and set aside for 15 minutes.
2. Use the mixture to form cutlets. Add cutlets to your fryer's basket and cook for 25 minutes. Serve with heavy cream and enjoy!
- **Nutrition Info:** Calories: 491.7 Cal Total Fat: 25.9 g Saturated Fat: 4.4 g Cholesterol: 42 mg Sodium: 364.3 mg Total Carbs: 40.4 g Fiber: 3.3 g Sugar: 0.7 g Protein: 21.8 g

197.Air Fryer Veggie Quesdillas

Servings: 4
Cooking Time: 40 Minutes
Ingredients:

- 4 sprouted whole-grain flour tortillas (6-in.)
- 1 cup sliced red bell pepper
- 4 ounces reduced-fat Cheddar cheese, shredded
- 1 cup sliced zucchini
- 1 cup canned black beans, drained and rinsed (no salt)
- Cooking spray
- 2 ounces plain 2% reduced-fat Greek yogurt
- 1 teaspoon lime zest
- 1 Tbsp. fresh juice (from 1 lime)
- ¼ tsp. ground cumin
- 2 tablespoons chopped fresh cilantro
- 1/2 cup drained refrigerated pico de gallo

Directions:

1. Place tortillas on work surface, sprinkle 2 tablespoons shredded cheese over half of each tortilla and top with cheese on each tortilla with 1/4 cup each red pepper slices, zucchini slices, and black beans. Sprinkle evenly with remaining 1/2 cup cheese.
2. Fold tortillas over to form half-moon shaped quesadillas, lightly coat with cooking spray, and secure with toothpicks.
3. Lightly spray air fryer basket with cooking spray. Place 2 quesadillas in the basket, and cook at 400°F for 10 minutes until tortillas are golden brown and slightly crispy, cheese is melted, and vegetables are slightly softened. Turn quesadillas over halfway through cooking.
4. Repeat with remaining quesadillas.
5. Meanwhile, stir yogurt, lime juice, lime zest and cumin in a small bowl.
6. Cut each quesadilla into wedges and sprinkle with cilantro.
7. Serve with 1 tablespoon cumin cream and 2 tablespoons pico de gallo each.
- **Nutrition Info:** Calories 291 Fat 8g Saturated fat 4g Unsaturated fat 3g Protein 17g Carbohydrate 36g Fiber 8g Sugars 3g Sodium 518mg Calcium 30% DV Potassium 6% DV

198.Ham Pinwheels

Servings: 4
Cooking Time: 11 Minutes
Ingredients:

- 1 puff pastry sheet
- 10 ham slices
- 1 cup Gruyere cheese, shredded plus more for sprinkling
- 4 teaspoons Dijon mustard

Directions:

1. Preheat the Air fryer to 375 degree F and grease an Air fryer basket.
2. Place the puff pastry onto a smooth surface and spread evenly with the mustard.
3. Top with the ham and ¾ cup cheese and roll the puff pastry.
4. Wrap the roll in plastic wrap and freeze for about 30 minutes.
5. Remove from the freezer and slice into ½-inch rounds.
6. Arrange the pinwheels in the Air fryer basket and cook for about 8 minutes.
7. Top with remaining cheese and cook for 3 more minutes.
8. Dish out in a platter and serve warm.
- **Nutrition Info:** Calories: 294, Fat: 19.4g, Carbohydrates: 8.4g, Sugar: 0.2g, Protein: 20.8g, Sodium: 1090mg

199.Five Spice Pork

Servings: 4
Cooking Time: 20 Minutes
Ingredients:

- 1-pound pork belly
- 2 tablespoons swerve
- 2 tablespoons dark soy sauce
- 1 tablespoon Shaoxing: cooking wine
- 2 teaspoons garlic, minced
- 2 teaspoons ginger, minced
- 1 tablespoon hoisin sauce
- 1 teaspoon Chinese Five Spice

Directions:

1. Preheat the Air fryer to 390 degree F and grease an Air fryer basket.
2. Mix all the ingredients in a bowl and place in the Ziplock bag.

3. Seal the bag, shake it well and refrigerate to marinate for about 1 hour.
4. Remove the pork from the bag and arrange it in the Air fryer basket.
5. Cook for about 15 minutes and dish out in a bowl to serve warm.
- **Nutrition Info:** Calories: 604, Fat: 30.6g, Carbohydrates: 1.4g, Sugar: 20.3g, Protein: 19.8g, Sodium: 834mg

200.Chili Pepper Lamb Chops

Servings: 6
Cooking Time: 10 Minutes
Ingredients:
- 21 oz. lamb chops
- 1 teaspoon chili pepper
- ½ teaspoon chili flakes
- 1 teaspoon onion powder
- 1 teaspoon garlic powder
- 1 teaspoon cayenne pepper
- 1 tablespoon olive oil
- 1 tablespoon butter
- ½ teaspoon lime zest

Directions:
1. Melt the butter and combine it with the olive oil.
2. Whisk the liquid and add chili pepper, chili flakes, onion powder, garlic powder, cayenne pepper, and lime zest.
3. Whisk it well
4. Then sprinkle the lamb chops with the prepared oily marinade.
5. Leave the meat for at least 5 minutes in the fridge.
6. Preheat the air fryer to 400 F.
7. Place the marinated lamb chops in the air fryer and cook them for 5 minutes.
8. After this, open the air fryer and turn the lamb chops into another side.
9. Cook the lamb chops for 5 minutes more.
10. When the meat is cooked – transfer it to the serving plates.
11. Enjoy!
- **Nutrition Info:** calories 227, fat 11.6, fiber 0.2, carbs 1, protein 28.1

201.Korean Beef Bowl

Servings: 4
Cooking Time: 18 Minutes
Ingredients:
- 1 tablespoon minced garlic
- 1 teaspoon ground ginger
- 4 oz chive stems, chopped
- 2 tablespoon apple cider vinegar
- 1 teaspoon stevia extract
- 1 tablespoon flax seeds
- 1 teaspoon olive oil
- 1 teaspoon olive oil
- 1-pound ground beef

- 4 tablespoon chicken stock

Directions:
1. Sprinkle the ground beef with the apple cider vinegar and stir the meat with the help of the spoon.
2. After this, sprinkle the ground beef with the ground ginger, minced garlic, and olive oil.
3. Mix it up.
4. Preheat the air fryer to 370 F.
5. Put the ground beef in the air fryer basket tray and cook it for 8 minutes.
6. After this, stir the ground beef carefully and sprinkle with the chopped chives, flax seeds, olive oil, and chicken stock.
7. Mix the dish up and cook it for 10 minutes more.
8. When the time is over – stir the dish carefully.
9. Serve Korean beef bowl immediately.
10. Enjoy!
- **Nutrition Info:** calories 258, fat 10.1, fiber 1.2, carbs 4.2, protein 35.3

202.Pepper Pork Chops

Servings: 2
Cooking Time: 6 Minutes
Ingredients:
- 2 pork chops
- 1 egg white
- ¾ cup xanthum gum
- ½ teaspoon sea salt
- ¼ teaspoon freshly ground black pepper
- 1 oil mister

Directions:
1. Preheat the Air fryer to 400 degree F and grease an Air fryer basket.
2. Whisk egg white with salt and black pepper in a bowl and dip the pork chops in it.
3. Cover the bowl and marinate for about 20 minutes.
4. Pour the xanthum gum over both sides of the chops and spray with oil mister.
5. Arrange the chops in the Air fryer basket and cook for about 6 minutes.
6. Dish out in a bowl and serve warm.
- **Nutrition Info:** Calories: 541, Fat: 34g, Carbohydrates: 3.4g, Sugar: 1g, Protein: 20.3g, Sodium: 547mg

203.Amazing Bacon And Potato Platter

Servings: 4
Cooking Time: 40 Minutes
Ingredients:
- 4 potatoes, halved
- 6 garlic cloves, squashed
- 4 streaky cut rashers bacon
- 2 sprigs rosemary
- 1 tbsp olive oil

Directions:

1. Preheat your air fryer to 392 f. In a mixing bowl, mix garlic, bacon, potatoes and rosemary; toss in oil. Place the mixture in your air fryer's cooking basket and roast for 25-30 minutes. Serve and enjoy!
- **Nutrition Info:** Calories: 336 Cal Total Fat: 18.5 g Saturated Fat: 0 g Cholesterol: 82 mg Sodium: 876 mg Total Carbs: 69.9 g Fiber: 0 g Sugar: 0 g Protein: 0 g

204.Beef Sausage With Grilled Broccoli

Servings: 4
Cooking Time: 20 Minutes
Ingredients:
- 1 pound beef Vienna sausage
- 1/2 cup mayonnaise
- 1 teaspoon yellow mustard
- 1 tablespoon fresh lemon juice
- 1 teaspoon garlic powder
- 1/4 teaspoon black pepper
- 1 pound broccoli

Directions:
1. Start by preheating your Air Fryer to 380 degrees F. Spritz the grill pan with cooking oil.
2. Cut the sausages into serving sized pieces. Cook the sausages for 15 minutes, shaking the basket occasionally to get all sides browned. Set aside.
3. In the meantime, whisk the mayonnaise with mustard, lemon juice, garlic powder, and black pepper. Toss the broccoli with the mayo mixture.
4. Turn up temperature to 400 degrees F. Cook broccoli for 6 minutes, turning halfway through the cooking time.
5. Serve the sausage with the grilled broccoli on the side.
- **Nutrition Info:** 477 Calories; 42g Fat; 3g Carbs; 19g Protein; 7g Sugars; 6g Fiber

205.Garlic Lamb Shank

Servings: 5
Cooking Time: 24 Minutes
Ingredients:
- 17 oz. lamb shanks
- 2 tablespoon garlic, peeled
- 1 teaspoon kosher salt
- 1 tablespoon dried parsley
- 4 oz chive stems, chopped
- ½ cup chicken stock
- 1 teaspoon butter
- 1 teaspoon dried rosemary
- 1 teaspoon nutmeg
- ½ teaspoon ground black pepper

Directions:
1. Chop the garlic roughly.
2. Make the cuts in the lamb shank and fill the cuts with the chopped garlic.
3. Then sprinkle the lamb shank with the kosher salt, dried parsley, dried rosemary, nutmeg, and ground black pepper.
4. Stir the spices on the lamb shank gently.
5. Then put the butter and chicken stock in the air fryer basket tray.
6. Preheat the air fryer to 380 F.
7. Put the chives in the air fryer basket tray.
8. Add the lamb shank and cook the meat for 24 minutes.
9. When the lamb shank is cooked – transfer it to the serving plate and sprinkle with the remaining liquid from the cooked meat.
10. Enjoy!
- **Nutrition Info:** calories 205, fat 8.2, fiber 0.8, carbs 3.8, protein 27.2

206.Flank Steak Beef

Servings: 4
Cooking Time: 20 Minutes
Ingredients:
- 1 pound flank steaks, sliced
- ¼ cup xanthum gum
- 2 teaspoon vegetable oil
- ½ teaspoon ginger
- ½ cup soy sauce
- 1 tablespoon garlic, minced
- ½ cup water
- ¾ cup swerve, packed

Directions:
1. Preheat the Air fryer to 390 degree F and grease an Air fryer basket.
2. Coat the steaks with xanthum gum on both the sides and transfer into the Air fryer basket.
3. Cook for about 10 minutes and dish out in a platter.
4. Meanwhile, cook rest of the ingredients for the sauce in a saucepan.
5. Bring to a boil and pour over the steak slices to serve.
- **Nutrition Info:** Calories: 372, Fat: 11.8g, Carbohydrates: 1.8g, Sugar: 27.3g, Protein: 34g, Sodium: 871mg

207.Fish Cakes With Horseradish Sauce

Servings: 4
Cooking Time: 20 Minutes
Ingredients:
- Halibut Cakes:
- 1 pound halibut
- 2 tablespoons olive oil
- 1/2 teaspoon cayenne pepper
- 1/4 teaspoon black pepper
- Salt, to taste
- 2 tablespoons cilantro, chopped
- 1 shallot, chopped
- 2 garlic cloves, minced
- 1 cup Romano cheese, grated

- 1 egg, whisked
- 1 tablespoon Worcestershire sauce
- Mayo Sauce:
- 1 teaspoon horseradish, grated
- 1/2 cup mayonnaise

Directions:

1. Start by preheating your Air Fryer to 380 degrees F. Spritz the Air Fryer basket with cooking oil.
2. Mix all ingredients for the halibut cakes in a bowl; knead with your hands until everything is well incorporated.
3. Shape the mixture into equally sized patties. Transfer your patties to the Air Fryer basket. Cook the fish patties for 10 minutes, turning them over halfway through.
4. Mix the horseradish and mayonnaise. Serve the halibut cakes with the horseradish mayo.
- **Nutrition Info:** 532 Calories; 32g Fat; 3g Carbs; 28g Protein; 3g Sugars; 6g Fiber

208.Baked Veggie Egg Rolls

Servings: 2
Cooking Time: 20 Minutes
Ingredients:

- 1/2 tablespoon olive or vegetable oil
- 2 cups thinly-sliced chard
- 1/4 cup grated carrot
- 1/2 cup chopped pea pods
- 3 shiitake mushrooms
- 2 scallions
- 2 medium cloves garlic
- 1/2 tablespoon fresh ginger
- 1/2 tablespoon soy sauce
- 6 egg roll wrappers
- Olive oil spray for cookie sheet and egg rolls

Directions:

1. Start by mincing mushrooms, garlic, and ginger and slicing scallions.
2. Heat oil on medium heat in a medium skillet and char peas, carrots, scallions, and mushrooms.
3. Cook 3 minutes, then add ginger. Stir in soy sauce and remove from heat.
4. Preheat toaster oven to 400°F and spray cookie sheet. Spoon even portions of vegetable mix over each egg roll wrapper, and wrap them up.
5. Place egg rolls on cookie sheet and spray with olive oil. Bake for 20 minutes until egg roll shells are browned.
- **Nutrition Info:** Calories: 421, Sodium: 1166 mg, Dietary Fiber: 8.2 g, Total Fat: 7.7 g, Total Carbs: 76.9 g, Protein: 13.7 g.

209.Zucchini Muffins

Servings: 8
Cooking Time: 20 Minutes

Ingredients:

- 6 eggs
- 4 drops stevia 1/4 cup Swerve
- 1/3 cup coconut oil, melted 1 cup zucchini, grated
- 3/4 cup coconut flour 1/4 tsp ground nutmeg 1 tsp ground cinnamon 1/2 tsp baking soda

Directions:

1. Preheat the air fryer to 325 F.
2. Add all ingredients except zucchini in a bowl and mix well.
3. Add zucchini and stir well.
4. Pour batter into the silicone muffin molds and place into the air fryer basket.
5. Cook muffins for 20 minutes.
6. Serve and enjoy.
- **Nutrition Info:** Calories 136 Fat 12 g Carbohydrates 1 g Sugar 0.6 g Protein 4 g Cholesterol 123 mg

210.Lamb Skewers

Servings: 4
Cooking Time: 20 Minutes
Ingredients:

- 2 lb. lamb meat; cubed
- 2 red bell peppers; cut into medium pieces
- ¼ cup olive oil
- 2 tbsp. lemon juice
- 1 tbsp. oregano; dried
- 1 tbsp. red vinegar
- 1 tbsp. garlic; minced
- ½ tsp. rosemary; dried
- A pinch of salt and black pepper

Directions:

1. Take a bowl and mix all the ingredients and toss them well.
2. Thread the lamb and bell peppers on skewers, place them in your air fryer's basket and cook at 380°F for 10 minutes on each side. Divide between plates and serve with a side salad
- **Nutrition Info:** Calories: 274; Fat: 12g; Fiber: 3g; Carbs: 6g; Protein: 16g

211.Zingy Dilled Salmon

Servings: 2
Cooking Time: 20 Minutes
Ingredients:

- 2 salmon steaks
- Coarse sea salt, to taste
- 1/4 teaspoon freshly ground black pepper, or more to taste
- 1 tablespoon sesame oil
- Zest of 1 lemon
- 1 tablespoon fresh lemon juice
- 1 teaspoon garlic, minced
- 1/2 teaspoon smoked cayenne pepper
- 1/2 teaspoon dried dill

Directions:
1. Preheat your Air Fryer to 380 degrees F. Pat dry the salmon steaks with a kitchen towel.
2. In a ceramic dish, combine the remaining ingredients until everything is well whisked.
3. Add the salmon steaks to the ceramic dish and let them sit in the refrigerator for 1 hour. Now, place the salmon steaks in the cooking basket. Reserve the marinade.
4. Cook for 12 minutes, flipping halfway through the cooking time.
5. Meanwhile, cook the marinade in a small sauté pan over a moderate flame. Cook until the sauce has thickened.
6. Pour the sauce over the steaks and serve.
- **Nutrition Info:** 476 Calories; 18g Fat; 2g Carbs; 47g Protein; 8g Sugars; 4g Fiber

212.Dinner Avocado Chicken Sliders

Servings: 4
Cooking Time: 20 Minutes
Ingredients:
- ½ pounds ground chicken meat 4 burger buns
- 1/2 cup Romaine lettuce, loosely packed
- ½ tsp. dried parsley flakes 1/3 tsp. mustard seeds
- 1 tsp. onion powder
- 1 ripe fresh avocado, mashed 1 tsp. garlic powder
- 1 ½ tablespoon extra-virgin olive oil
- 1 cloves garlic, minced Nonstick cooking spray
- Salt and cracked black pepper (peppercorns, to taste)

Directions:
1. Firstly, spritz an air fryer cooking basket with a nonstick cooking spray.
2. Mix ground chicken meat, mustard seeds, garlic powder, onion powder, parsley, salt, and black pepper until everything is thoroughly combined. Make sure not to overwork the meat to avoid tough chicken burgers.
3. Shape the meat mixture into patties and roll them in breadcrumbs; transfer your burgers to the prepared cooking basket. Brush the patties with the cooking spray.
4. Air-fry at 355 F for 9 minutes, working in batches. Slice burger buns into halves. In the meantime, combine olive oil with mashed avocado and pressed garlic.
5. To finish, lay Romaine lettuce and avocado spread on bun bottoms; now, add burgers and bun tops.
- **Nutrition Info:** 321 Calories; 18.7g Fat; 15.8g Carbs; 1.2g Sugars

213.Coconut Crusted Shrimp

Servings: 3

Cooking Time: 40 Minutes
Ingredients:
- 8 ounces coconut milk
- ½ cup sweetened coconut, shredded
- ½ cup panko breadcrumbs
- 1 pound large shrimp, peeled and deveined
- Salt and black pepper, to taste

Directions:
1. Preheat the Air fryer to 350-degree F and grease an Air fryer basket.
2. Place the coconut milk in a shallow bowl.
3. Mix coconut, breadcrumbs, salt, and black pepper in another bowl.
4. Dip each shrimp into coconut milk and finally, dredge in the coconut mixture.
5. Arrange half of the shrimps into the Air fryer basket and cook for about 20 minutes.
6. Dish out the shrimps onto serving plates and repeat with the remaining mixture to serve.
- **Nutrition Info:** Calories: 408, Fats: 23.7g, Carbohydrates: 11.7g, Sugar: 3.4g, Proteins: 31g, Sodium: 253mg

214.Morning Ham And Cheese Sandwich

Servings: 4
Cooking Time: 15 Minutes
Ingredients:
- 8 slices whole wheat bread
- 4 slices lean pork ham
- 4 slices cheese
- 8 slices tomato

Directions:
1. Preheat your air fryer to 360 f. Lay four slices of bread on a flat surface. Spread the slices with cheese, tomato, turkey and ham. Cover with the remaining slices to form sandwiches. Add the sandwiches to the air fryer cooking basket and cook for 10 minutes.
- **Nutrition Info:** Calories: 361 Cal Total Fat: 16.7 g Saturated Fat: 0 g Cholesterol: 0 mg Sodium: 1320 mg Total Carbs: 32.5 g Fiber: 2.3 g Sugar: 5.13 g Protein: 19.3 g

215.Homemade Pork Ratatouille

Servings: 4
Cooking Time: 25 Minutes
Ingredients:
- 4 pork sausages
- For ratatouille
- 1 pepper, chopped
- 2 zucchinis, chopped
- 1 eggplant, chopped
- 1 medium red onion, chopped
- 1 tbsp olive oil
- 1-ounce butterbean, drained
- 15 oz tomatoes, chopped
- 2 sprigs fresh thyme

- 1 tbsp balsamic vinegar
- 2 garlic cloves, minced
- 1 red chili, chopped

Directions:

1. Preheat your air fryer to 392 f. Mix pepper, eggplant, oil, onion, zucchinis, and add to the cooking basket. Roast for 20 minutes. Set aside to cool. Reduce air fryer temperature to 356 f. In a saucepan, mix prepared vegetables and the remaining ratatouille ingredients, and bring to a boil over medium heat.
2. Let the mixture simmer for 10 minutes; season with salt and pepper. Add sausages to your air fryer's basket and cook for 10-15 minutes. Serve the sausages with ratatouille.
- **Nutrition Info:** Calories: 232.3 Cal Total Fat: 11.5 g Saturated Fat: 4.0 g Cholesterol: 58.2 mg Sodium: 611 mg Total Carbs: 9.2 g Fiber: 1.7 g Sugar: 4.4 g Protein: 23.1 g

216.Rice Flour Coated Shrimp

Servings: 3
Cooking Time: 20 Minutes
Ingredients:

- 3 tablespoons rice flour
- 1 pound shrimp, peeled and deveined
- 2 tablespoons olive oil
- 1 teaspoon powdered sugar
- Salt and black pepper, as required

Directions:

1. Preheat the Air fryer to 325 ºF and grease an Air fryer basket.
2. Mix rice flour, olive oil, sugar, salt, and black pepper in a bowl.
3. Stir in the shrimp and transfer half of the shrimp to the Air fryer basket.
4. Cook for about 10 minutes, flipping once in between.
5. Dish out the mixture onto serving plates and repeat with the remaining mixture.
- **Nutrition Info:** Calories: 299, Fat: 12g, Carbohydrates: 11.1g, Sugar: 0.8g, Protein: 35g, Sodium: 419mg

217.Roasted Lamb

Servings: 4
Cooking Time: 1 Hour 30 Minutes
Ingredients:

- 2½ pounds half lamb leg roast, slits carved
- 2 garlic cloves, sliced into smaller slithers
- 1 tablespoon dried rosemary
- 1 tablespoon olive oil
- Cracked Himalayan rock salt and cracked peppercorns, to taste

Directions:

1. Preheat the Air fryer to 400 degree F and grease an Air fryer basket.
2. Insert the garlic slithers in the slits and brush with rosemary, oil, salt, and black pepper.
3. Arrange the lamb in the Air fryer basket and cook for about 15 minutes.
4. Set the Air fryer to 350 degree F on the Roast mode and cook for 1 hour and 15 minutes.
5. Dish out the lamb chops and serve hot.
- **Nutrition Info:** Calories: 246, Fat: 7.4g, Carbohydrates: 9.4g, Sugar: 6.5g, Protein: 37.2g, Sodium: 353mg

218.Tasty Sausage Bacon Rolls

Servings: 4
Cooking Time: 1 Hour 44 Minutes
Ingredients:

- Sausage:
- 8 bacon strips
- 8 pork sausages
- Relish:
- 8 large tomatoes
- 1 clove garlic, peeled
- 1 small onion, peeled
- 3 tbsp chopped parsley
- A pinch of salt
- A pinch of pepper
- 2 tbsp sugar
- 1 tsp smoked paprika
- 1 tbsp white wine vinegar

Directions:

1. Start with the relish; add the tomatoes, garlic, and onion in a food processor. Blitz them for 10 seconds until the mixture is pulpy. Pour the pulp into a saucepan, add the vinegar, salt, pepper, and place it over medium heat.
2. Bring to simmer for 10 minutes; add the paprika and sugar. Stir with a spoon and simmer for 10 minutes until pulpy and thick. Turn off the heat, transfer the relish to a bowl and chill it for an hour. In 30 minutes after putting the relish in the refrigerator, move on to the sausages. Wrap each sausage with a bacon strip neatly and stick in a bamboo skewer at the end of the sausage to secure the bacon ends.
3. Open the Air Fryer, place 3 to 4 wrapped sausages in the fryer basket and cook for 12 minutes at 350 F. Ensure that the bacon is golden and crispy before removing them. Repeat the cooking process for the remaining wrapped sausages. Remove the relish from the refrigerator. Serve the sausages and relish with turnip mash.
- **Nutrition Info:** 346 Calories; 11g Fat; 4g Carbs; 32g Protein; 1g Sugars; 1g Fiber

219.Lobster Lasagna Maine Style

Servings: 6
Cooking Time: 50 Minutes
Ingredients:

- 1/2 (15 ounces) container ricotta cheese
- 1 egg
- 1 cup shredded Cheddar cheese
- 1/2 cup shredded mozzarella cheese
- 1/2 cup grated Parmesan cheese
- 1/2 medium onion, minced
- 1-1/2 teaspoons minced garlic
- 1 tablespoon chopped fresh parsley
- 1/2 teaspoon freshly ground black pepper
- 1 (16 ounces) jar Alfredo pasta sauce
- 8 no-boil lasagna noodles
- 1 pound cooked and cubed lobster meat
- 5-ounce package baby spinach leaves

Directions:

1. Mix well half of Parmesan, half of the mozzarella, half of cheddar, egg, and ricotta cheese in a medium bowl. Stir in pepper, parsley, garlic, and onion.
2. Place the instant pot air fryer lid on, lightly grease baking pan of the instant pot with cooking spray.
3. On the bottom of the pan, spread ½ of the Alfredo sauce, top with a single layer of lasagna noodles. Followed by 1/3 of lobster meat, 1/3 of ricotta cheese mixture, 1/3 of spinach. Repeat layering process until all ingredients are used up.
4. Sprinkle remaining cheese on top. Shake pan to settle lasagna and burst bubbles. Cover pan with foil and place the baking pan in the instant pot.
5. Close the air fryer lid and cook at 360 ºF for 30 minutes
6. Remove foil and cook for 10 minutes at 390 ºF until tops are lightly browned.
7. Let it stand for 10 minutes.
8. Serve and enjoy.
- **Nutrition Info:** Calories: 558; Carbs: 20.4g; Protein: 36.8g; Fat: 36.5g

220.Cheesy Shrimp

Servings: 4
Cooking Time: 20 Minutes
Ingredients:

- 2/3 cup Parmesan cheese, grated
- 2 pounds shrimp, peeled and deveined
- 4 garlic cloves, minced
- 2 tablespoons olive oil
- 1 teaspoon dried basil
- ½ teaspoon dried oregano
- 1 teaspoon onion powder
- ½ teaspoon red pepper flakes, crushed
- Ground black pepper, as required
- 2 tablespoons fresh lemon juice

Directions:

1. Preheat the Air fryer to 350 degree F and grease an Air fryer basket.
2. Mix Parmesan cheese, garlic, olive oil, herbs, and spices in a large bowl.
3. Arrange half of the shrimp into the Air fryer basket in a single layer and cook for about 10 minutes.
4. Dish out the shrimps onto serving plates and drizzle with lemon juice to serve hot.
- **Nutrition Info:** Calories: 386, Fat: 14.2g, Carbohydrates: 5.3g, Sugar: 0.4g, Protein: 57.3g, Sodium: 670mg

221.Fried Spicy Tofu

Servings: 4
Cooking Time: 20 Minutes
Ingredients:

- 16 ounces firm tofu, pressed and cubed
- 1 tablespoon vegan oyster sauce
- 1 tablespoon tamari sauce
- 1 teaspoon cider vinegar
- 1 teaspoon pure maple syrup
- 1 teaspoon sriracha
- 1/2 teaspoon shallot powder
- 1/2 teaspoon porcini powder
- 1 teaspoon garlic powder
- 1 tablespoon sesame oil
- 2 tablespoons golden flaxseed meal

Directions:

1. Toss the tofu with the oyster sauce, tamari sauce, vinegar, maple syrup, sriracha, shallot powder, porcini powder, garlic powder, and sesame oil. Let it marinate for 30 minutes.
2. Toss the marinated tofu with the flaxseed meal.
3. Cook at 360 degrees F for 10 minutes; turn them over and cook for 12 minutes more.
- **Nutrition Info:** 173 Calories; 13g Fat; 5g Carbs; 12g Protein; 8g Sugars; 1g Fiber

222.Beef Pieces With Tender Broccoli

Servings: 4
Cooking Time: 13 Minutes
Ingredients:

- 6 oz. broccoli
- 10 oz. beef brisket
- 4 oz chive stems
- 1 teaspoon paprika
- 1/3 cup water
- 1 teaspoon olive oil
- 1 teaspoon butter
- 1 tablespoon flax seeds
- ½ teaspoon chili flakes

Directions:

1. Cut the beef brisket into the medium/convenient pieces.
2. Sprinkle the beef pieces with the paprika and chili flakes.

3. Mix the meat up with the help of the hands.
4. Then preheat the air fryer to 360 F.
5. Spray the air fryer basket tray with the olive oil.
6. Put the beef pieces in the air fryer basket tray and cook the meat for 7 minutes.
7. Stir it once during the cooking.
8. Meanwhile, separate the broccoli into the florets.
9. When the time is over – add the broccoli florets in the air fryer basket tray.
10. Sprinkle the ingredients with the flax seeds and butter.
11. Add water.
12. Dice the chives and add them in the air fryer basket tray too.
13. Stir it gently using the wooden spatula.
14. Then cook the dish at 265 F for 6 minutes more.
15. When the broccoli is tender – the dish is cooked.
16. Serve the dish little bit chilled.
17. Enjoy!
- **Nutrition Info:** calories 187, fat 7.3, fiber 2.4, carbs 6.2, protein 23.4

223.Award Winning Breaded Chicken

Servings: 4
Cooking Time: 20 Minutes
Ingredients:
- 1 1/2 tsp.s olive oil
- 1 tsp. red pepper flakes, crushed 1/3 tsp. chicken bouillon granules 1/3 tsp. shallot powder
- 1 1/2 tablespoons tamari soy sauce 1/3 tsp. cumin powder
- 1½ tablespoons mayo 1 tsp. kosher salt
- For the chicken:
- 2 beaten eggs Breadcrumbs
- 1½ chicken breasts, boneless and skinless 1 ½ tablespoons plain flour

Directions:
1. Margarine fly the chicken breasts, and then, marinate them for at least 55 minutes. Coat the chicken with plain flour; then, coat with the beaten eggs; finally, roll them in the breadcrumbs.
2. Lightly grease the cooking basket. Air-fry the breaded chicken at 345 °F for 12 minutes, flipping them halfway.
- **Nutrition Info:** 262 Calories; 14.9g Fat; 2.7g Carbs; 27.5g Protein; 0.3g Sugars

224.Paprika Crab Burgers

Servings: 3
Cooking Time: 20 Minutes
Ingredients:
- 2 eggs, beaten
- 1 shallot, chopped
- 2 garlic cloves, crushed
- 1 tablespoon olive oil
- 1 teaspoon yellow mustard
- 1 teaspoon fresh cilantro, chopped
- 10 ounces crab meat
- 1 teaspoon smoked paprika
- 1/2 teaspoon ground black pepper
- Sea salt, to taste
- 3/4 cup parmesan cheese

Directions:
1. In a mixing bowl, thoroughly combine the eggs, shallot, garlic, olive oil, mustard, cilantro, crab meat, paprika, black pepper, and salt. Mix until well combined.
2. Shape the mixture into 6 patties. Roll the crab patties over grated parmesan cheese, coating well on all sides. Place in your refrigerator for 2 hours.
3. Spritz the crab patties with cooking oil on both sides. Cook in the preheated Air Fryer at 360 degrees F for 14 minutes. Serve on dinner rolls if desired.
- **Nutrition Info:** 279 Calories; 14g Fat; 7g Carbs; 23g Protein; 5g Sugars; 6g Fiber

225.Party Stuffed Pork Chops

Servings: 4
Cooking Time: 40 Minutes
Ingredients:
- 8 pork chops
- ¼ tsp pepper
- 4 cups stuffing mix
- ½ tsp salt
- 2 tbsp olive oil
- 4 garlic cloves, minced
- 2 tbsp sage leaves

Directions:
1. Preheat your air fryer to 350 f. cut a hole in pork chops and fill chops with stuffing mix. In a bowl, mix sage leaves, garlic cloves, oil, salt and pepper. Cover chops with marinade and let marinate for 10 minutes. Place the chops in your air fryer's cooking basket and cook for 25 minutes. Serve and enjoy!
- **Nutrition Info:** Calories: 364 Cal Total Fat: 13 g Saturated Fat: 4 g Cholesterol: 119 mg Sodium: 349 mg Total Carbs: 19 g Fiber: 3 g Sugar: 6 g Protein: 40 g

226.Portuguese Bacalao Tapas

Servings: 4
Cooking Time: 26 Minutes
Ingredients:
- 1-pound codfish fillet, chopped
- 2 Yukon Gold potatoes, peeled and diced
- 2 tablespoon butter
- 1 yellow onion, thinly sliced
- 1 clove garlic, chopped, divided
- 1/4 cup chopped fresh parsley, divided

- 1/4 cup olive oil
- 3/4 teaspoon red pepper flakes
- freshly ground black pepper to taste
- 2 hard-cooked eggs, chopped
- 5 pitted green olives
- 5 pitted black olives

Directions:
1. Place the instant pot air fryer lid on, lightly grease baking pan of the instant pot with cooking spray. Add butter and place the baking pan in the instant pot.
2. Close the air fryer lid and melt butter at 360 ºF. Stir in onions and cook for 6 minutes until caramelized.
3. Stir in black pepper, red pepper flakes, half of the parsley, garlic, olive oil, diced potatoes, and chopped fish. For 10 minutes, cook on 360 ºF. Halfway through cooking time, stir well to mix.
4. Cook for 10 minutes at 390 ºF until tops are lightly browned.
5. Garnish with remaining parsley, eggs, black and green olives.
6. Serve and enjoy with chips.
- **Nutrition Info:** Calories: 691; Carbs: 25.2g; Protein: 77.1g; Fat: 31.3g

227.Creole Beef Meatloaf

Servings: 6
Cooking Time: 15 Minutes
Ingredients:
- 1 lb. ground beef
- 1/2 tablespoon butter
- 1 red bell pepper diced
- 1/3 cup red onion diced
- 1/3 cup cilantro diced
- 1/3 cup zucchini diced
- 1 tablespoon creole seasoning
- 1/2 teaspoon turmeric
- 1/2 teaspoon cumin
- 1/2 teaspoon coriander
- 2 garlic cloves minced
- Salt and black pepper to taste

Directions:

1. Mix the beef minced with all the meatball ingredients in a bowl.
2. Make small meatballs out of this mixture and place them in the Air fryer basket.
3. Press "Power Button" of Air Fry Oven and turn the dial to select the "Air Fry" mode.
4. Press the Time button and again turn the dial to set the cooking time to 15 minutes.
5. Now push the Temp button and rotate the dial to set the temperature at 370 degrees F.
6. Once preheated, place the Air fryer basket in the oven and close its lid.
7. Slice and serve warm.
- **Nutrition Info:** Calories: 331 Cal Total Fat: 2.5 g Saturated Fat: 0.5 g Cholesterol: 35 mg Sodium: 595 mg Total Carbs: 69 g Fiber: 12.2 g Sugar: 12.5 g Protein: 26.7 g

228.Scallops With Capers Sauce

Servings: 2
Cooking Time: 6 Minutes
Ingredients:
- 10: 1-ouncesea scallops, cleaned and patted very dry
- 2 tablespoons fresh parsley, finely chopped
- 2 teaspoons capers, finely chopped
- Salt and ground black pepper, as required
- ¼ cup extra-virgin olive oil
- 1 teaspoon fresh lemon zest, finely grated
- ½ teaspoon garlic, finely chopped

Directions:
1. Preheat the Air fryer to 390 degree F and grease an Air fryer basket.
2. Season the scallops evenly with salt and black pepper.
3. Arrange the scallops in the Air fryer basket and cook for about 6 minutes.
4. Mix parsley, capers, olive oil, lemon zest and garlic in a bowl.
5. Dish out the scallops in a platter and top with capers sauce.
- **Nutrition Info:** Calories: 344, Fat: 26.3g, Carbohydrates: 4.2g, Sugar: 0.1g, Protein: 24g, Sodium: 393mg

229.Rosemary Turkey Scotch Eggs

Servings:4
Cooking Time: 12 Minutes
Ingredients:
- 1 egg
- 1 cup panko bread crumbs
- ½ teaspoon rosemary
- 1 pound (454 g) ground turkey
- 4 hard-boiled eggs, peeled
- Salt and ground black pepper, to taste
- Cooking spray

Directions:
1. Spritz the air fryer basket with cooking spray.
2. Whisk the egg with salt in a bowl. Combine the bread crumbs with rosemary in a shallow dish.
3. Stir the ground turkey with salt and ground black pepper in a separate large bowl, then divide the ground turkey into four portions.
4. Wrap each hard-boiled egg with a portion of ground turkey. Dredge in the whisked egg, then roll over the breadcrumb mixture.
5. Place the wrapped eggs in the basket and spritz with cooking spray.
6. Put the air fryer basket on the baking pan and slide into Rack Position 2, select Air Fry, set temperature to 400ºF (205ºC) and set time to 12 minutes.
7. Flip the eggs halfway through.
8. When cooking is complete, the scotch eggs should be golden brown and crunchy.
9. Serve immediately.

230.Mango Marinated Chicken Breasts

Servings: 2
Cooking Time: 20 Minutes + Marinating Time
Ingredients:
- 2 chicken breasts, cubed
- 1 large mango, cubed
- 1 red pepper, chopped
- 2 tbsp balsamic vinegar
- 5 tbsp olive oil
- 2 garlic cloves, minced
- 1 tbsp fresh parsley, chopped
- Salt to taste

Directions:
1. In a bowl, mix mango, garlic, red pepper, olive oil, salt, and balsamic vinegar. Add the mixture to a blender and pulse until smooth. Transfer to a bowl and add in the chicken cubes. Toss to coat and place in the fridge for 30 minutes.
2. Preheat on Air Fry function to 360 F. Remove the chicken from the fridge and place cubes in the greased basket. Fit in the baking tray and cook in the air fryer oven for 12 minutes, shaking once. Garnish with parsley and serve.

231.Pork Sausage With Cauliflower Mash

Servings:6
Cooking Time: 27 Minutes
Ingredients:
- 1 pound (454 g) cauliflower, chopped
- 6 pork sausages, chopped
- ½ onion, sliced
- 3 eggs, beaten
- $^1/_3$ cup Colby cheese
- 1 teaspoon cumin powder
- ½ teaspoon tarragon
- ½ teaspoon sea salt
- ½ teaspoon ground black pepper
- Cooking spray

Directions:
1. Spritz the baking pan with cooking spray.
2. In a saucepan over medium heat, boil the cauliflower until tender. Place the boiled cauliflower in a food processor and pulse until puréed. Transfer to a large bowl and combine with remaining ingredients until well blended.
3. Pour the cauliflower and sausage mixture into the pan.
4. Slide the baking pan into Rack Position 1, select Convection Bake, set temperature to 365ºF (185ºC) and set time to 27 minutes.
5. When cooking is complete, the sausage should be lightly browned.
6. Divide the mixture among six serving dishes and serve warm.

232.Pork Leg Roast With Candy Onions

Servings:4
Cooking Time: 52 Minutes
Ingredients:
- 2 teaspoons sesame oil
- 1 teaspoon dried sage, crushed
- 1 teaspoon cayenne pepper
- 1 rosemary sprig, chopped
- 1 thyme sprig, chopped
- Sea salt and ground black pepper, to taste
- 2 pounds (907 g) pork leg roast, scored
- ½ pound (227 g) candy onions, sliced
- 4 cloves garlic, finely chopped
- 2 chili peppers, minced

Directions:
1. In a mixing bowl, combine the sesame oil, sage, cayenne pepper, rosemary, thyme, salt and black pepper until well mixed. In another bowl, place the pork leg and brush with the seasoning mixture.
2. Place the seasoned pork leg in the baking pan. Put the baking pan into Rack Position 2,

select Air Fry, set temperature to 400ºF (205ºC) and set time to 40 minutes.
3. After 20 minutes, remove from the oven. Flip the pork leg. Return the pan to the oven and continue cooking.
4. After another 20 minutes, add the candy onions, garlic, and chili peppers to the pan and air fry for another 12 minutes.
5. When cooking is complete, the pork leg should be browned.
6. Transfer the pork leg to a plate. Let cool for 5 minutes and slice. Spread the juices left in the pan over the pork and serve warm with the candy onions.

233.Easy Cocktail Franks Rolls

Servings:4
Cooking Time: 20 Minutes
Ingredients:
- 12 oz cocktail franks
- 8 oz can crescent rolls

Directions:
1. Cut the dough in 1 by 5-inch rectangles with a knife. Gently roll the franks in the strips, making sure the ends are visible Place in freezer for 5 minutes.
2. Preheat oven to 330 F on AirFry function. Take the franks out of the freezer and place them in the frying basket. Press Start and cook for 8-10 minutes. Increase temperature to 390 F, and cook for another 3 minutes until a fine golden texture appears.

234.Fried Chicken Tenderloins

Servings: 4
Cooking Time: 15 Minutes
Ingredients:
- 8 chicken tenderloins
- 2 tbsp butter, softened
- 2 oz breadcrumbs
- 1 large egg, whisked

Directions:
1. Preheat on Air Fry function to 380 F. Combine butter and breadcrumbs in a bowl. Keep mixing and stirring until the mixture gets crumbly. Dip the chicken in the egg, then in the crumb mix. Place in the greased basket and fit in the baking tray; cook for 10 minutes, flipping once until crispy. Set on Broil function for crispier taste. Serve.

235.Copycat Taco Bell Crunch Wraps

Servings: 6
Cooking Time: 2 Minutes
Ingredients:
- 6 wheat tostadas
- 2 C. sour cream
- 2 C. Mexican blend cheese
- 2 C. shredded lettuce
- 12 ounces low-sodium nacho cheese
- 3 Roma tomatoes
- 6 12-inch wheat tortillas
- 1 1/3 C. water
- 2 packets low-sodium taco seasoning
- 2 pounds of lean ground beef

Directions:
1. Preparing the Ingredients. Ensure your air fryer oven is preheated to 400 degrees.
2. Make beef according to taco seasoning packets.
3. Place 2/3 C. prepared beef, 4 tbsp. cheese, 1 tostada, 1/3 C. sour cream, 1/3 C. lettuce, 1/6th of tomatoes and 1/3 C. cheese on each tortilla.
4. Fold up tortillas edges and repeat with remaining ingredients.
5. Lay the folded sides of tortillas down into the air fryer oven and spray with olive oil.
6. Air Frying. Set temperature to 400°F, and set time to 2 minutes. Cook 2 minutes till browned.
- **Nutrition Info:** CALORIES: 311; FAT: 9G; PROTEIN:22G; SUGAR:2

236.Garlic Pork Roast

Servings: 4
Cooking Time: 55 Minutes
Ingredients:
- 2 lbs pork sirloin roast
- 6 garlic cloves, sliced
- 2 tbsp olive oil
- 1/2 tsp pepper
- 1 tsp salt

Directions:
1. Fit the oven with the rack in position
2. Using a sharp knife make slits on top of the roast and stuff sliced garlic in each slit.
3. Season pork roast with pepper and salt.
4. Heat oil in a pan over medium-high heat.
5. Place roast in a pan and brown from all the sides.
6. Transfer roast in a baking pan.
7. Set to bake at 300 F for 60 minutes. After 5 minutes place the baking pan in the preheated oven.
8. Slice and serve.
- **Nutrition Info:** Calories 537 Fat 28.4 g Carbohydrates 1.7 g Sugar 0.1 g Protein 65 g Cholesterol 195 mg

237.Sumptuous Beef And Pork Sausage Meatloaf

Servings:4
Cooking Time: 25 Minutes
Ingredients:
- ¾ pound (340 g) ground chuck
- 4 ounces (113 g) ground pork sausage

- 2 eggs, beaten
- 1 cup Parmesan cheese, grated
- 1 cup chopped shallot
- 3 tablespoons plain milk
- 1 tablespoon oyster sauce
- 1 tablespoon fresh parsley
- 1 teaspoon garlic paste
- 1 teaspoon chopped porcini mushrooms
- ½ teaspoon cumin powder
- Seasoned salt and crushed red pepper flakes, to taste

Directions:
1. In a large bowl, combine all the ingredients until well blended.
2. Place the meat mixture in the baking pan. Use a spatula to press the mixture to fill the pan.
3. Slide the baking pan into Rack Position 1, select Convection Bake, set temperature to 360ºF (182ºC) and set time to 25 minutes.
4. When cooking is complete, the meatloaf should be well browned.
5. Let the meatloaf rest for 5 minutes. Transfer to a serving dish and slice. Serve warm.

238.Paprika Chicken Breasts With Ham & Cheese

Servings:4
Cooking Time: 35 Minutes
Ingredients:
- 4 chicken breasts
- 4 ham slices
- 4 Swiss cheese slices
- 3 tbsp all-purpose flour
- 4 tbsp butter
- 1 tbsp paprika
- 1 tbsp chicken bouillon granules
- ½ cup dry white wine
- 1 cup heavy whipping cream
- 1 tbsp cornstarch

Directions:
1. Preheat on AirFry function to 380 F. Pound the chicken breasts and put a slice of ham on each of the chicken breasts. Fold the edges over the filling and secure with toothpicks.
2. In a bowl, combine paprika and flour and coat in the chicken. Press Start and fry the chicken for 14-16 minutes.
3. Melt the butter in a skillet and add the bouillon and wine. Stir to combine and reduce the heat to low. Remove the chicken from the oven and place in the skillet. Let simmer for 5 minutes.

239.Baked Sweet & Tangy Pork Chops

Servings: 2
Cooking Time: 35 Minutes
Ingredients:

- 2 pork chops
- 2 tbsp brown sugar
- 2 tbsp ketchup
- 2 onion sliced
- Pepper
- Salt

Directions:
1. Fit the oven with the rack in position
2. Season pork chops with pepper and salt.
3. Place pork chops in a baking dish.
4. Mix ketchup and brown sugar and pour over pork chops.
5. Top with onion slices.
6. Set to bake at 375 F for 40 minutes. After 5 minutes place the baking dish in the preheated oven.
7. Serve and enjoy.
- **Nutrition Info:** Calories 308 Fat 19.9 g Carbohydrates 13.5 g Sugar 12.5 g Protein 18.4 g Cholesterol 69 mg

240.Stuffed Pork Chops

Servings: 4
Cooking Time: 35 Minutes
Ingredients:
- 4 pork chops, boneless and thick-cut
- 2 tbsp olives, chopped
- 3 tbsp sun-dried tomatoes, chopped
- 1/2 cup goat cheese, crumbled
- 3 garlic cloves, minced
- 2 tbsp fresh parsley, chopped

Directions:
1. Fit the oven with the rack in position
2. In a bowl, combine together cheese, garlic, parsley, olives, and sun-dried tomatoes.
3. Stuff cheese mixture all the pork chops.
4. Season pork chops with pepper and salt and place in baking pan.
5. Set to bake at 375 F for 40 minutes. After 5 minutes place the baking pan in the preheated oven.
6. Serve and enjoy.
- **Nutrition Info:** Calories 295 Fat 22.6 g Carbohydrates 1.6 g Sugar 0.4 g Protein 20.2 g Cholesterol 75 mg

241.Parmesan Chicken Fingers With Plum Sauce

Servings: 2
Cooking Time: 20 Minutes
Ingredients:
- 2 chicken breasts, cut in strips
- 3 tbsp Parmesan cheese, grated
- ¼ tbsp fresh chives, chopped
- ⅓ cup breadcrumbs
- 1 egg white
- 2 tbsp plum sauce, optional
- ½ tbsp fresh thyme, chopped
- ½ tbsp black pepper

- 1 tbsp water

Directions:
1. Preheat on Air Fry function to 360 F. Mix the chives, Parmesan cheese, thyme, pepper and breadcrumbs. In another bowl, whisk the egg white and mix with the water. Dip the chicken strips into the egg mixture and then in the breadcrumb mixture. Place the strips in the greased basket and fit in the baking tray. Cook for 10 minutes, flipping once. Serve with plum sauce.

242.Cripsy Crusted Pork Chops

Servings: 4
Cooking Time: 40 Minutes
Ingredients:
- 4 pork chops, boneless
- 1 cup parmesan cheese
- 1 tbsp olive oil
- 1 tsp garlic powder
- 1 cup breadcrumbs
- 1/2 tsp Italian seasoning
- Pepper
- Salt

Directions:
1. Fit the oven with the rack in position
2. In a shallow dish, mix breadcrumbs, parmesan cheese, Italian seasoning, garlic powder, pepper, and salt.
3. Brush pork chops with oil and coat with breadcrumb mixture.
4. Place coated pork chops in a baking pan.
5. Set to bake at 350 F for 45 minutes. After 5 minutes place the baking pan in the preheated oven.
6. Serve and enjoy.
- **Nutrition Info:** Calories 469 Fat 29.8 g Carbohydrates 20.8 g Sugar 1.9 g Protein 28.9 g Cholesterol 85 mg

243.Chili Chicken Strips With Aioli

Servings:4
Cooking Time: 20 Minutes
Ingredients:
- 1 lb chicken breasts, cut into strips
- 2 tbsp olive oil
- 1 cup breadcrumbs
- ½ tbsp garlic powder
- ½ tbsp chili powder
- ½ cup mayonnaise

Directions:
1. Preheat on AirFry function to 350 F. Mix breadcrumbs, garlic powder, and chili in a plate. Coat the strips in the breadcrumb mixture. Drizzle with olive oil.
2. Arrange the chicken strips on the basket and press Start. Cook for 12-14 minutes. To prepare the aioli: combine mayo with ground chili. Serve with the chicken strips.

244.Mustard Chicken Tenders

Servings: 4
Cooking Time: 20 Minutes
Ingredients:
- ½ C. coconut flour
- 1 tbsp. spicy brown mustard
- 2 beaten eggs
- 1 pound of chicken tenders

Directions:
1. Preparing the Ingredients. Season tenders with pepper and salt.
2. Place a thin layer of mustard onto tenders and then dredge in flour and dip in egg.
3. Air Frying. Add to the air fryer oven, set temperature to 390°F, and set time to 20 minutes.
- **Nutrition Info:** CALORIES: 403; FAT: 20G; PROTEIN:22G; SUGAR:4G

245.Herby Stuffed Turkey Breast

Servings: 4
Cooking Time: 35 Minutes
Ingredients:
- 1 pound turkey breast
- 1 ham slice
- 1 slice cheddar cheese
- 2 oz breadcrumbs
- 1 tbsp cream cheese
- ½ tsp garlic powder
- 1 tbsp fresh thyme, chopped
- 1 tbsp fresh tarragon, chopped
- 1 egg, beaten
- Salt and black pepper to taste

Directions:
1. Preheat on Air Fry function to 350 F. Cut the turkey in the middle; that way so you can add ingredients in the center. Season with salt, pepper, thyme, and tarragon. Combine cream cheese and garlic powder in a bowl.
2. Spread the mixture on the inside of the breast. Place half cheddar slice and half ham slice in the center of each breast. Dip in the egg first, then sprinkle with breadcrumbs. Cook on the baking tray for 30 minutes, flipping once.

246.Delicious Turkey Cutlets

Servings: 4
Cooking Time: 25 Minutes
Ingredients:
- 1 egg
- 1 1/2 lbs turkey cutlets
- 1/2 tsp garlic powder
- 1/2 tsp onion powder
- 1/2 tsp dried parsley
- 1/4 cup parmesan cheese, grated
- 1/2 cup almond flour

- 1/4 tsp pepper
- 1/2 tsp salt

Directions:
1. Fit the oven with the rack in position
2. Add egg in a small bowl and whisk well.
3. In a shallow dish, mix almond flour, parmesan cheese, parsley, onion powder, garlic powder, pepper, and salt.
4. Dip turkey cutlet into the egg and coat with almond flour mixture.
5. Place coated turkey cutlets into the baking pan.
6. Set to bake at 350 F for 30 minutes. After 5 minutes place the baking pan in the preheated oven.
7. Serve and enjoy.
- **Nutrition Info:** Calories 346 Fat 12.6 g Carbohydrates 1.6 g Sugar 0.4 g Protein 53.9 g Cholesterol 174 mg

247.Sweet Pork Meatballs With Cheddar Cheese

Servings:4
Cooking Time: 25 Minutes
Ingredients:
- 1 lb ground pork
- 1 large onion, chopped
- ½ tsp maple syrup
- 2 tsp yellow mustard
- ½ cup fresh basil leaves, chopped
- Salt and black pepper to taste
- 2 tbsp Cheddar cheese, grated

Directions:
1. In a bowl, add ground pork, onion, maple syrup, mustard, basil, salt, pepper, and cheddar cheese; mix well. Form balls. Place in the frying basket. Select AirFry function, adjust the temperature to 400 F, and press Start. Cook for 10 minutes, shake, and cook for 5 minutes.

248.Olive Caper Chicken

Servings: 4
Cooking Time: 18 Minutes
Ingredients:
- 4 chicken breast, boneless and halves
- 12 olives, pitted and halved
- 2 cups cherry tomatoes
- 3 tbsp olive oil
- 3 tbsp capers, rinsed and drained
- Pepper
- Salt

Directions:
1. Fit the oven with the rack in position
2. In a bowl, toss tomatoes, capers, olives with 2 tablespoons of oil. Set aside.
3. Season chicken with pepper and salt.
4. Heat remaining oil in a pan over high heat.
5. Place chicken in the pan and cook for 4 minutes.
6. Transfer chicken in baking dish. Top with tomato mixture.
7. Set to bake at 450 F for 23 minutes. After 5 minutes place the baking dish in the preheated oven.
8. Serve and enjoy.
- **Nutrition Info:** Calories 251 Fat 15 g Carbohydrates 4.7 g Sugar 2.4 g Protein 24.8 g Cholesterol 72 mg

249.Greek Chicken Paillard

Servings: 8
Cooking Time: 25 Minutes
Ingredients:
- 4 chicken breasts, skinless and boneless
- 1/2 cup olives, diced
- 1 small onion, sliced
- 1 fennel bulb, sliced
- 28 oz can tomatoes, diced
- 1/4 cup fresh basil, chopped
- 1/4 cup fresh parsley, chopped
- 1/4 cup pine nuts
- 2 tbsp olive oil
- Pepper
- Salt

Directions:
1. Fit the oven with the rack in position
2. Season chicken with pepper and salt and place in baking dish. Drizzle with oil.
3. In a bowl, mix together olives, tomatoes, pine nuts, onion, fennel, pepper, and salt.
4. Pour olive mixture over chicken.
5. Set to bake at 450 F for 30 minutes. After 5 minutes place the baking dish in the preheated oven.
6. Garnish with basil and parsley and serve.
- **Nutrition Info:** Calories 242 Fat 12.8 g Carbohydrates 9.3 g Sugar 3.9 g Protein 23.2 g Cholesterol 65 mg

250.Lime Chicken With Cilantro

Servings:4
Cooking Time: 10 Minutes
Ingredients:
- 4 (4-ounce / 113-g) boneless, skinless chicken breasts
- ½ cup chopped fresh cilantro
- Juice of 1 lime
- Chicken seasoning or rub, to taste
- Salt and ground black pepper, to taste
- Cooking spray

Directions:
1. Put the chicken breasts in the large bowl, then add the cilantro, lime juice, chicken seasoning, salt, and black pepper. Toss to coat well.

2. Wrap the bowl in plastic and refrigerate to marinate for at least 30 minutes.
3. Spritz the air fryer basket with cooking spray.
4. Remove the marinated chicken breasts from the bowl and place in the basket. Spritz with cooking spray.
5. Put the air fryer basket on the baking pan and slide into Rack Position 2, select Air Fry, set temperature to 400ºF (205ºC) and set time to 10 minutes.
6. Flip the breasts halfway through.
7. When cooking is complete, the internal temperature of the chicken should reach at least 165ºF (74ºC).
8. Serve immediately.

251.Air Fryer Herb Pork Chops

Servings: 4
Cooking Time: 15 Minutes
Ingredients:
- 4 pork chops
- 2 tsp oregano
- 2 tsp thyme
- 2 tsp sage
- 1 tsp garlic powder
- 1 tsp paprika
- 1 tsp rosemary
- Pepper
- Salt

Directions:
1. Fit the oven with the rack in position 2.
2. Line the air fryer basket with parchment paper.
3. Mix garlic powder, paprika, rosemary, oregano, thyme, sage, pepper, and salt and rub over pork chops.
4. Place pork chops in the air fryer basket then place an air fryer basket in the baking pan.
5. Place a baking pan on the oven rack. Set to air fry at 360 F for 15 minutes.
6. Serve and enjoy.
- **Nutrition Info:** Calories 266 Fat 20.2 g Carbohydrates 2 g Sugar 0.3 g Protein 18.4 g Cholesterol 69 mg

252.Citrus Carnitas

Servings:6
Cooking Time: 25 Minutes
Ingredients:
- 2½ pounds (1.1 kg) boneless country-style pork ribs, cut into 2-inch pieces
- 3 tablespoons olive brine
- 1 tablespoon minced fresh oregano leaves
- $^1/_3$ cup orange juice
- 1 teaspoon ground cumin
- 1 tablespoon minced garlic
- 1 teaspoon salt
- 1 teaspoon ground black pepper

- Cooking spray

Directions:
1. Combine all the ingredients in a large bowl. Toss to coat the pork ribs well. Wrap the bowl in plastic and refrigerate for at least an hour to marinate.
2. Spritz the air fryer basket with cooking spray.
3. Arrange the marinated pork ribs in the pan and spritz with cooking spray.
4. Put the air fryer basket on the baking pan and slide into Rack Position 2, select Air Fry, set temperature to 400ºF (205ºC) and set time to 25 minutes.
5. Flip the ribs halfway through.
6. When cooking is complete, the ribs should be well browned.
7. Serve immediately.

253.Spiced Pork Roast

Servings: 8
Cooking Time: 50 Minutes
Ingredients:
- Nonstick cooking spray
- 3 1/3 tbsp. brown sugar
- 2/3 tbsp. sugar
- 1 ½ tsp pepper
- 1 tsp salt
- 1 tsp ginger
- ¾ tsp garlic powder
- ¾ tsp onion salt
- ½ tbsp. dry mustard
- ¼ tsp cayenne pepper
- ¼ tsp crushed red pepper flakes
- ¼ tsp cumin
- ¼ tsp paprika
- ¾ tsp thyme
- 2 ½ lb. pork loin roast, boneless

Directions:
1. Place baking pan in position 1 of the oven. Spray the fryer basket with cooking spray.
2. In a small bowl, combine sugars and spices, mix well.
3. Rub spice mixture into all sides of the pork roast. Place roast in the basket.
4. Set oven to convection bake on 300°F for 60 minutes. After 5 minutes, place the basket on the pan and cook 45-50 minutes.
5. Remove from oven and let rest 10 minutes before slicing and serving.
- **Nutrition Info:** Calories 224, Total Fat 6g, Saturated Fat 2g, Total Carbs 8g, Net Carbs 8g, Protein 32g, Sugar 8g, Fiber 0g, Sodium 362mg, Potassium 549mg, Phosphorus 321mg

254.Sticky Chinese-style Chicken

Servings: 3
Cooking Time: 25 Minutes

Ingredients:

- 1 lb chicken wingettes
- 1 tbsp cilantro leaves, chopped
- Salt and black pepper, to taste
- 1 tbsp roasted peanuts, chopped
- ½ tbsp apple cider vinegar
- 1 garlic clove, minced
- ½ tbsp chili sauce
- 1 ginger, minced
- 1 ½ tbsp soy sauce
- 2 ½ tbsp honey

Directions:

1. In a bowl, mix ginger, garlic, chili sauce, honey, soy sauce, cilantro, salt, pepper, and vinegar. Add in the chicken toss to coat. Place the prepared chicken onto the greased basket and fit in the baking tray; cook for 20 minutes at 360 F on Air Fry function. Serve sprinkled with peanuts.

255.Pork Schnitzels With Sour Cream And Dill Sauce

Servings:4 To 6
Cooking Time: 4 Minutes
Ingredients:

- ½ cup flour
- 1½ teaspoons salt
- Freshly ground black pepper, to taste
- 2 eggs
- ½ cup milk
- 1½ cups toasted bread crumbs
- 1 teaspoon paprika
- 6 boneless, center cut pork chops (about 1½ pounds / 680 g), fat trimmed, pound to ½-inch thick
- 2 tablespoons olive oil
- 3 tablespoons melted butter
- Lemon wedges, for serving
- Sour Cream and Dill Sauce:
- 1 cup chicken stock
- 1½ tablespoons cornstarch
- $^{1}/_{3}$ cup sour cream
- 1½ tablespoons chopped fresh dill
- Salt and ground black pepper, to taste

Directions:

1. Combine the flour with salt and black pepper in a large bowl. Stir to mix well. Whisk the egg with milk in a second bowl. Stir the bread crumbs and paprika in a third bowl.
2. Dredge the pork chops in the flour bowl, then in the egg milk, and then into the bread crumbs bowl. Press to coat well. Shake the excess off.
3. Arrange the pork chop in the basket, then brush with olive oil and butter on all sides.
4. Put the air fryer basket on the baking pan and slide into Rack Position 2, select Air Fry,

set temperature to 400ºF (205ºC) and set time to 4 minutes.
5. After 2 minutes, remove from the oven. Flip the pork. Return to the oven and continue cooking.
6. When cooking is complete, the pork chop should be golden brown and crispy.
7. Meanwhile, combine the chicken stock and cornstarch in a small saucepan and bring to a boil over medium-high heat. Simmer for 2 more minutes.
8. Turn off the heat, then mix in the sour cream, fresh dill, salt, and black pepper.
9. Remove the schnitzels from the oven to a plate and baste with sour cream and dill sauce. Squeeze the lemon wedges over and slice to serve.

256.Asian Pork Shoulder

Servings: 4
Cooking Time: 15 Minutes
Ingredients:

- 1 lb pork shoulder, boneless
- 1 tbsp wine
- 1 tbsp sugar
- 2 tbsp soy sauce
- 4 tbsp honey
- 1 tsp Chinese five-spice
- 2 tsp ginger, minced
- 2 tsp garlic, minced

Directions:

1. Fit the oven with the rack in position 2.
2. Add all ingredients except pork into the large zip-lock bag and mix well.
3. Add pork and seal the bag and place it in the fridge overnight.
4. Remove pork from marinade and place in an air fryer basket then place an air fryer basket in baking pan.
5. Place a baking pan on the oven rack. Set to air fry at 390 F for 15 minutes.
6. Serve and enjoy.
- **Nutrition Info:** Calories 419 Fat 24.3 g Carbohydrates 22.1 g Sugar 20.5 g Protein 27.1 g Cholesterol 102 mg

257.Beef Steak Oregano Fingers

Servings:x
Cooking Time:x
Ingredients:

- 1 lb. boneless beef steak cut into Oregano Fingers
- 2 cup dry breadcrumbs
- 4 tbsp. lemon juice
- 2 tsp. salt
- 1 tsp. pepper powder
- 1 tsp. red chili powder
- 6 tbsp. corn flour
- 4 eggs

- 2 tsp. oregano
- 2 tsp. red chili flakes
- 1 ½ tbsp. ginger-garlic paste

Directions:
1. Mix all the ingredients for the marinade and put the beef Oregano Fingers inside and let it rest overnight. Mix the breadcrumbs, oregano and red chili flakes well and place the marinated Oregano Fingers on this mixture. Cover it with plastic wrap and leave it till right before you serve to cook. Pre heat the oven at 160 degrees Fahrenheit for 5 minutes. Place the Oregano Fingers in the fry basket and close it. Let them cook at the same temperature for another 15 minutes or so. Toss the Oregano Fingers well so that they are cooked uniformly.

258.Meatballs(13)

Servings: 4
Cooking Time: 20 Minutes
Ingredients:
- 1 lb ground turkey
- 1/4 cup basil, chopped
- 3 tbsp scallions, chopped
- 1 egg, lightly beaten
- 1/2 cup almond flour
- 1/2 tsp red pepper, crushed
- 1 tbsp lemongrass, chopped
- 1 1/2 tbsp fish sauce
- 2 garlic cloves, minced

Directions:
1. Fit the oven with the rack in position 2.
2. Line the air fryer basket with parchment paper.
3. Add all ingredients into a large bowl and mix until well combined.
4. Make small balls from meat mixture and place in the air fryer basket then place the air fryer basket in the baking pan.
5. Place a baking pan on the oven rack. Set to air fry at 380 F for 20 minutes.
6. Serve and enjoy.
- **Nutrition Info:** Calories 269 Fat 15.4 g Carbohydrates 3.4 g Sugar 1.3 g Protein 33.9 g Cholesterol 157 mg

259.Super Lemon Chicken

Servings:6
Cooking Time: 35 Minutes
Ingredients:
- 3 (8-ounce / 227-g) boneless, skinless chicken breasts, halved, rinsed
- 1 cup dried bread crumbs
- ¼ cup olive oil
- ¼ cup chicken broth
- Zest of 1 lemon
- 3 medium garlic cloves, minced
- ½ cup fresh lemon juice
- ½ cup water
- ¼ cup minced fresh oregano
- 1 medium lemon, cut into wedges
- ¼ cup minced fresh parsley, divided
- Cooking spray

Directions:
1. Pour the bread crumbs in a shadow dish, then roll the chicken breasts in the bread crumbs to coat.
2. Spritz a skillet with cooking spray, and brown the coated chicken breasts over medium heat about 3 minutes on each side. Transfer the browned chicken to the baking pan.
3. In a small bowl, combine the remaining ingredients, except the lemon and parsley. Pour the sauce over the chicken.
4. Slide the baking pan into Rack Position 1, select Convection Bake, set the temperature to 325ºF (163ºC) and set the time to 30 minutes.
5. After 15 minutes, remove the pan from the oven. Flip the breasts. Return the pan to the oven and continue cooking.
6. When cooking is complete, the chicken should no longer pink.
7. Transfer to a serving platter, and spoon the sauce over the chicken. Garnish with the lemon and parsley.

260.Garlic Butter Wings

Servings: 4
Cooking Time: 25 Minutes
Ingredients:
- 1 lb chicken wings
- 1 tsp garlic powder
- 1/4 tsp pepper
- 1/2 tsp Italian seasoning
- 1/2 tsp salt
- For sauce:
- 1 tbsp butter, melted
- 1/8 tsp garlic powder

Directions:
1. Fit the oven with the rack in position 2.
2. In a large bowl, toss chicken wings with Italian seasoning, garlic powder, pepper, and salt.
3. Arrange chicken wings in the air fryer basket then place an air fryer basket in the baking pan.
4. Place a baking pan on the oven rack. Set to air fry at 390 F for 25 minutes.
5. In a bowl, mix melted butter and garlic powder.
6. Add chicken wings and toss until well coated.
7. Serve and enjoy.

- **Nutrition Info:** Calories 246 Fat 11.5 g Carbohydrates 0.7 g Sugar 0.2 g Protein 33 g Cholesterol 109 mg

261.Chicken Schnitzel

Servings:4
Cooking Time: 5 Minutes
Ingredients:
- ½ cup all-purpose flour
- 1 teaspoon marjoram
- ½ teaspoon thyme
- 1 teaspoon dried parsley flakes
- ½ teaspoon salt
- 1 egg
- 1 teaspoon lemon juice
- 1 teaspoon water
- 1 cup bread crumbs
- 4 chicken tenders, pounded thin, cut in half lengthwise
- Cooking spray

Directions:
1. Spritz the air fryer basket with cooking spray.
2. Combine the flour, marjoram, thyme, parsley, and salt in a shallow dish. Stir to mix well.
3. Whisk the egg with lemon juice and water in a large bowl. Pour the bread crumbs in a separate shallow dish.
4. Roll the chicken halves in the flour mixture first, then in the egg mixture, and then roll over the bread crumbs to coat well. Shake the excess off.
5. Arrange the chicken halves in the basket and spritz with cooking spray on both sides.
6. Put the air fryer basket on the baking pan and slide into Rack Position 2, select Air Fry, set temperature to 390ºF (199ºC) and set time to 5 minutes.
7. Flip the halves halfway through.
8. When cooking is complete, the chicken halves should be golden brown and crispy.
9. Serve immediately.

262.Ranch Beef Patties

Servings: 4
Cooking Time: 12 Minutes
Ingredients:
- 1 lb ground beef
- 1/2 tsp onion powder
- 1/2 tsp garlic powder
- 2 tsp dried parsley
- 1/8 tsp dried dill
- 1/2 tsp paprika
- 1/2 tsp dried dill
- Pepper
- Salt

Directions:
1. Fit the oven with the rack in position 2.
2. Line the air fryer basket with parchment paper.
3. Add all ingredients into the large bowl and mix until well combined.
4. Make four even shape patties from the meat mixture and place in the air fryer basket then place an air fryer basket in the baking pan.
5. Place a baking pan on the oven rack. Set to air fry at 350 F for 12 minutes.
6. Serve and enjoy.
- **Nutrition Info:** Calories 214 Fat 7.1 g Carbohydrates 0.8 g Sugar 0.2 g Protein 34.6 g Cholesterol 101 mg

263.Dijon Garlic Pork Tenderloin

Servings: 6
Cooking Time: 10 Minutes
Ingredients:
- 1 C. breadcrumbs
- Pinch of cayenne pepper
- 3 crushed garlic cloves
- 2 tbsp. ground ginger
- 2 tbsp. Dijon mustard
- 2 tbsp. raw honey
- 4 tbsp. water
- 2 tsp. salt
- 1 pound pork tenderloin, sliced into 1-inch rounds

Directions:
1. Preparing the Ingredients. With pepper and salt, season all sides of tenderloin.
2. Combine cayenne pepper, garlic, ginger, mustard, honey, and water until smooth.
3. Dip pork rounds into the honey mixture and then into breadcrumbs, ensuring they all get coated well.
4. Place coated pork rounds into your air fryer oven.
5. Air Frying. Set temperature to 400°F, and set time to 10 minutes. Cook 10 minutes at 400 degrees. Flip and then cook an additional 5 minutes until golden in color.
- **Nutrition Info:** CALORIES: 423; FAT: 18G; PROTEIN:31G; SUGAR:3G

264.Dijon Pork Tenderloin

Servings:4
Cooking Time: 15 Minutes
Ingredients:
- 3 tablespoons Dijon mustard
- 3 tablespoons honey
- 1 teaspoon dried rosemary
- 1 tablespoon olive oil
- 1 pound (454 g) pork tenderloin, rinsed and drained
- Salt and freshly ground black pepper, to taste

Directions:

1. In a small bowl, combine the Dijon mustard, honey, and rosemary. Stir to combine.
2. Rub the pork tenderloin with salt and pepper on all sides on a clean work surface.
3. Heat the olive oil in an oven-safe skillet over high heat. Sear the pork loin on all sides in the skillet for 6 minutes or until golden brown. Flip the pork halfway through.
4. Remove from the heat and spread honey-mustard mixture evenly to coat the pork loin.
5. Select Bake of the oven, set temperature to 425ºF (220ºC) and set time to 15 minutes.
6. When cooking is complete, an instant-read thermometer inserted in the pork should register at least 145ºF (63ºC).
7. Remove from the oven and allow to rest for 3 minutes. Slice the pork into ½-inch slices and serve.

265.Homemade Teriyaki Pork Ribs

Servings:4
Cooking Time: 30 Minutes
Ingredients:
- ¼ cup soy sauce
- ¼ cup honey
- 1 teaspoon garlic powder
- 1 teaspoon ground dried ginger
- 4 (8-ounce / 227-g) boneless country-style pork ribs
- Cooking spray

Directions:
1. Spritz the air fryer basket with cooking spray.
2. Make the teriyaki sauce: combine the soy sauce, honey, garlic powder, and ginger in a bowl. Stir to mix well.
3. Brush the ribs with half of the teriyaki sauce, then arrange the ribs in the pan. Spritz with cooking spray.
4. Put the air fryer basket on the baking pan and slide into Rack Position 2, select Air Fry, set temperature to 350ºF (180ºC) and set time to 30 minutes.
5. After 15 minutes, remove from the oven. Flip the ribs and brush with remaining teriyaki sauce. Return to the oven and continue cooking.
6. When cooking is complete, the internal temperature of the ribs should reach at least 145ºF (63ºC).
7. Serve immediately.

266.Chicken Mexican Burritos

Servings:x
Cooking Time:x
Ingredients:
- ½ lb. chicken (You will need to cut the chicken into small pieces)
- 2 carrots (Cut in to long thin slices)
- 1-2 lettuce leaves shredded.
- 1 or 2 spring onions chopped finely. Also cut the greens.
- Take one tomato. Remove the seeds and chop it into small pieces.
- 1 green chili chopped.
- 1 tbsp. Olive oil
- 1 medium onion finely sliced
- 3 flakes garlic crushed
- 1 tsp. white wine
- A pinch of salt to taste
- ½ tsp. red chili flakes
- 1 cup of cheddar cheese grated.
- 1 cup boiled rice (not necessary).
- A few flour tortillas to put the filing in.
- ½ small onion chopped
- 1 tbsp. olive oil
- 2 tbsp. tomato puree
- ¼ tsp. red chili powder
- 1 tsp. of salt to taste
- 4-5 flour tortillas

Directions:
1. Cook the chicken, onions and garlic in two cups of water. You will need to cook till the chicken pieces have turned very soft. Now, mash the beans very fine.
2. In a pan, add oil and a few more onions to the pan and cook till the onions have turned translucent. Add the tomato puree and the cooked chicken and stir. Add the chili powder and salt to the pan and continue to cook till you get a thick paste. Set it aside.
3. For the filling, you will need to sauté the onions and garlic in oil. Add the French beans and the chopped carrots. You will need to stir-fry for a few minutes and add the remaining ingredients for the filling. Cook for another ten minutes and take the pan off the flame.
4. Mix it well and add the jalapenos. To make the salad, toss the ingredients together. Place a tortilla and add a layer of the French beans to it.
5. Cover the edges using the chicken paste. Put the filling in the center of the tortilla along with the salad and some boiled rice. Roll up the tortilla using the chicken sauce to help you hold it together. Pre-heat the oven for around 5 minutes at 200 Fahrenheit. Open the fry basket and keep the burritos inside. Close the basket properly.
6. Let the oven remain at 200 Fahrenheit for another 15 minutes or so. Halfway through, remove the basket and turn all the burritos over in order to get a uniform cook. You can either serve the burritos as they are or you can cut them into pieces so that they are easier to eat. Recommended sides are salsa or some salad.

267. Chuck And Sausage Subs

Servings:4
Cooking Time: 24 Minutes
Ingredients:

- 1 large egg
- ¼ cup whole milk
- 24 saltines, crushed but not pulverized
- 1 pound (454 g) ground chuck
- 1 pound (454 g) Italian sausage, casings removed
- 4 tablespoons grated Parmesan cheese, divided
- 1 teaspoon kosher salt
- 4 sub rolls, split
- 1 cup Marinara sauce
- ¾ cup shredded Mozzarella cheese

Directions:

1. In a large bowl, whisk the egg into the milk, then stir in the crackers. Let sit for 5 minutes to hydrate.
2. With your hands, break the ground chuck and sausage into the milk mixture, alternating beef and sausage. When you've added half of the meat, sprinkle 2 tablespoons of the grated Parmesan and the salt over it, then continue breaking up the meat until it's all in the bowl. Gently mix everything together. Try not to overwork the meat, but get it all combined.
3. Form the mixture into balls about the size of a golf ball. You should get about 24 meatballs. Flatten the balls slightly to prevent them from rolling, then place them in the baking pan, about 2 inches apart.
4. Slide the baking pan into Rack Position 2, select Roast, set temperature to 400ºF (205ºC), and set time to 20 minutes.
5. After 10 minutes, remove from the oven and turn over the meatballs. Return to the oven and continue cooking.
6. When cooking is complete, remove from the oven. Place the meatballs on a rack. Wipe off the baking pan.
7. Open the rolls, cut-side up, on the baking pan. Place 3 to 4 meatballs on the base of each roll, and top each sandwich with ¼ cup of marinara sauce. Divide the Mozzarella among the top halves of the buns and sprinkle the remaining Parmesan cheese over the Mozzarella.
8. Select Convection Broil, set temperature to High, and set time to 4 minutes.
9. Check the sandwiches after 2 minutes; the Mozzarella cheese should be melted and bubbling slightly.
10. When cooking is complete, remove from the oven. Close the sandwiches and serve.

268. Baked Zucchini Chicken Tenders

Servings: 4
Cooking Time: 30 Minutes
Ingredients:

- 2 lbs chicken tenders
- 1 large zucchini
- 2 tbsp feta cheese, crumbled
- 1 tbsp fresh lemon juice
- 1 tbsp fresh dill, chopped
- 1 cup grape tomatoes
- 2 tbsp olive oil

Directions:

1. Fit the oven with the rack in position
2. Coat chicken with oil and place in baking pan along with zucchini, dill, and tomatoes. Season with salt.
3. Set to bake at 400 F for 35 minutes. After 5 minutes place the baking dish in the preheated oven.
4. Drizzle with lemon juice and top with feta cheese.
5. Serve and enjoy.
- **Nutrition Info:** Calories 527 Fat 25.1 g Carbohydrates 5.2 g Sugar 2.9 g Protein 67.9 g Cholesterol 206 mg

269. Lettuce Chicken Tacos With Peanut Sauce

Servings:4
Cooking Time: 6 Minutes
Ingredients:

- 1 pound (454 g) ground chicken
- 2 cloves garlic, minced
- ¼ cup diced onions
- ¼ teaspoon sea salt
- Cooking spray
- Peanut Sauce:
- ¼ cup creamy peanut butter, at room temperature
- 2 tablespoons tamari
- 1½ teaspoons hot sauce
- 2 tablespoons lime juice
- 2 tablespoons grated fresh ginger
- 2 tablespoons chicken broth
- 2 teaspoons sugar
- For Serving:
- 2 small heads butter lettuce, leaves separated
- Lime slices (optional)

Directions:

1. Spritz the baking pan with cooking spray.
2. Combine the ground chicken, garlic, and onions in the baking pan, then sprinkle with salt. Use a fork to break the ground chicken and combine them well.
3. Slide the baking pan into Rack Position 1, select Convection Bake, set temperature to 350ºF (180ºC) and set time to 5 minutes.

4. Stir them halfway through the cooking time.
5. When cooking is complete, the chicken should be lightly browned.
6. Meanwhile, combine the ingredients for the sauce in a small bowl. Stir to mix well.
7. Pour the sauce in the pan of chicken, then bake for 1 more minute or until heated through.
8. Unfold the lettuce leaves on a large serving plate, then divide the chicken mixture on the lettuce leaves. Drizzle with lime juice and serve immediately.

270.Stuffed Bell Peppers

Servings: 6
Cooking Time: 15 Minutes
Ingredients:
- 6 green bell peppers, cut off tops & remove seeds
- 1 lb. lean ground beef
- 1 tbsp. olive oil
- ¼ cup green onion, chopped
- ¼ cup fresh parsley, chopped
- ½ tsp sage
- ½ tsp garlic salt
- 1 cup rice, cooked
- 1 cup marinara sauce
- Nonstick cooking spray
- ¼ cup mozzarella cheese, grated

Directions:
1. Heat a medium skillet over med-high heat. Add ground beef and cook, breaking up with spatula, until no longer pink. Drain off fat.
2. Add oil, onion, and seasonings and stir to mix.
3. Stir in rice and marinara and mix well.
4. Spoon beef mixture into the bell peppers.
5. Place the baking pan in position 2 of the oven. Lightly spray fryer basket with cooking spray.
6. Place peppers in basket and place on baking pan. Set oven to air fry on 355°F for 10 minutes.
7. Remove basket and sprinkle cheese over tops of peppers. Return to oven and cook another 5 minutes, or until peppers are tended and cheese is melted. Serve immediately.
- **Nutrition Info:** Calories 398, Total Fat 16g, Saturated Fat 5g, Total Carbs 35g, Net Carbs 31g, Protein 26g, Sugar 4g, Fiber 4g, Sodium 114mg, Potassium 674mg, Phosphorus 272mg

271.Crispy Crusted Chicken

Servings: 4
Cooking Time: 30 Minutes
Ingredients:
- 4 chicken breasts, skinless and boneless
- 2 tbsp butter, melted
- 3 cups corn flakes, crushed
- 1 tsp poultry seasoning
- 1 tsp water
- 1 egg, lightly beaten
- Pepper
- Salt

Directions:
1. Fit the oven with the rack in position
2. Season chicken with poultry seasoning, pepper, and salt.
3. In a shallow dish, whisk together egg and water.
4. In a separate shallow dish, mix crushed cornflakes and melted butter.
5. Dip chicken into the egg mixture then coats with crushed cornflakes.
6. Place the coated chicken into the parchment-lined baking pan.
7. Set to bake at 400 F for 35 minutes. After 5 minutes place the baking pan in the preheated oven.
8. Serve and enjoy.
- **Nutrition Info:** Calories 421 Fat 17.7 g Carbohydrates 18.6 g Sugar 1.5 g Protein 45.1 g Cholesterol 186 mg

272.Mixed Meat Balls

Servings: 8
Cooking Time: 15 Minutes
Ingredients:
- 1 lb. ground beef
- 1 lb. mild Italian sausage
- ¼ cup onion, chopped fine
- 2 cloves garlic, chopped fine
- 2 tbsp. fresh parsley, chopped
- 2 eggs
- 1½ cup parmesan cheese, grated
- ½ tsp salt
- ¼ tsp pepper
- ½ tsp crushed red pepper flakes
- ½ tsp Italian seasoning
- Nonstick cooking spray

Directions:
1. In a large bowl, combine all ingredients thoroughly.
2. Form mixture into 1-inch balls.
3. Place baking pan in position 2 of the oven. Lightly spray fryer basket with cooking spray.
4. Add meatballs in a single layer, these will need to be cooked in batches, to the basket.
5. Place basket on the baking pan and set oven to air fryer on 350°F for 15 minutes. Turn meatballs over halfway through cooking time. Serve immediately.
- **Nutrition Info:** Calories 406, Total Fat 30g, Saturated Fat 12g, Total Carbs 4g, Net Carbs

4g, Protein 30g, Sugar 0g, Fiber 0g, Sodium 951mg, Potassium 379mg, Phosphorus 335mg

273.Roasted Pork Tenderloin

Servings: 4
Cooking Time: 1 Hour
Ingredients:
- 1 (3-pound) pork tenderloin
- 2 tablespoons extra-virgin olive oil
- 2 garlic cloves, minced
- 1 teaspoon dried basil
- 1 teaspoon dried oregano
- 1 teaspoon dried thyme
- Salt
- Pepper

Directions:
1. Preparing the Ingredients. Drizzle the pork tenderloin with the olive oil.
2. Rub the garlic, basil, oregano, thyme, and salt and pepper to taste all over the tenderloin.
3. Air Frying. Place the tenderloin in the air fryer oven. Cook for 45 minutes.
4. Use a meat thermometer to test for doneness
5. Open the air fryer oven and flip the pork tenderloin. Cook for an additional 15 minutes.
6. Remove the cooked pork from the air fryer oven and allow it to rest for 10 minutes before cutting.
- **Nutrition Info:** CALORIES: 283; FAT: 10G; PROTEIN:48

274.Cheesy Chicken Casserole

Servings: 4
Cooking Time: 20 Minutes
Ingredients:
- 1 lb cooked chicken, shredded
- 1/2 cup salsa
- 4 oz cream cheese, softened
- 4 cups cauliflower florets
- 1/4 cup Greek yogurt
- 1 cup cheddar cheese, shredded
- 1/8 tsp pepper
- 1/2 tsp kosher salt

Directions:
1. Fit the oven with the rack in position
2. Add cauliflower into the boiling water and cook until tender. Drain well.
3. In a mixing bowl, mix cauliflower, salsa, cream cheese, chicken, yogurt, pepper, and salt.
4. Pour cauliflower mixture into the greased casserole dish and top with shredded cheddar cheese.
5. Set to bake at 375 F for 25 minutes. After 5 minutes place the casserole dish in the preheated oven.
6. Serve and enjoy.
- **Nutrition Info:** Calories 427 Fat 23.1 g Carbohydrates 9 g Sugar 4.1 g Protein 45.8 g Cholesterol 149 mg

275.Stuffed Pork Loin

Servings: 8
Cooking Time: 35 Minutes
Ingredients:
- 3 tbsp. butter
- 2 onions, sliced thin
- ½ cup beef broth
- 3 lb. pork loin, center cut
- 2 tbsp. extra virgin olive oil
- 1 tsp salt
- 1/4 tsp pepper
- 1 tsp Italian seasoning
- 2 cups gruyere cheese, grated
- Nonstick cooking spray

Directions:
1. Melt butter in a large skillet over med-high heat. Add onions and broth and cook until onions are brown and tender, about 15 minutes. Transfer to bowl and keep warm.
2. Butterfly the pork making sure you do not cut all the way through. Open up the tenderloin, cover with plastic wrap and pound to 1/3-inch thick.
3. In a small bowl, combine salt, pepper, and Italian seasoning. Rub both sides of pork with mixture.
4. Spread half the cooked onions on one side of pork and top with half the cheese. Tightly roll up pork and tie with butcher string.
5. Heat oil in skillet. Add the tenderloin and brown on all sides.
6. Set the oven to convection bake on 425°F for 35 minutes.
7. Lightly spray the baking pan with cooking spray and place pork on it. After the oven has preheated for 5 minutes, place the baking pan in position 1 and cook 30 minutes. Basting occasionally with juice from the pan.
8. Top pork with remaining onions and cheese. Increase heat to broil and cook another 5 minutes, or until cheese is melted and golden brown. Let rest 5 minutes before slicing and serving.
- **Nutrition Info:** Calories 448, Total Fat 24g, Saturated Fat 11g, Total Carbs 3g, Net Carbs 0g, Protein 55g, Sugar 1g, Fiber 0g, Sodium 715mg, Potassium 795mg, Phosphorus 665mg

276.Country Fried Steak

Servings: 2
Cooking Time: 12 Minutes
Ingredients:
- 1 tsp. pepper
- 2 C. almond milk
- 2 tbsp. almond flour
- 6 ounces ground sausage meat
- 1 tsp. pepper
- 1 tsp. salt
- 1 tsp. garlic powder
- 1 tsp. onion powder
- 1 C. panko breadcrumbs
- 1 C. almond flour
- 3 beaten eggs
- 6 ounces sirloin steak, pounded till thin

Directions:
1. Preparing the Ingredients. Season panko breadcrumbs with spices.
2. Dredge steak in flour, then egg, and then seasoned panko mixture.
3. Place into air fryer rack/basket.
4. Air Frying. Set temperature to 370°F, and set time to 12 minutes.
5. To make sausage gravy, cook sausage and drain off fat, but reserve 2 tablespoons.
6. Add flour to sausage and mix until incorporated. Gradually mix in milk over medium to high heat till it becomes thick.
7. Season mixture with pepper and cook 3 minutes longer.
8. Serve steak topped with gravy and enjoy!
- **Nutrition Info:** CALORIES: 395; FAT: 11G; PROTEIN:39G; SUGAR:5G

277.Chicken Ciabatta Sandwiches

Servings:4
Cooking Time: 13 Minutes
Ingredients:
- 2 (8-ounce / 227-g) boneless, skinless chicken breasts
- 1 teaspoon kosher salt, divided
- 1 cup all-purpose flour
- 1 teaspoon Italian seasoning
- 2 large eggs
- 2 tablespoons plain yogurt
- 2 cups panko bread crumbs
- $1^1/_3$ cups grated Parmesan cheese, divided
- 2 tablespoons olive oil
- 4 ciabatta rolls, split in half
- ½ cup marinara sauce
- ½ cup shredded Mozzarella cheese

Directions:
1. Lay the chicken breasts on a cutting board and cut each one in half parallel to the board so you have 4 fairly even, flat fillets. Place a piece of plastic wrap over the chicken pieces and use a rolling pin to gently pound them to an even thickness, about ½-inch thick. Season the chicken on both sides with ½ teaspoon of kosher salt.
2. Place the flour on a plate and add the remaining kosher salt and the Italian seasoning. Mix with a fork to distribute evenly. In a wide bowl, whisk together the eggs with the yogurt. In a small bowl combine the panko, 1 cup of Parmesan cheese, and olive oil. Place this in a shallow bowl.
3. Lightly dredge both sides of the chicken pieces in the seasoned flour, and then dip them in the egg wash to coat completely, letting the excess drip off. Finally, dredge the chicken in the bread crumbs. Carefully place the breaded chicken pieces in the basket.
4. Put the air fryer basket on the baking pan and slide into Rack Position 2, select Air Fry, set temperature to 375ºF (190ºC), and set time to 10 minutes.
5. After 5 minutes, remove from the oven. Carefully turn the chicken over. Return to the oven and continue cooking. When cooking is complete, remove from the oven.
6. Unfold the rolls on the basket and spread each half with 1 tablespoon of marinara sauce. Place a chicken breast piece on the bottoms of the buns and sprinkle the remaining Parmesan cheese over the chicken pieces. Divide the Mozzarella among the top halves of the buns.
7. Select Convection Broil, set temperature to High, and set time to 3 minutes.
8. Check the sandwiches halfway through. When cooking is complete, the Mozzarella cheese should be melted and bubbly.
9. Remove from the oven and close the sandwiches and serve.

278.Quail Marinade Cutlet

Servings:x
Cooking Time:x
Ingredients:
- ½ cup mint leaves
- 4 tsp. fennel
- 2 tbsp. ginger-garlic paste
- 1 small onion
- 6-7 flakes garlic (optional)
- Salt to taste
- 2 cups sliced quail
- 1 big capsicum (Cut this capsicum into big cubes)
- 1 onion (Cut it into quarters. Now separate the layers carefully.)
- 5 tbsp. gram flour
- A pinch of salt to taste
- For the filling:

- 2 cup fresh green coriander
- 3 tbsp. lemon juice

Directions:
1. You will first need to make the sauce. Add the ingredients to a blender and make a thick paste. Slit the pieces of quail and stuff half the paste into the cavity obtained.
2. Take the remaining paste and add it to the gram flour and salt. Toss the pieces of quail in this mixture and set aside.
3. Apply a little bit of the mixture on the capsicum and onion. Place these on a stick along with the quail pieces.
4. Pre heat the oven at 290 Fahrenheit for around 5 minutes. Open the basket. Arrange the satay sticks properly. Close the basket. Keep the sticks with the quail at 180 degrees for around half an hour while the sticks with the vegetables are to be kept at the same temperature for only 7 minutes.
5. Turn the sticks in between so that one side does not get burnt and also to provide a uniform cook.

279.Rosemary Turkey Breast

Servings:6
Cooking Time: 30 Minutes
Ingredients:
- ½ teaspoon dried rosemary
- 2 minced garlic cloves
- 2 teaspoons salt
- 1 teaspoon ground black pepper
- ¼ cup olive oil
- 2½ pounds (1.1 kg) turkey breast
- ¼ cup pure maple syrup
- 1 tablespoon stone-ground brown mustard
- 1 tablespoon melted vegan butter

Directions:
1. Combine the rosemary, garlic, salt, ground black pepper, and olive oil in a large bowl. Stir to mix well.
2. Dunk the turkey breast in the mixture and wrap the bowl in plastic. Refrigerate for 2 hours to marinate.
3. Remove the bowl from the refrigerator and let sit for half an hour before cooking.
4. Spritz the air fryer basket with cooking spray.
5. Remove the turkey from the marinade and place in the basket.
6. Put the air fryer basket on the baking pan and slide into Rack Position 2, select Air Fry, set temperature to 400ºF (205ºC) and set time to 20 minutes.
7. Flip the breast halfway through.
8. When cooking is complete, the breast should be well browned.
9. Meanwhile, combine the remaining ingredients in a small bowl. Stir to mix well.

10. Pour half of the butter mixture over the turkey breast in the oven and air fry for 10 more minutes. Flip the breast and pour the remaining half of butter mixture over halfway through.
11. Transfer the turkey on a plate and slice to serve.

280.Simple Air Fried Chicken Wings

Servings:4
Cooking Time: 15 Minutes
Ingredients:
- 1 tablespoon olive oil
- 8 whole chicken wings
- Chicken seasoning or rub, to taste
- 1 teaspoon garlic powder
- Freshly ground black pepper, to taste

Directions:
1. Grease the basket with olive oil.
2. On a clean work surface, rub the chicken wings with chicken seasoning and rub, garlic powder, and ground black pepper.
3. Arrange the well-coated chicken wings in the basket.
4. Put the air fryer basket on the baking pan and slide into Rack Position 2, select Air Fry, set temperature to 400ºF (205ºC) and set time to 15 minutes.
5. Flip the chicken wings halfway through.
6. When cooking is complete, the internal temperature of the chicken wings should reach at least 165ºF (74ºC).
7. Remove the chicken wings from the oven. Serve immediately.

281.Peach And Cherry Chicken

Servings:4
Cooking Time: 15 Minutes
Ingredients:
- $^1/_3$ cup peach preserves
- 1 teaspoon ground rosemary
- ½ teaspoon black pepper
- ½ teaspoon salt
- ½ teaspoon marjoram
- 1 teaspoon light olive oil
- 1 pound (454 g) boneless chicken breasts, cut in 1½-inch chunks
- 1 (10-ounce / 284-g) package frozen dark cherries, thawed and drained
- Cooking spray

Directions:
1. In a medium bowl, mix peach preserves, rosemary, pepper, salt, marjoram, and olive oil.
2. Stir in chicken chunks and toss to coat well with the preserve mixture.
3. Spritz the baking pan with cooking spray and lay chicken chunks in the pan.

4. Slide the baking pan into Rack Position 1, select Convection Bake, set the temperature to 400ºF (205ºC) and set the time to 15 minutes.
5. After 7 minutes, remove from the oven and flip the chicken chunks. Return the pan to the oven and continue cooking.
6. When cooking is complete, the chicken should no longer pink and the juices should run clear.
7. Scatter the cherries over and cook for an additional minute to heat cherries.
8. Serve immediately.

282.Barbecue Pork Club Sandwich With Mustard

Servings:x
Cooking Time:x
Ingredients:
- 2 slices of white bread
- 1 tbsp. softened butter
- ½ lb. cut pork (Get the meat cut into cubes)
- 1 small capsicum
- ¼ tbsp. red chili sauce
- 1 tbsp. tomato ketchup
- ½ cup water.
- ¼ tbsp. Worcestershire sauce
- ½ tsp. olive oil
- ½ flake garlic crushed
- ¼ cup chopped onion
- ¼ tsp. mustard powder
- ½ tbsp. sugar
- A pinch of salt and black pepper to taste

Directions:
1. Take the slices of bread and remove the edges. Now cut the slices horizontally. Cook the ingredients for the sauce and wait till it thickens. Now, add the pork to the sauce and stir till it obtains the flavors. Roast the capsicum and peel the skin off. Cut the capsicum into slices.
2. Mix the ingredients together and apply it to the bread slices.
3. Pre-heat the oven for 5 minutes at 300 Fahrenheit. Open the basket of the Fryer and place the prepared Classic Sandwiches in it such that no two Classic Sandwiches are touching each other. Now keep the fryer at 250 degrees for around 15 minutes.
4. Turn the Classic Sandwiches in between the cooking process to cook both slices. Serve the Classic Sandwiches with tomato ketchup or mint sauce.

283.Simple Jerk Chicken Wings

Servings: 2
Cooking Time: 20 Minutes
Ingredients:
- 1 lb chicken wings
- 1 tbsp jerk seasoning
- 1 tsp olive oil
- 1 tbsp cornstarch
- Pepper
- Salt

Directions:
1. Fit the oven with the rack in position 2.
2. In a large bowl, add chicken wings.
3. Add remaining ingredients on top of chicken wings and toss to coat.
4. Add chicken wings to the air fryer basket then place an air fryer basket in the baking pan.
5. Place a baking pan on the oven rack. Set to air fry at 380 F for 20 minutes.
6. Serve and enjoy.
- **Nutrition Info:** Calories 466 Fat 19.1 g Carbohydrates 3.7 g Sugar 0 g Protein 65.6 g Cholesterol 202 mg

284.Pork Fried Rice With Scrambled Egg

Servings:4
Cooking Time: 12 Minutes
Ingredients:
- 3 scallions, diced (about ½ cup)
- ½ red bell pepper, diced (about ½ cup)
- 2 teaspoons sesame oil
- ½ pound (227 g) pork tenderloin, diced
- ½ cup frozen peas, thawed
- ½ cup roasted mushrooms
- ½ cup soy sauce
- 2 cups cooked rice
- 1 egg, beaten

Directions:
1. Place the scallions and red pepper in the baking pan. Drizzle with the sesame oil and toss the vegetables to coat them in the oil.
2. Slide the baking pan into Rack Position 2, select Roast, set temperature to 375ºF (190ºC), and set time to 12 minutes.
3. While the vegetables are cooking, place the pork in a large bowl. Add the peas, mushrooms, soy sauce, and rice and toss to coat the ingredients with the sauce.
4. After about 4 minutes, remove from the oven. Place the pork mixture on the pan and stir the scallions and peppers into the pork and rice. Return the pan to the oven and continue cooking.
5. After another 6 minutes, remove from the oven. Move the rice mixture to the sides to create an empty circle in the middle of the pan. Pour the egg in the circle. Return the pan to the oven and continue cooking.
6. When cooking is complete, remove from the oven and stir the egg to scramble it. Stir the egg into the fried rice mixture. Serve immediately.

285.Worcestershire Ribeye Steaks

Servings:2 To 4
Cooking Time: 10 To 12 Minutes
Ingredients:

- 2 (8-ounce / 227-g) boneless ribeye steaks
- 4 teaspoons Worcestershire sauce
- ½ teaspoon garlic powder
- Salt and ground black pepper, to taste
- 4 teaspoons olive oil

Directions:

1. Brush the steaks with Worcestershire sauce on both sides. Sprinkle with garlic powder and coarsely ground black pepper. Drizzle the steaks with olive oil. Allow steaks to marinate for 30 minutes.
2. Transfer the steaks into the basket.
3. Put the air fryer basket on the baking pan and slide into Rack Position 2, select Roast, set the temperature to 400ºF (205ºC) and set time to 4 minutes.
4. After 2 minutes, remove from the oven. Flip the steaks. Return to the oven and continue cooking.
5. When cooking is complete, the steaks should be well browned.
6. Remove the steaks from the basket and let sit for 5 minutes. Salt and serve.

286.Crispy Cheesy Fish Fingers

Servings: 4
Cooking Time: 20 Minutes
Ingredients:
- Large codfish filet, approximately 6-8 ounces, fresh or frozen and thawed, cut into 1 ½-inch strips
- 2 raw eggs
- ½ cup of breadcrumbs (we like Panko, but any brand or home recipe will do)
- 2 tablespoons of shredded or powdered parmesan cheese
- 1 tablespoons of shredded cheddar cheese
- Pinch of salt and pepper

Directions:
1. Preparing the Ingredients. Cover the basket of the air fryer oven with a lining of tin foil, leaving the edges uncovered to allow air to circulate through the basket.
2. Preheat the air fryer oven to 350 degrees.
3. In a large mixing bowl, beat the eggs until fluffy and until the yolks and whites are fully combined.
4. Dunk all the fish strips in the beaten eggs, fully submerging.
5. In a separate mixing bowl, combine the bread crumbs with the parmesan, cheddar, and salt and pepper, until evenly mixed.
6. One by one, coat the egg-covered fish strips in the mixed dry ingredients so that they're fully covered, and place on the foil-lined Oven rack/basket. Place the Rack on the middle-shelf of the air fryer oven.
7. Air Frying. Set the air-fryer timer to 20 minutes.
8. Halfway through the cooking time, shake the handle of the air-fryer so that the breaded fish jostles inside and fry-coverage is even.
9. After 20 minutes, when the fryer shuts off, the fish strips will be perfectly cooked and their breaded crust golden-brown and delicious! Using tongs, remove from the air fryer oven and set on a serving dish to cool.

287.Browned Shrimp Patties

Servings:4
Cooking Time: 12 Minutes
Ingredients:
- ½ pound (227 g) raw shrimp, shelled, deveined, and chopped finely
- 2 cups cooked sushi rice
- ¼ cup chopped red bell pepper
- ¼ cup chopped celery
- ¼ cup chopped green onion
- 2 teaspoons Worcestershire sauce
- ½ teaspoon salt

- ½ teaspoon garlic powder
- ½ teaspoon Old Bay seasoning
- ½ cup plain bread crumbs
- Cooking spray

Directions:
1. Put all the ingredients except the bread crumbs and oil in a large bowl and stir to incorporate.
2. Scoop out the shrimp mixture and shape into 8 equal-sized patties with your hands, no more than ½-inch thick. Roll the patties in the bread crumbs on a plate and spray both sides with cooking spray. Place the patties in the air fryer basket.
3. Put the air fryer basket on the baking pan and slide into Rack Position 2, select Air Fry, set temperature to 390ºF (199ºC), and set time to 12 minutes.
4. Flip the patties halfway through the cooking time.
5. When cooking is complete, the outside should be crispy brown. Divide the patties among four plates and serve warm.

288.Tasty Lemon Pepper Basa

Servings: 4
Cooking Time: 12 Minutes
Ingredients:
- 4 basa fish fillets
- 8 tsp olive oil
- 2 tbsp fresh parsley, chopped
- 1/4 cup green onion, sliced
- 1/2 tsp garlic powder
- 1/4 tsp lemon pepper seasoning
- 4 tbsp fresh lemon juice
- Pepper
- Salt

Directions:
1. Fit the oven with the rack in position
2. Place fish fillets in a baking dish.
3. Pour remaining ingredients over fish fillets.
4. Set to bake at 425 F for 12 minutes. After 5 minutes place the baking dish in the preheated oven.
5. Serve and enjoy.
- **Nutrition Info:** Calories 308 Fat 21.4 g Carbohydrates 5.5 g Sugar 3.4 g Protein 24.1 g Cholesterol 0 mg

289.Lobster Spicy Lemon Kebab

Servings:x
Cooking Time:x
Ingredients:
- 1 lb. lobster (Shelled and cubed)
- 3 onions chopped
- 5 green chilies-roughly chopped
- 1 ½ tbsp. ginger paste
- 1 ½ tsp garlic paste

- 1 ½ tsp salt
- 3 tsp lemon juice
- 2 tsp garam masala
- 4 tbsp. chopped coriander
- 3 tbsp. cream
- 2 tbsp. coriander powder
- 4 tbsp. fresh mint chopped
- 3 tbsp. chopped capsicum
- 3 eggs
- 2 ½ tbsp. white sesame seeds

Directions:

1. Take all the ingredients mentioned under the first heading and mix them in a bowl. Grind them thoroughly to make a smooth paste.
2. Take the eggs in a different bowl and beat them. Add a pinch of salt and leave them aside.
3. Take a flat plate and in it mix the sesame seeds and breadcrumbs.
4. Dip the lobster cubes in the egg and salt mixture and then in the mixture of
5. breadcrumbs and sesame seeds. Leave these kebabs in the fridge for an hour or so to set.
6. Pre heat the oven at 160 degrees Fahrenheit for around 5 minutes. Place the kebabs in the basket and let them cook for another 25 minutes at the same temperature. Turn the kebabs over in between the cooking process to get a uniform cook. Serve the kebabs with mint sauce.

290.Panko Crab Sticks With Mayo Sauce

Servings:4
Cooking Time: 12 Minutes
Ingredients:

- Crab Sticks:
- 2 eggs
- 1 cup flour
- $^1/_3$ cup panko bread crumbs
- 1 tablespoon old bay seasoning
- 1 pound (454 g) crab sticks
- Cooking spray
- Mayo Sauce:
- ½ cup mayonnaise
- 1 lime, juiced
- 2 garlic cloves, minced

Directions:

1. In a bowl, beat the eggs. In a shallow bowl, place the flour. In another shallow bowl, thoroughly combine the panko bread crumbs and old bay seasoning.
2. Dredge the crab sticks in the flour, shaking off any excess, then in the beaten eggs, finally press them in the bread crumb mixture to coat well.
3. Arrange the crab sticks in the air fryer basket and spray with cooking spray.
4. Put the air fryer basket on the baking pan and slide into Rack Position 2, select Air Fry, set temperature to 390ºF (199ºC), and set time to 12 minutes.
5. Flip the crab sticks halfway through the cooking time.
6. Meanwhile, make the sauce by whisking together the mayo, lime juice, and garlic in a small bowl.
7. When cooking is complete, remove from the oven. Serve the crab sticks with the mayo sauce on the side.

291.Breaded Fish Fillets

Servings:4
Cooking Time: 7 Minutes
Ingredients:

- 1 pound (454 g) fish fillets
- 1 tablespoon coarse brown mustard
- 1 teaspoon Worcestershire sauce
- ½ teaspoon hot sauce
- Salt, to taste
- Cooking spray
- Crumb Coating:
- ¾ cup panko bread crumbs
- ¼ cup stone-ground cornmeal
- ¼ teaspoon salt

Directions:

1. On your cutting board, cut the fish fillets crosswise into slices, about 1 inch wide.
2. In a small bowl, stir together the mustard, Worcestershire sauce, and hot sauce to make a paste and rub this paste on all sides of the fillets. Season with salt to taste.
3. In a shallow bowl, thoroughly combine all the ingredients for the crumb coating and spread them on a sheet of wax paper.
4. Roll the fish fillets in the crumb mixture until thickly coated. Spritz all sides of the fish with cooking spray, then arrange them in the air fryer basket in a single layer.
5. Put the air fryer basket on the baking pan and slide into Rack Position 2, select Air Fry, set temperature to 400ºF (205ºC), and set time to 7 minutes.
6. When cooking is complete, the fish should flake apart with a fork. Remove from the oven and serve warm.

292.Cajun And Lemon Pepper Cod

Servings: 2 Cod Fillets
Cooking Time: 12 Minutes
Ingredients:

- 1 tablespoon Cajun seasoning
- 1 teaspoon salt
- ½ teaspoon lemon pepper
- ½ teaspoon freshly ground black pepper

- 2 (8-ounce / 227-g) cod fillets, cut to fit into the air fryer basket
- Cooking spray
- 2 tablespoons unsalted butter, melted
- 1 lemon, cut into 4 wedges

Directions:
1. Spritz the baking pan with cooking spray.
2. Thoroughly combine the Cajun seasoning, salt, lemon pepper, and black pepper in a small bowl. Rub this mixture all over the cod fillets until completely coated.
3. Put the fillets in the prepared pan and brush the melted butter over both sides of each fillet.
4. Slide the baking pan into Rack Position 1, select Convection Bake, set temperature to 360ºF (182ºC), and set time to 12 minutes.
5. Flip the fillets halfway through the cooking time.
6. When cooking is complete, the fish should flake apart with a fork. Remove the fillets from the oven and serve with fresh lemon wedges.

293.Spicy Catfish

Servings: 4
Cooking Time: 15 Minutes
Ingredients:
- 1 lb catfish fillets, cut 1/2-inch thick
- 1 tsp crushed red pepper
- 2 tsp onion powder
- 1 tbsp dried oregano, crushed
- 1/2 tsp ground cumin
- 1/2 tsp chili powder
- Pepper
- Salt

Directions:
1. Fit the oven with the rack in position
2. In a small bowl, mix cumin, chili powder, crushed red pepper, onion powder, oregano, pepper, and salt.
3. Rub fish fillets with the spice mixture and place in baking dish.
4. Set to bake at 350 F for 20 minutes. After 5 minutes place the baking dish in the preheated oven.
5. Serve and enjoy.
- **Nutrition Info:** Calories 164 Fat 8.9 g Carbohydrates 2.3 g Sugar 0.6 g Protein 18 g Cholesterol 53 mg

294.Rosemary & Garlic Prawns

Servings:2
Cooking Time: 15 Minutes + Chilling Time
Ingredients:
- 8 large prawns
- 2 garlic cloves, minced
- 1 rosemary sprig, chopped
- 1 tbsp butter, melted
- Salt and black pepper to taste

Directions:
1. Combine garlic, butter, rosemary, salt, and pepper in a bowl. Add in the prawns and mix to coat. Cover the bowl and refrigerate for 1 hour. Preheat on AirFry function to 350 F. Remove the prawns from the fridge and transfer to the frying basket. Cook for 6-8 minutes.

295.Italian Cod

Servings: 4
Cooking Time: 20 Minutes
Ingredients:
- 1 1/2 lbs cod fillet
- 1/4 cup olives, sliced
- 1 lb cherry tomatoes, halved
- 2 garlic cloves, crushed
- 1 small onion, chopped
- 1 tbsp olive oil
- 1/4 cup of water
- 1 tsp Italian seasoning
- Pepper
- Salt

Directions:
1. Fit the oven with the rack in position
2. Place fish fillets, olives, tomatoes, garlic, and onion in a baking dish. Drizzle with oil.
3. Sprinkle with Italian seasoning, pepper, and salt. Pour water into the dish.
4. Set to bake at 400 F for 25 minutes. After 5 minutes place the baking dish in the preheated oven.
5. Serve and enjoy.
- **Nutrition Info:** Calories 210 Fat 6.5 g Carbohydrates 7.2 g Sugar 3.8 g Protein 31.7 g Cholesterol 84 mg

296.Lemon-honey Snapper With Fruit

Servings:4
Cooking Time: 12 Minutes
Ingredients:
- 4 (4-ounce / 113-g) red snapper fillets
- 2 teaspoons olive oil
- 3 plums, halved and pitted
- 3 nectarines, halved and pitted
- 1 cup red grapes
- 1 tablespoon freshly squeezed lemon juice
- 1 tablespoon honey
- ½ teaspoon dried thyme

Directions:
1. Arrange the red snapper fillets in the air fryer basket and drizzle the olive oil over the top.
2. Put the air fryer basket on the baking pan and slide into Rack Position 2, select Air Fry, set temperature to 390ºF (199ºC), and set time to 12 minutes.

3. After 4 minutes, remove from the oven. Top the fillets with the plums and nectarines. Scatter the red grapes all over the fillets. Drizzle with the lemon juice and honey and sprinkle the thyme on top. Return the pan to the oven and continue cooking for 8 minutes, or until the fish is flaky.
4. When cooking is complete, remove from the oven and serve warm.

297.Savory Cod Fish In Soy Sauce

Servings: 4
Cooking Time: 20 Minutes
Ingredients:
- 4 cod fish fillets
- 4 tbsp chopped cilantro
- Salt to taste
- 2 green onions, chopped
- 1 cup water
- 4 slices of ginger
- 4 tbsp light soy sauce
- 3 tbsp oil
- 1 tsp dark soy sauce
- 4 cubes rock sugar

Directions:
1. Sprinkle the cod with salt and cilantro and drizzle with olive oil. Place in the cooking basket and fit in the baking tray; cook for 15 minutes at 360 F on Air Fry function.
2. Place the remaining ingredients in a frying pan over medium heat and cook for 5 minutes until sauce reaches desired consistency. Pour the sauce over the fish and serve.

298.Prawn Grandma's Easy To Cook Wontons

Servings:x
Cooking Time:x
Ingredients:
- 1 ½ cup all-purpose flour
- ½ tsp. salt
- 5 tbsp. water
- 2 cups minced prawn
- 2 tbsp. oil
- 2 tsp. ginger-garlic paste
- 2 tsp. soya sauce
- 2 tsp. vinegar

Directions:
1. Squeeze the dough and cover it with plastic wrap and set aside. Next, cook the ingredients for the filling and try to ensure that the prawn is covered well with the sauce. Roll the dough and place the filling in the center.
2. Now, wrap the dough to cover the filling and pinch the edges together. Pre heat the oven at 200° F for 5 minutes. Place the wontons in the fry basket and close it. Let

them cook at the same temperature for another 20 minutes. Recommended sides are chili sauce or ketchup.

299.Teriyaki Salmon

Servings:4
Cooking Time: 15 Minutes
Ingredients:
- ¾ cup Teriyaki sauce, divided
- 4 (6-ounce / 170-g) skinless salmon fillets
- 4 heads baby bok choy, root ends trimmed off and cut in half lengthwise through the root
- 1 teaspoon sesame oil
- 1 tablespoon vegetable oil
- 1 tablespoon toasted sesame seeds

Directions:
1. Set aside ¼ cup of Teriyaki sauce and pour the remaining sauce into a resealable plastic bag. Put the salmon into the bag and seal, squeezing as much air out as possible. Allow the salmon to marinate for at least 10 minutes.
2. Arrange the bok choy halves in the baking pan. Drizzle the oils over the vegetables, tossing to coat. Drizzle about 1 tablespoon of the reserved Teriyaki sauce over the bok choy, then push them to the sides of the pan.
3. Put the salmon fillets in the middle of the pan.
4. Slide the baking pan into Rack Position 2, select Roast, set temperature to 375ºF (190ºC), and set time to 15 minutes.
5. When done, remove the pan and brush the salmon with the remaining Teriyaki sauce. Serve garnished with the sesame seeds.

300.Carp Best Homemade Croquette

Servings:x
Cooking Time:x
Ingredients:
- 1 lb. Carp filets
- 3 onions chopped
- 5 green chilies-roughly chopped
- 1 ½ tbsp. ginger paste
- 1 ½ tsp garlic paste
- 1 ½ tsp salt
- 3 tsp lemon juice
- 2 tsp garam masala
- 4 tbsp. chopped coriander
- 3 tbsp. cream
- 2 tbsp. coriander powder
- 4 tbsp. fresh mint chopped
- 3 tbsp. chopped capsicum
- 3 eggs
- 2 ½ tbsp. white sesame seeds

Directions:
1. Take all the ingredients mentioned under the first heading and mix them in a bowl.

Grind them thoroughly to make a smooth paste. Take the eggs in a different bowl and beat them. Add a pinch of salt and leave them aside. Mold the fish mixture into small balls and flatten them into round and flat Best Homemade Croquettes. Dip these Best Homemade Croquettes in the egg and salt mixture and then in the mixture of breadcrumbs and sesame seeds.

2. Leave these Best Homemade Croquettes in the fridge for an hour or so to set. Pre heat the oven at 160 degrees Fahrenheit for around 5 minutes. Place the Best Homemade Croquettes in the basket and let them cook for another 25 minutes at the same temperature. Turn the Best Homemade Croquettes over in between the cooking process to get a uniform cook. Serve the Best Homemade Croquettes with mint sauce.

301.Lobster Grandma's Easy To Cook Wontons

Servings:x
Cooking Time:x
Ingredients:
- 1 ½ cup all-purpose flour
- ½ tsp. salt
- 5 tbsp. water
- For filling:
- 2 cups minced lobster
- 2 tbsp. oil
- 2 tsp. ginger-garlic paste
- 2 tsp. soya sauce
- 2 tsp. vinegar

Directions:
1. Squeeze the dough and cover it with plastic wrap and set aside. Next, cook the ingredients for the filling and try to ensure that the lobster is covered well with the sauce.
2. Roll the dough and place the filling in the center. Now, wrap the dough to cover the filling and pinch the edges together.
3. Pre heat the oven at 200° F for 5 minutes. Place the wontons in the fry basket and close it. Let them cook at the same temperature for another 20 minutes. Recommended sides are chili sauce or ketchup.

302.Chili Tuna Casserole

Servings:4
Cooking Time: 16 Minutes
Ingredients:
- ½ tablespoon sesame oil
- $^1/_3$ cup yellow onions, chopped
- ½ bell pepper, deveined and chopped
- 2 cups canned tuna, chopped
- Cooking spray
- 5 eggs, beaten
- ½ chili pepper, deveined and finely minced
- 1½ tablespoons sour cream
- $^1/_3$ teaspoon dried basil
- $^1/_3$ teaspoon dried oregano
- Fine sea salt and ground black pepper, to taste

Directions:
1. Heat the sesame oil in a nonstick skillet over medium heat until it shimmers.
2. Add the onions and bell pepper and sauté for 4 minutes, stirring occasionally, or until tender.
3. Add the canned tuna and keep stirring until the tuna is heated through.
4. Meanwhile, coat the baking pan lightly with cooking spray.
5. Transfer the tuna mixture to the baking pan, along with the beaten eggs, chili pepper, sour cream, basil, and oregano. Stir to combine well. Season with sea salt and black pepper.
6. Slide the baking pan into Rack Position 1, select Convection Bake, set temperature to 325ºF (160ºC), and set time to 12 minutes.
7. When cooking is complete, the eggs should be completely set and the top lightly browned. Remove from the oven and serve on a plate.

303.Easy Shrimp And Vegetable Paella

Servings:4
Cooking Time: 16 Minutes
Ingredients:
- 1 (10-ounce / 284-g) package frozen cooked rice, thawed
- 1 (6-ounce / 170-g) jar artichoke hearts, drained and chopped
- ¼ cup vegetable broth
- ½ teaspoon dried thyme
- ½ teaspoon turmeric
- 1 cup frozen cooked small shrimp
- ½ cup frozen baby peas
- 1 tomato, diced

Directions:
1. Mix together the cooked rice, chopped artichoke hearts, vegetable broth, thyme, and turmeric in the baking pan and stir to combine.
2. Slide the baking pan into Rack Position 1, select Convection Bake, set temperature to 340ºF (171ºC), and set time to 16 minutes.
3. After 9 minutes, remove from the oven and add the shrimp, baby peas, and diced tomato to the baking pan. Mix well. Return the pan to the oven and continue cooking for 7 minutes more, or until the shrimp are done and the paella is bubbling.

4. When cooking is complete, remove from the oven. Cool for 5 minutes before serving.

304. Lemon Salmon

Servings: 2
Cooking Time: 20 Minutes
Ingredients:
- 2 salmon fillets
- Salt to taste
- Zest of 1 lemon

Directions:
1. Rub the fillets with salt and lemon zest. Place them in the frying basket and spray with cooking spray. Press Start and cook the salmon in the preheated oven for 14 minutes at 360 F on AirFry function. Serve with steamed asparagus and a drizzle of lemon juice.

305. Salmon Beans & Mushrooms

Servings: 6
Cooking Time: 25 Minutes
Ingredients:
- 4 salmon fillets
- 2 tbsp fresh parsley, minced
- 1/4 cup fresh lemon juice
- 1 tsp garlic, minced
- 1 tbsp olive oil
- 1/2 lb mushrooms, sliced
- 1/2 lb green beans, trimmed
- 1/2 cup parmesan cheese, grated
- Pepper
- Salt

Directions:
1. Fit the oven with the rack in position
2. Heat oil in a small saucepan over medium-high heat.
3. Add garlic and sauté for 30 seconds.
4. Remove from heat and stir in lemon juice, parsley, pepper, and salt.
5. Arrange fish fillets, mushrooms, and green beans in baking pan and drizzle with oil mixture.
6. Sprinkle with grated parmesan cheese.
7. Set to bake at 400 F for 30 minutes. After 5 minutes place the baking pan in the preheated oven.
8. Serve and enjoy.
- **Nutrition Info:** Calories 225 Fat 11.5 g Carbohydrates 4.7 g Sugar 1.4 g Protein 27.5 g Cholesterol 58 mg

306. Lemon Tilapia

Servings: 4
Cooking Time: 12 Minutes
Ingredients:
- 1 tablespoon olive oil
- 1 tablespoon lemon juice
- 1 teaspoon minced garlic
- ½ teaspoon chili powder
- 4 tilapia fillets

Directions:
1. Line the baking pan with parchment paper.
2. In a shallow bowl, stir together the olive oil, lemon juice, garlic, and chili powder to make a marinade. Put the tilapia fillets in the bowl, turning to coat evenly.
3. Place the fillets in the baking pan in a single layer.
4. Put the air fryer basket on the baking pan and slide into Rack Position 2, select Air Fry, set temperature to 375ºF (190ºC), and set time to 12 minutes.
5. When cooked, the fish will flake apart with a fork. Remove from the oven to a plate and serve hot.

307. Crispy Crab And Fish Cakes

Servings: 4
Cooking Time: 12 Minutes
Ingredients:
- 8 ounces (227 g) imitation crab meat
- 4 ounces (113 g) leftover cooked fish (such as cod, pollock, or haddock)
- 2 tablespoons minced celery
- 2 tablespoons minced green onion
- 2 tablespoons light mayonnaise
- 1 tablespoon plus 2 teaspoons Worcestershire sauce
- ¾ cup crushed saltine cracker crumbs
- 2 teaspoons dried parsley flakes
- 1 teaspoon prepared yellow mustard
- ½ teaspoon garlic powder
- ½ teaspoon dried dill weed, crushed
- ½ teaspoon Old Bay seasoning
- ½ cup panko bread crumbs
- Cooking spray

Directions:
1. Pulse the crab meat and fish in a food processor until finely chopped.
2. Transfer the meat mixture to a large bowl, along with the celery, green onion, mayo, Worcestershire sauce, cracker crumbs, parsley flakes, mustard, garlic powder, dill weed, and Old Bay seasoning. Stir to mix well.
3. Scoop out the meat mixture and form into 8 equal-sized patties with your hands.
4. Place the panko bread crumbs on a plate. Roll the patties in the bread crumbs until they are evenly coated on both sides. Put the patties in the baking pan and spritz them with cooking spray.
5. Slide the baking pan into Rack Position 1, select Convection Bake, set temperature to 390ºF (199ºC), and set time to 12 minutes.
6. Flip the patties halfway through the cooking time.

7. When cooking is complete, they should be golden brown and cooked through. Remove the pan from the oven. Divide the patties among four plates and serve.

308.Easy Scallops

Servings:2
Cooking Time: 4 Minutes
Ingredients:
- 12 medium sea scallops, rinsed and patted dry
- 1 teaspoon fine sea salt
- ¾ teaspoon ground black pepper, plus more for garnish
- Fresh thyme leaves, for garnish (optional)
- Avocado oil spray

Directions:
1. Coat the air fryer basket with avocado oil spray.
2. Place the scallops in a medium bowl and spritz with avocado oil spray. Sprinkle the salt and pepper to season.
3. Transfer the seasoned scallops to the basket, spacing them apart.
4. Put the air fryer basket on the baking pan and slide into Rack Position 2, select Air Fry, set temperature to 390ºF (199ºC), and set time to 4 minutes.
5. Flip the scallops halfway through the cooking time.
6. When cooking is complete, the scallops should reach an internal temperature of just 145ºF (63ºC) on a meat thermometer. Sprinkle the pepper and thyme leaves on top for garnish, if desired. Serve immediately.

309.Parmesan Shrimp

Servings: 4
Cooking Time: 10 Minutes
Ingredients:
- 2 tbsp. olive oil
- 1 tsp. onion powder
- 1 tsp. basil
- ½ tsp. oregano
- 1 tsp. pepper
- 2/3 C. grated parmesan cheese
- 4 minced garlic cloves
- pounds of jumbo cooked shrimp (peeled/deveined)

Directions:
1. Preparing the Ingredients. Mix all seasonings together and gently toss shrimp with the mixture.
2. Air Frying. Spray olive oil into the Oven rack/basket and add seasoned shrimp. Place the Rack on the middle-shelf of the air fryer oven. Cook 8-10 minutes at 350 degrees. Squeeze lemon juice over shrimp right before devouring!
- **Nutrition Info:** CALORIES: 351; FAT:11G; PROTEIN:19G; SUGAR:1G

310.Grilled Soy Salmon Fillets

Servings: 4
Cooking Time: 8 Minutes
Ingredients:
- 4 salmon fillets
- 1/4 teaspoon ground black pepper
- 1/2 teaspoon cayenne pepper
- 1/2 teaspoon salt
- 1 teaspoon onion powder
- 1 tablespoon fresh lemon juice
- 1/2 cup soy sauce
- 1/2 cup water
- 1 tablespoon honey
- 2 tablespoons extra-virgin olive oil

Directions:
1. Preparing the Ingredients. Firstly, pat the salmon fillets dry using kitchen towels. Season the salmon with black pepper, cayenne pepper, salt, and onion powder.
2. To make the marinade, combine together the lemon juice, soy sauce, water, honey, and olive oil. Marinate the salmon for at least 2 hours in your refrigerator.
3. Arrange the fish fillets on a grill basket in your air fryer oven.
4. Air Frying. Bake at 330 degrees for 8 to 9 minutes, or until salmon fillets are easily flaked with a fork.
5. Work with batches and serve warm.

311.Cajun Red Snapper

Servings: 2
Cooking Time: 12 Minutes
Ingredients:
- 8 oz red snapper fillets
- 2 tbsp parmesan cheese, grated
- 1/4 cup breadcrumbs
- 1/2 tsp Cajun seasoning
- 1/4 tsp Worcestershire sauce
- 1 garlic clove, minced
- 1/4 cup butter

Directions:
1. Fit the oven with the rack in position
2. Melt butter in a pan over low heat. Add Cajun seasoning, garlic, and Worcestershire sauce into the melted butter and stir well.
3. Brush fish fillets with melted butter and place into the baking dish.
4. Mix together parmesan cheese and breadcrumbs and sprinkle over fish fillets.
5. Set to bake at 400 F for 17 minutes. After 5 minutes place the baking dish in the preheated oven.
6. Serve and enjoy.

6. Put the air fryer basket on the baking pan and slide into Rack Position 2, select Air Fry, set temperature to 390ºF (199ºC), and set time to 8 minutes.
7. Flip the fish chunks halfway through the cooking time.
8. When cooking is complete, they should be no longer translucent in the center and golden brown. Remove the fish chunks from the oven to a plate. Serve warm.

321.Caesar Shrimp Salad

Servings:4
Cooking Time: 15 Minutes
Ingredients:
- ½ baguette, cut into 1-inch cubes (about 2½ cups)
- 4 tablespoons extra-virgin olive oil, divided
- ¼ teaspoon granulated garlic
- ¼ teaspoon kosher salt
- ¾ cup Caesar dressing, divided
- 2 romaine lettuce hearts, cut in half lengthwise and ends trimmed
- 1 pound (454 g) medium shrimp, peeled and deveined
- 2 ounces (57 g) Parmesan cheese, coarsely grated

Directions:
1. Make the croutons: Put the bread cubes in a medium bowl and drizzle 3 tablespoons of olive oil over top. Season with granulated garlic and salt and toss to coat. Transfer to the air fryer basket in a single layer.
2. Put the air fryer basket on the baking pan and slide into Rack Position 2, select Air Fry, set temperature to 400ºF (205ºC), and set time to 4 minutes.
3. Toss the croutons halfway through the cooking time.
4. When done, remove from the oven and set aside.
5. Brush 2 tablespoons of Caesar dressing on the cut side of the lettuce. Set aside.
6. Toss the shrimp with the ¼ cup of Caesar dressing in a large bowl until well coated. Set aside.
7. Coat the baking pan with the remaining 1 tablespoon of olive oil. Arrange the romaine halves on the coated pan, cut side down. Brush the tops with the remaining 2 tablespoons of Caesar dressing.
8. Slide the baking pan into Rack Position 2, select Roast, set temperature to 375ºF (190ºC), and set time to 10 minutes.
9. After 5 minutes, remove from the oven and flip the romaine halves. Spoon the shrimp around the lettuce. Return the pan to the oven and continue cooking.
10. When done, remove from the oven. If they are not quite cooked through, roast for another 1 minute.
11. On each of four plates, put a romaine half. Divide the shrimp among the plates and top with croutons and grated Parmesan cheese. Serve immediately.

322.Old Bay Seasoned Scallops

Servings: 4
Cooking Time: 4 Minutes
Ingredients:
- 1 lb sea scallops
- 1/2 tsp garlic powder
- 1/2 cup crushed crackers
- 2 tbsp butter, melted
- 1/2 tsp old bay seasoning

Directions:
1. Fit the oven with the rack in position 2.
2. In a shallow dish, mix crushed crackers, garlic powder, and old bay seasoning.
3. Add melted butter in a separate shallow dish.
4. Dip scallops in melted butter and coat with crushed crackers.
5. Place coated scallops in air fryer basket then place air fryer basket in baking pan.
6. Place a baking pan on the oven rack. Set to air fry at 390 F for 4 minutes.
7. Serve and enjoy.
- **Nutrition Info:** Calories 167 Fat 7.4 g Carbohydrates 4.8 g Sugar 0.5 g Protein 19.5 g Cholesterol 53 mg

323.Spicy Lemon Cod

Servings: 2
Cooking Time: 10 Minutes
Ingredients:
- 1 lb cod fillets
- 1/4 tsp chili powder
- 1 tbsp fresh parsley, chopped
- 1 1/2 tbsp olive oil
- 1 tbsp fresh lemon juice
- 1/8 tsp cayenne pepper
- 1/4 tsp salt

Directions:
1. Fit the oven with the rack in position
2. Arrange fish fillets in a baking dish. Drizzle with oil and lemon juice.
3. Sprinkle with chili powder, salt, and cayenne pepper.
4. Set to bake at 400 F for 15 minutes. After 5 minutes place the baking dish in the preheated oven.
5. Garnish with parsley and serve.
- **Nutrition Info:** Calories 276 Fat 12.7 g Carbohydrates 0.5 g Sugar 0.2 g Protein 40.7 g Cholesterol 111 mg

324.Herb Fish Fillets

Servings: 2
Cooking Time: 5 Minutes
Ingredients:
- 2 salmon fillets
- 1/4 tsp smoked paprika
- 1 tsp herb de Provence
- 1 tbsp butter, melted
- 2 tbsp olive oil
- Pepper
- Salt

Directions:
1. Fit the oven with the rack in position 2.
2. Brush salmon fillets with oil and sprinkle with paprika, herb de Provence, pepper, and salt.
3. Place salmon fillets in the air fryer basket then place an air fryer basket in the baking pan.
4. Place a baking pan on the oven rack. Set to air fry at 390 F for 5 minutes.
5. Drizzle melted butter over salmon and serve.
- **Nutrition Info:** Calories 413 Fat 31.1 g Carbohydrates 0.2 g Sugar 0 g Protein 35.4 g Cholesterol 94 mg

325.Coconut Chili Fish Curry

Servings:4
Cooking Time: 22 Minutes
Ingredients:
- 2 tablespoons sunflower oil, divided
- 1 pound (454 g) fish, chopped
- 1 ripe tomato, pureéd
- 2 red chilies, chopped
- 1 shallot, minced
- 1 garlic clove, minced
- 1 cup coconut milk
- 1 tablespoon coriander powder
- 1 teaspoon red curry paste
- ½ teaspoon fenugreek seeds
- Salt and white pepper, to taste

Directions:
1. Coat the air fryer basket with 1 tablespoon of sunflower oil. Place the fish in the basket.
2. Put the air fryer basket on the baking pan and slide into Rack Position 2, select Air Fry, set temperature to 380ºF (193ºC), and set time to 10 minutes.
3. Flip the fish halfway through the cooking time.
4. When cooking is complete, transfer the cooked fish to the baking pan greased with the remaining 1 tablespoon of sunflower oil. Stir in the remaining ingredients.
5. Put the air fryer basket on the baking pan and slide into Rack Position 2, select Air Fry, set temperature to 350ºF (180ºC), and set time to 12 minutes.

6. When cooking is complete, they should be heated through. Cool for 5 to 8 minutes before serving.

326.Cheesy Tilapia Fillets

Servings: 4
Cooking Time: 15 Minutes
Ingredients:
- ¾ cup grated Parmesan cheese
- 1 tbsp olive oil
- 2 tsp paprika
- 1 tbsp chopped parsley
- ¼ tsp garlic powder
- 4 tilapia fillets

Directions:
1. Preheat on Air Fry function to 350 F. Mix parsley, Parmesan cheese, garlic, and paprika in a bowl. Brush the olive oil over the fillets and then coat with the Parmesan mixture. Place the tilapia onto a lined baking sheet and cook for 8-10 minutes, turning once. Serve.

327.Baked Tilapia

Servings: 4
Cooking Time: 10 Minutes
Ingredients:
- 1 1/4 lbs tilapia fillets
- 2 tsp onion powder
- 2 tbsp olive oil
- 1/2 tsp garlic powder
- 1/2 tsp dried thyme
- 1/2 tsp oregano
- 1/2 tsp chili powder
- 2 tbsp sweet paprika
- 1 tsp pepper
- 1/2 tsp salt

Directions:
1. Fit the oven with the rack in position
2. Brush fish fillets with oil and place in baking dish.
3. Mix together spices and sprinkle over the fish fillets.
4. Set to bake at 425 F for 15 minutes. After 5 minutes place the baking dish in the preheated oven.
5. Serve and enjoy.
- **Nutrition Info:** Calories 195 Fat 8.9 g Carbohydrates 3.9 g Sugar 0.9 g Protein 27.2 g Cholesterol 69 mg

328.Asian-inspired Swordfish Steaks

Servings:4
Cooking Time: 8 Minutes
Ingredients:
- 4 (4-ounce / 113-g) swordfish steaks
- ½ teaspoon toasted sesame oil
- 1 jalapeño pepper, finely minced
- 2 garlic cloves, grated

- 2 tablespoons freshly squeezed lemon juice
- 1 tablespoon grated fresh ginger
- ½ teaspoon Chinese five-spice powder
- ⅛ teaspoon freshly ground black pepper

Directions:
1. On a clean work surface, place the swordfish steaks and brush both sides of the fish with the sesame oil.
2. Combine the jalapeño, garlic, lemon juice, ginger, five-spice powder, and black pepper in a small bowl and stir to mix well. Rub the mixture all over the fish until completely coated. Allow to sit for 10 minutes.
3. When ready, arrange the swordfish steaks in the air fryer basket.
4. Put the air fryer basket on the baking pan and slide into Rack Position 2, select Air Fry, set temperature to 380ºF (193ºC), and set time to 8 minutes.
5. Flip the steaks halfway through.
6. When cooking is complete, remove from the oven and cool for 5 minutes before serving.

329.Fish And Chips

Servings: 4
Cooking Time: 20 Minutes
Ingredients:
- 4 (4-ounce) fish fillets
- Pinch salt
- Freshly ground black pepper
- ½ teaspoon dried thyme
- 1 egg white
- ¾ cup crushed potato chips
- 2 tablespoons olive oil, divided
- 1 russet potatoes, peeled and cut into strips

Directions:
1. Preparing the Ingredients. Pat the fish fillets dry and sprinkle with salt, pepper, and thyme. Set aside.
2. In a shallow bowl, beat the egg white until foamy. In another bowl, combine the potato chips and 1 tablespoon of olive oil and mix until combined.
3. Dip the fish fillets into the egg white, then into the crushed potato chip mixture to coat.
4. Toss the fresh potato strips with the remaining 1 tablespoon olive oil.
5. Air Frying. Use your separator to divide the Oven rack/basket in half, then fry the chips and fish. The chips will take about 20 minutes; the fish will take about 10 to 12 minutes to cook.
- **Nutrition Info:** CALORIES: 374; FAT:16G; PROTEIN:30G; FIBER:4G

330.Garlic-butter Catfish

Servings: 2
Cooking Time: 20 Minutes

Ingredients:
- 2 catfish fillets
- 2 tsp blackening seasoning
- Juice of 1 lime
- 2 tbsp butter, melted
- 1 garlic clove, mashed
- 2 tbsp cilantro

Directions:
1. In a bowl, blend in garlic, lime juice, cilantro, and butter. Pour half of the mixture over the fillets and sprinkle with blackening seasoning. Place the fillets in the basket and fit in the baking tray; cook for 15 minutes at 360 F on Air Fry function. Serve the fish with remaining sauce.

331.Crab Cakes

Servings: 4
Cooking Time: 10 Minutes
Ingredients:
- 8 ounces jumbo lump crabmeat
- 1 tablespoon Old Bay Seasoning
- ⅓ cup bread crumbs
- ¼ cup diced red bell pepper
- ¼ cup diced green bell pepper
- 1 egg
- ¼ cup mayonnaise
- Juice of ½ lemon
- 1 teaspoon flour
- Cooking oil

Directions:
1. Preparing the Ingredients. In a large bowl, combine the crabmeat, Old Bay Seasoning, bread crumbs, red bell pepper, green bell pepper, egg, mayo, and lemon juice. Mix gently to combine.
2. Form the mixture into 4 patties. Sprinkle ¼ teaspoon of flour on top of each patty.
3. Air Frying. Place the crab cakes in the air fryer oven. Spray them with cooking oil. Cook for 10 minutes.
4. Serve.

332.Parmesan-crusted Salmon Patties

Servings:4
Cooking Time: 13 Minutes
Ingredients:
- 1 pound (454 g) salmon, chopped into ½-inch pieces
- 2 tablespoons coconut flour
- 2 tablespoons grated Parmesan cheese
- 1½ tablespoons milk
- ½ white onion, peeled and finely chopped
- ½ teaspoon butter, at room temperature
- ½ teaspoon chipotle powder
- ½ teaspoon dried parsley flakes
- $^1/_3$ teaspoon ground black pepper
- $^1/_3$ teaspoon smoked cayenne pepper
- 1 teaspoon fine sea salt

Directions:

1. Put all the ingredients for the salmon patties in a bowl and stir to combine well.
2. Scoop out 2 tablespoons of the salmon mixture and shape into a patty with your palm, about ½ inch thick. Repeat until all the mixture is used. Transfer to the refrigerator for about 2 hours until firm.
3. When ready, arrange the salmon patties in the baking pan.
4. Slide the baking pan into Rack Position 1, select Convection Bake, set temperature to 395ºF (202ºC), and set time to 13 minutes.
5. Flip the patties halfway through the cooking time.
6. When cooking is complete, the patties should be golden brown. Remove from the oven and cool for 5 minutes before serving.

333.Baked Halibut Steaks With Parsley

Servings: 4
Cooking Time: 10 Minutes
Ingredients:

- 1 pound (454 g) halibut steaks
- ¼ cup vegetable oil
- 2½ tablespoons Worcester sauce
- 2 tablespoons honey
- 2 tablespoons vermouth
- 1 tablespoon freshly squeezed lemon juice
- 1 tablespoon fresh parsley leaves, coarsely chopped
- Salt and pepper, to taste
- 1 teaspoon dried basil

Directions:

1. Put all the ingredients in a large mixing dish and gently stir until the fish is coated evenly. Transfer the fish to the baking pan.
2. Slide the baking pan into Rack Position 1, select Convection Bake, set temperature to 375ºF (190ºC), and set time to 10 minutes.
3. Flip the fish halfway through cooking time.
4. When cooking is complete, the fish should reach an internal temperature of at least 145ºF (63ºC) on a meat thermometer. Remove from the oven and let the fish cool for 5 minutes before serving.

334.Easy Baked Fish Fillet

Servings: 4
Cooking Time: 15 Minutes
Ingredients:

- 1 lb white fish fillets
- 2 tbsp dried parsley
- 1/4 tsp red chili flakes
- 2 tbsp garlic, minced
- 2 tbsp olive oil
- Pepper
- Salt

Directions:

1. Fit the oven with the rack in position
2. Place fish fillets in a baking dish and drizzle with oil.
3. Sprinkle with chili flakes, parsley, and garlic. Season with pepper and salt.
4. Set to bake at 400 F for 20 minutes. After 5 minutes place the baking dish in the preheated oven.
5. Serve and enjoy.
- **Nutrition Info:** Calories 262 Fat 15.6 g Carbohydrates 1.5 g Sugar 0.1 g Protein 28.1 g Cholesterol 87 mg

335.Parmesan-crusted Halibut Fillets

Servings:4
Cooking Time: 10 Minutes
Ingredients:

- 2 medium-sized halibut fillets
- Dash of tabasco sauce
- 1 teaspoon curry powder
- ½ teaspoon ground coriander
- ½ teaspoon hot paprika
- Kosher salt and freshly cracked mixed peppercorns, to taste
- 2 eggs
- 1½ tablespoons olive oil
- ½ cup grated Parmesan cheese

Directions:

1. On a clean work surface, drizzle the halibut fillets with the tabasco sauce. Sprinkle with the curry powder, coriander, hot paprika, salt, and cracked mixed peppercorns. Set aside.
2. In a shallow bowl, beat the eggs until frothy. In another shallow bowl, combine the olive oil and Parmesan cheese.
3. One at a time, dredge the halibut fillets in the beaten eggs, shaking off any excess, then roll them over the Parmesan cheese until evenly coated.
4. Arrange the halibut fillets in the air fryer basket in a single layer.
5. Put the air fryer basket on the baking pan and slide into Rack Position 2, select Roast, set temperature to 365ºF (185ºC), and set time to 10 minutes.
6. When cooking is complete, the fish should be golden brown and crisp. Cool for 5 minutes before serving.

336.Chili Prawns

Servings:2
Cooking Time: 8 Minutes
Ingredients:

- 8 prawns, cleaned
- Salt and black pepper, to taste
- ½ teaspoon ground cayenne pepper
- ½ teaspoon garlic powder
- ½ teaspoon ground cumin

- ½ teaspoon red chili flakes
- Cooking spray

Directions:

1. Spritz the air fryer basket with cooking spray.
2. Toss the remaining ingredients in a large bowl until the prawns are well coated.
3. Spread the coated prawns evenly in the basket and spray them with cooking spray.
4. Put the air fryer basket on the baking pan and slide into Rack Position 2, select Air Fry, set temperature to 340ºF (171ºC), and set time to 8 minutes.
5. Flip the prawns halfway through the cooking time.
6. When cooking is complete, the prawns should be pink. Remove the prawns from the oven to a plate.

337.Quick Tuna Patties

Servings: 10
Cooking Time: 10 Minutes
Ingredients:

- 15 oz can tuna, drained and flaked
- 3 tbsp parmesan cheese, grated
- 1/2 cup breadcrumbs
- 1 tbsp lemon juice
- 2 eggs, lightly beaten
- 1/2 tsp dried mixed herbs
- 1/2 tsp garlic powder
- 2 tbsp onion, minced
- 1 celery stalk, chopped
- Pepper
- Salt

Directions:

1. Fit the oven with the rack in position 2.
2. Add all ingredients into the mixing bowl and mix until well combined.
3. Make patties from mixture and place in the air fryer basket then place the air fryer basket in the baking pan.
4. Place a baking pan on the oven rack. Set to air fry at 360 F for 10 minutes.
5. Serve and enjoy.
- **Nutrition Info:** Calories 90 Fat 1.8 g Carbohydrates 4.4 g Sugar 0.6 g Protein 13.2 g Cholesterol 47 mg

338.Paprika Cod

Servings: 4
Cooking Time: 15 Minutes
Ingredients:

- 4 cod fillets
- 1 tsp smoked paprika
- 1/2 cup parmesan cheese, grated
- 1/2 tbsp olive oil
- 1 tsp parsley
- Pepper
- Salt

Directions:

1. Fit the oven with the rack in position
2. Brush fish fillets with oil and season with pepper and salt.
3. In a shallow dish, mix parmesan cheese, paprika, and parsley.
4. Coat fish fillets with cheese mixture and place into the baking dish.
5. Set to bake at 400 F for 20 minutes. After 5 minutes place the baking dish in the preheated oven.
6. Serve and enjoy.
- **Nutrition Info:** Calories 125 Fat 5 g Carbohydrates 0.7 g Sugar 0.1 g Protein 19.8 g Cholesterol 52 mg

339.Sweet & Spicy Lime Salmon

Servings: 6
Cooking Time: 15 Minutes
Ingredients:

- 1 1/2 lbs salmon fillets
- 3 tbsp brown sugar
- 2 tbsp fresh lime juice
- 1/3 cup olive oil
- 1/2 tsp red pepper flakes
- 2 garlic cloves, minced
- Pepper
- Salt

Directions:

1. Fit the oven with the rack in position
2. Place salmon on a prepared baking sheet and season with pepper and salt.
3. In a small bowl, whisk oil, red pepper flakes, garlic, brown sugar, and lime juice.
4. Pour oil mixture over salmon.
5. Set to bake at 350 F for 20 minutes. After 5 minutes place the baking dish in the preheated oven.
6. Serve and enjoy.
- **Nutrition Info:** Calories 269 Fat 18.3 g Carbohydrates 6.1 g Sugar 4.7 g Protein 22.2 g Cholesterol 50 mg

340.Air Fry Prawns

Servings: 4
Cooking Time: 6 Minutes
Ingredients:

- 24 prawns
- 6 tbsp mayonnaise
- 1 1/2 tsp chili powder
- 2 tbsp vinegar
- 2 tbsp ketchup
- 1 tsp red chili flakes
- 1/2 tsp sea salt

Directions:

1. Fit the oven with the rack in position 2.
2. In a bowl, toss prawns with chili flakes, chili powder, and salt.

3. Add shrimp to the air fryer basket then place an air fryer basket in the baking pan.
4. Place a baking pan on the oven rack. Set to air fry at 350 F for 6 minutes.
5. In a small bowl, mix mayonnaise, vinegar, and ketchup and serve with shrimp.
- **Nutrition Info:** Calories 255 Fat 9.8 g Carbohydrates 9.8 g Sugar 3.2 g Protein 30.5 g Cholesterol 284 mg

341.Prawn French Cuisine Galette

Servings:x
Cooking Time:x
Ingredients:
- 2 tbsp. garam masala
- 1 lb. minced prawn
- 3 tsp ginger finely chopped
- 1-2 tbsp. fresh coriander leaves
- 2 or 3 green chilies finely chopped
- 1 ½ tbsp. lemon juice
- Salt and pepper to taste

Directions:
1. Mix the ingredients in a clean bowl.
2. Mold this mixture into round and flat French Cuisine Galettes.
3. Wet the French Cuisine Galettes slightly with water.
4. Pre heat the oven at 160 degrees Fahrenheit for 5 minutes. Place the French Cuisine Galettes in the fry basket and let them cook for another 25 minutes at the same temperature. Keep rolling them over

to get a uniform cook. Serve either with mint sauce or ketchup.

342.Greek Cod With Asparagus

Servings: 2
Cooking Time: 20 Minutes
Ingredients:
- 1 lb cod, cut into 4 pieces
- 8 asparagus spears
- 1 leek, sliced
- 1 onion, quartered
- 2 tomatoes, halved
- 1/2 tsp oregano
- 1/2 tsp red chili flakes
- 1/2 cup olives, chopped
- 2 tbsp olive oil
- 1/4 tsp pepper
- 1/4 tsp salt

Directions:
1. Fit the oven with the rack in position
2. Arrange fish pieces, olives, asparagus, leek, onion, and tomatoes in a baking dish.
3. Season with oregano, chili flakes, pepper, and salt and drizzle with olive oil.
4. Set to bake at 400 F for 25 minutes. After 5 minutes place the baking dish in the preheated oven.
5. Serve and enjoy.
- **Nutrition Info:** Calories 489 Fat 20.2 g Carbohydrates 22.5 g Sugar 9.1 g Protein 56.6 g Cholesterol 125 mg

343.Vegetable And Cheese Stuffed Tomatoes

Servings:4
Cooking Time: 18 Minutes
Ingredients:
- 4 medium beefsteak tomatoes, rinsed
- ½ cup grated carrot
- 1 medium onion, chopped
- 1 garlic clove, minced
- 2 teaspoons olive oil
- 2 cups fresh baby spinach
- ¼ cup crumbled low-sodium feta cheese
- ½ teaspoon dried basil

Directions:
1. On your cutting board, cut a thin slice off the top of each tomato. Scoop out a ¼- to ½-inch-thick tomato pulp and place the tomatoes upside down on paper towels to drain. Set aside.
2. Stir together the carrot, onion, garlic, and olive oil in the baking pan.
3. Slide the baking pan into Rack Position 1, select Convection Bake, set temperature to 350ºF (180ºC) and set time to 5 minutes.
4. Stir the vegetables halfway through.
5. When cooking is complete, the carrot should be crisp-tender.
6. Remove from the oven and stir in the spinach, feta cheese, and basil.
7. Spoon ¼ of the vegetable mixture into each tomato and transfer the stuffed tomatoes to the oven. Set time to 13 minutes.
8. When cooking is complete, the filling should be hot and the tomatoes should be lightly caramelized.
9. Let the tomatoes cool for 5 minutes and serve.

344.Mushroom Marinade Cutlet

Servings:x
Cooking Time:x
Ingredients:
- 2 cup fresh green coriander
- ½ cup mint leaves
- 4 tsp. fennel
- 2 tbsp. ginger-garlic paste
- 1 small onion
- 6-7 flakes garlic (optional)
- Salt to taste
- 2 cups sliced mushrooms
- 1 big capsicum (Cut this capsicum into big cubes)
- 1 onion (Cut it into quarters. Now separate the layers carefully.)
- 5 tbsp. gram flour
- A pinch of salt to taste

- 3 tbsp. lemon juice

Directions:
1. Take a clean and dry container. Put into it the coriander, mint, fennel, and ginger, onion/garlic, salt and lemon juice. Mix them.
2. Pour the mixture into a grinder and blend until you get a thick paste. Slit the mushroom almost till the end and leave them aside. Now stuff all the pieces with the paste and set aside. Take the sauce and add to it the gram flour and some salt. Mix them together properly. Rub this mixture all over the stuffed mushroom.
3. Now, to the leftover sauce, add the capsicum and onions. Apply the sauce generously on each of the pieces of capsicum and onion. Now take satay sticks and arrange the cottage cheese pieces and vegetables on separate sticks.
4. Pre heat the oven at 290 Fahrenheit for around 5 minutes. Open the basket. Arrange the satay sticks properly. Close the basket. Keep the sticks with the mushroom at 180 degrees for around half an hour while the sticks with the vegetables are to be kept at the same temperature for only 7 minutes. Turn the sticks in between so that one side does not get burnt and also to provide a uniform cook.

345.Pumpkin French Cuisine Galette

Servings:x
Cooking Time:x
Ingredients:
- 2 or 3 green chilies finely chopped
- 1 ½ tbsp. lemon juice
- Salt and pepper to taste
- 2 tbsp. garam masala
- 1 cup sliced pumpkin
- 3 tsp. ginger finely chopped
- 1-2 tbsp. fresh coriander leaves

Directions:
1. Mix the ingredients in a clean bowl.
2. Mold this mixture into round and flat French Cuisine Galettes.
3. Wet the French Cuisine Galettes slightly with water.
4. Pre heat the oven at 160 degrees Fahrenheit for 5 minutes. Place the French Cuisine Galettes in the fry basket and let them cook for another 25 minutes at the same temperature. Keep rolling them over to get a uniform cook. Serve either with mint sauce or ketchup.

346.Cumin Sweet Potatoes Wedges

Servings:4
Cooking Time: 30 Minutes

Ingredients:
- ½ tsp garlic powder
- ½ tsp cayenne pepper powder
- ¼ tsp ground cumin
- 3 tbsp olive oil
- 3 sweet potatoes, cut into ½-inch thick wedges
- 2 tbsp fresh parsley, chopped
- Sea salt to taste

Directions:
1. In a bowl, mix salt, garlic powder, cayenne pepper powder, and cumin. Whisk in olive oil and coat in the potatoes. Arrange them on the basket, without overcrowding and press Start. Cook for 20-25 minutes at 380 F on AirFry function. Sprinkle with parsley and sea salt and serve.

347.Mushroom Patties

Servings:x
Cooking Time:x
Ingredients:
- 1 tsp. lemon juice
- 1 tbsp. fresh coriander leaves
- ¼ tsp. red chili powder
- ¼ tsp. cumin powder
- 1 cup minced mushroom
- A pinch of salt to taste
- ¼ tsp. ginger finely chopped
- 1 green chili finely chopped

Directions:
1. Mix the ingredients together and ensure that the flavors are right. You will now make round patties with the mixture and roll them out well.
2. Pre heat the oven at 250 Fahrenheit for 5 minutes. Open the basket of the Fryer and arrange the patties in the basket. Close it carefully. Keep the fryer at 150 degrees for around 10 or 12 minutes. In between the cooking process, turn the patties over to get a uniform cook. Serve hot with mint sauce.

348.Cheesy Rice And Olives Stuffed Peppers

Servings:4
Cooking Time: 16 To 17 Minutes
Ingredients:
- 4 red bell peppers, tops sliced off
- 2 cups cooked rice
- 1 cup crumbled feta cheese
- 1 onion, chopped
- ¼ cup sliced kalamata olives
- ¾ cup tomato sauce
- 1 tablespoon Greek seasoning
- Salt and black pepper, to taste
- 2 tablespoons chopped fresh dill, for serving

Directions:

1. Microwave the red bell peppers for 1 to 2 minutes until tender.
2. When ready, transfer the red bell peppers to a plate to cool.
3. Mix the cooked rice, feta cheese, onion, kalamata olives, tomato sauce, Greek seasoning, salt, and pepper in a medium bowl and stir until well combined.
4. Divide the rice mixture among the red bell peppers and transfer to a greased baking pan.
5. Slide the baking pan into Rack Position 1, select Convection Bake, set temperature to 360ºF (182ºC) and set time to 15 minutes.
6. When cooking is complete, the rice should be heated through and the vegetables should be soft.
7. Remove from the oven and serve with the dill sprinkled on top.

349.Radish Flat Cakes

Servings:x
Cooking Time:x
Ingredients:
- 1-2 tbsp. fresh coriander leaves
- 2 or 3 green chilies finely chopped
- 1 ½ tbsp. lemon juice
- Salt and pepper to taste
- 2 tbsp. garam masala
- 2 cups sliced radish
- 3 tsp. ginger finely chopped

Directions:
1. Mix the ingredients in a clean bowl and add water to it. Make sure that the paste is not too watery but is enough to apply on the radish.
2. Pre heat the oven at 160 degrees Fahrenheit for 5 minutes. Place the French Cuisine Galettes in the fry basket and let them cook for another 25 minutes at the same temperature. Keep rolling them over to get a uniform cook. Serve either with mint sauce or ketchup.

350.Garlic Stuffed Mushrooms

Servings:2
Cooking Time: 12 Minutes
Ingredients:
- 18 medium-sized white mushrooms
- 1 small onion, peeled and chopped
- 4 garlic cloves, peeled and minced
- 2 tablespoons olive oil
- 2 teaspoons cumin powder
- A pinch ground allspice
- Fine sea salt and freshly ground black pepper, to taste

Directions:

1. On a clean work surface, remove the mushroom stems. Using a spoon, scoop out the mushroom gills and discard.
2. Thoroughly combine the onion, garlic, olive oil, cumin powder, allspice, salt, and pepper in a mixing bowl. Stuff the mushrooms evenly with the mixture.
3. Place the stuffed mushrooms in the air fryer basket.
4. Put the air fryer basket on the baking pan and slide into Rack Position 2, select Roast, set temperature to 345ºF (174ºC) and set time to 12 minutes.
5. When cooking is complete, the mushroom should be browned.
6. Cool for 5 minutes before serving.

351.Spicy Thai-style Vegetables

Servings:4
Cooking Time: 8 Minutes
Ingredients:
- 1 small head Napa cabbage, shredded, divided
- 1 medium carrot, cut into thin coins
- 8 ounces (227 g) snow peas
- 1 red or green bell pepper, sliced into thin strips
- 1 tablespoon vegetable oil
- 2 tablespoons soy sauce
- 1 tablespoon sesame oil
- 2 tablespoons brown sugar
- 2 tablespoons freshly squeezed lime juice
- 2 teaspoons red or green Thai curry paste
- 1 serrano chile, deseeded and minced
- 1 cup frozen mango slices, thawed
- ½ cup chopped roasted peanuts or cashews

Directions:
1. Put half the Napa cabbage in a large bowl, along with the carrot, snow peas, and bell pepper. Drizzle with the vegetable oil and toss to coat. Spread them evenly in the air fryer basket.
2. Put the air fryer basket on the baking pan and slide into Rack Position 2, select Roast, set temperature to 375ºF (190ºC), and set time to 8 minutes.
3. Meanwhile, whisk together the soy sauce, sesame oil, brown sugar, lime juice, and curry paste in a small bowl.
4. When done, the vegetables should be tender and crisp. Remove from the oven and put the vegetables back into the bowl. Add the chile, mango slices, and the remaining cabbage. Pour over the dressing and toss to coat. Top with the roasted nuts and serve.

352.Vegetable Fried Mix Chips

Servings: 4
Cooking Time: 45 Minutes
Ingredients:
- 1 large eggplant
- 4 potatoes
- 3 zucchinis
- ½ cup cornstarch
- ½ cup olive oil
- Salt to season

Directions:
1. Preheat on Air Fry function to 390 F. Cut the eggplant and zucchini in long 3-inch strips. Peel and cut the potatoes into 3-inch strips; set aside.
2. In a bowl, stir in cornstarch, ½ cup of water, salt, pepper, oil, eggplant, zucchini, and potatoes. Place one-third of the veggie strips in the basket and fit in the baking tray; cook for 12 minutes, shaking once.
3. Once ready, transfer them to a serving platter. Repeat the cooking process for the remaining veggie strips. Serve warm.

353.Air Fried Winter Vegetables

Servings:2
Cooking Time: 16 Minutes
Ingredients:
- 1 parsnip, sliced
- 1 cup sliced butternut squash
- 1 small red onion, cut into wedges
- ½ chopped celery stalk
- 1 tablespoon chopped fresh thyme
- 2 teaspoons olive oil
- Salt and black pepper, to taste

Directions:
1. Toss all the ingredients in a large bowl until the vegetables are well coated.
2. Transfer the vegetables to the air fryer basket.
3. Put the air fryer basket on the baking pan and slide into Rack Position 2, select Air Fry, set temperature to 380ºF (193ºC), and set time to 16 minutes.
4. Stir the vegetables halfway through the cooking time.
5. When cooking is complete, the vegetables should be golden brown and tender. Remove from the oven and serve warm.

354.Cottage Cheese Best Homemade Croquette(2)

Servings:x
Cooking Time:x
Ingredients:
- 1 big capsicum (Cut this capsicum into big cubes)
- 1 onion (Cut it into quarters. Now separate the layers carefully.)
- 5 tbsp. gram flour
- A pinch of salt to taste
- 2 cup fresh green coriander

- ½ cup mint leaves
- 4 tsp. fennel
- 1 small onion
- 2 tbsp. ginger-garlic paste
- 6-7 garlic flakes (optional)
- 3 tbsp. lemon juice
- 2 cups cottage cheese cut into slightly thick and long pieces (similar to
- French fries)
- Salt

Directions:
1. Take a clean and dry container. Put into it the coriander, mint, fennel, and ginger, onion/garlic, salt and lemon juice. Mix them.
2. Pour the mixture into a grinder and blend until you get a thick paste. Now move on to the cottage cheese pieces.
3. Slit these pieces almost till the end and leave them aside. Now stuff all the pieces with the paste that was obtained from the previous step. Now leave the stuffed cottage cheese aside. Take the sauce and add to it the gram flour and some salt.
4. Mix them together properly. Rub this mixture all over the stuffed cottage cheese pieces. Now leave the cottage cheese aside. Now, to the leftover sauce, add the capsicum and onions. Apply the sauce generously on each of the pieces of capsicum and onion.
5. Now take satay sticks and arrange the cottage cheese pieces and vegetables on separate sticks. Pre heat the oven at 290 Fahrenheit for around 5 minutes. Open the basket. Arrange the satay sticks properly. Close the basket.
6. Keep the sticks with the cottage cheese at 180 degrees for around half an hour while the sticks with the vegetables are to be kept at the same temperature for only 7 minutes. Turn the sticks in between so that one side does not get burnt and also to provide a uniform cook.

355.Mushroom Club Sandwich

Servings:x
Cooking Time:x
Ingredients:
- ¼ tbsp. Worcestershire sauce
- ½ tsp. olive oil
- ½ flake garlic crushed
- ¼ cup chopped onion
- ¼ tbsp. red chili sauce
- ½ cup water
- 2 slices of white bread
- 1 tbsp. softened butter
- 1 cup minced mushroom
- 1 small capsicum

Directions:

1. Take the slices of bread and remove the edges. Now cut the slices horizontally.
2. Cook the ingredients for the sauce and wait till it thickens. Now, add the mushroom to the sauce and stir till it obtains the flavors. Roast the capsicum and peel the skin off. Cut the capsicum into slices. Apply the sauce on the slices.
3. Pre-heat the oven for 5 minutes at 300 Fahrenheit. Open the basket of the Fryer and place the prepared Classic Sandwiches in it such that no two Classic Sandwiches are touching each other. Now keep the fryer at 250 degrees for around 15 minutes. Turn the Classic Sandwiches in between the cooking process to cook both slices. Serve the Classic Sandwiches with tomato ketchup or mint sauce.

356.Spicy Sweet Potato Friespotato Fries

Servings: 4
Cooking Time: 37 Minutes
Ingredients:
- 2 tbsp. sweet potato fry seasoning mix
- 2 tbsp. olive oil
- 2 sweet potatoes
- Seasoning Mix:
- 2 tbsp. salt
- 1 tbsp. cayenne pepper
- 1 tbsp. dried oregano
- 1 tbsp. fennel
- 2 tbsp. coriander

Directions:
1. Preparing the Ingredients. Slice both ends off sweet potatoes and peel. Slice lengthwise in half and again crosswise to make four pieces from each potato.
2. Slice each potato piece into 2-3 slices, then slice into fries.
3. Grind together all of seasoning mix ingredients and mix in the salt.
4. Ensure the air fryer oven is preheated to 350 degrees.
5. Toss potato pieces in olive oil, sprinkling with seasoning mix and tossing well to coat thoroughly.
6. Air Frying. Add fries to air fryer rack/basket. Set temperature to 350°F, and set time to 27 minutes. Select START/STOP to begin.
7. Take out the basket and turn fries. Turn off air fryer oven and let cook 10-12 minutes till fries are golden.
- **Nutrition Info:** CALORIES: 89; FAT: 14G; PROTEIN: 8Gs; SUGAR:3

357.Parmesan Cabbage With Blue Cheese Sauce

Servings:4
Cooking Time: 25 Minutes

Ingredients:

- ½ head cabbage, cut into wedges
- 2 cups Parmesan cheese, chopped
- 4 tbsp butter, melted
- Salt and black pepper to taste
- ½ cup blue cheese sauce

Directions:

1. Drizzle cabbage wedges with butter and coat with Parmesan cheese. Place them in the frying basket and cook for 20 minutes at 380 F on AirFry setting. Serve topped with blue cheese sauce.

358.Crispy Potato Lentil Nuggets

Servings: 4
Cooking Time: 10 Minutes
Ingredients:

- Nonstick cooking spray
- 1 cup red lentils
- 1 tbsp. olive oil
- 1 cup onion, grated
- 1 cup carrot, grated
- 1 cup potato, grated
- ½ cup flour
- ½ tsp salt
- ½ tsp garlic powder
- ¾ tsp paprika
- ¼ tsp pepper

Directions:

1. Place baking pan in position 2. Lightly spray fryer basket with cooking spray.
2. Soak lentils in just enough water to cover them for 25 minutes.
3. Heat oil in a large skillet over medium heat. Add onion, carrot, and potato. Cook, stirring frequently until vegetables are tender, 12-15 minutes.
4. Drain the lentils and place them in a food processor. Add flour and spices and pulse to combine, leave some texture to the mixture.
5. Add cooked veggies to the food processor and pulse just until combined. Mixture will be sticky, so oil your hands. Form mixture into nugget shapes and add to the fryer basket in a single layer.
6. Place basket in the oven and set air fry on 350°F for 10 minutes. Turn nuggets over halfway through cooking time. Repeat with remaining mixture. Serve with your favorite dipping sauce.

- **Nutrition Info:** Calories 317, Total Fat 5g, Saturated Fat 1g, Total Carbs 54g, Net Carbs 46g, Protein 14g, Sugar 3g, Fiber 8g, Sodium 317mg, Potassium 625mg, Phosphorus 197mg

359.Herbed Broccoli With Cheese

Servings:4
Cooking Time: 18 Minutes

Ingredients:

- 1 large-sized head broccoli, stemmed and cut into small florets
- 2½ tablespoons canola oil
- 2 teaspoons dried basil
- 2 teaspoons dried rosemary
- Salt and ground black pepper, to taste
- $^1/_3$ cup grated yellow cheese

Directions:

1. Bring a pot of lightly salted water to a boil. Add the broccoli florets to the boiling water and let boil for about 3 minutes.
2. Drain the broccoli florets well and transfer to a large bowl. Add the canola oil, basil, rosemary, salt, and black pepper to the bowl and toss until the broccoli is fully coated. Place the broccoli in the air fryer basket.
3. Put the air fryer basket on the baking pan and slide into Rack Position 2, select Air Fry, set temperature to 390ºF (199ºC), and set time to 15 minutes.
4. Stir the broccoli halfway through the cooking time.
5. When cooking is complete, the broccoli should be crisp. Serve the broccoli warm with grated cheese sprinkled on top.

360.Speedy Vegetable Pizza

Servings: 1
Cooking Time: 15 Minutes
Ingredients:

- 1 ½ tbsp tomato paste
- ¼ cup grated cheddar cheese
- ¼ cup grated mozzarella cheese
- 1 tbsp cooked sweet corn
- 4 zucchini slices
- 4 eggplant slices
- 4 red onion rings
- ½ green bell pepper, chopped
- 3 cherry tomatoes, quartered
- 1 pizza crust
- ¼ tsp basil
- ¼ tsp oregano

Directions:

1. Preheat on Bake function to 350 F. Spread the tomato paste on the pizza crust. Top with zucchini and eggplant slices first, then green peppers, and onion rings. Cover with cherry tomatoes and scatter the corn. Sprinkle with oregano and basil and sprinkle with cheddar and mozzarella cheeses. Cook for 10-12 minutes until golden brown on top. Serve.

361.Asparagus Spicy Lemon Kebab

Servings:x
Cooking Time:x
Ingredients:

- 3 tsp. lemon juice
- 2 tsp. garam masala
- 3 eggs
- 2 ½ tbsp. white sesame seeds
- 2 cups sliced asparagus
- 3 onions chopped
- 5 green chilies-roughly chopped
- 1 ½ tbsp. ginger paste
- 1 ½ tsp. garlic paste
- 1 ½ tsp. salt

Directions:

1. Grind the ingredients except for the egg and form a smooth paste. Coat the asparagus in the paste. Now, beat the eggs and add a little salt to it.
2. Dip the coated apricots in the egg mixture and then transfer to the sesame seeds and coat the asparagus. Place the vegetables on a stick.
3. Pre heat the oven at 160 degrees Fahrenheit for around 5 minutes. Place the sticks in the basket and let them cook for another 25 minutes at the same temperature. Turn the sticks over in between the cooking process to get a uniform cook.

362. Garlicky Veggie Bake

Servings: 3
Cooking Time: 25 Minutes
Ingredients:

- 3 turnips, sliced
- 1 large red onion, cut into rings
- 1 large zucchini, sliced
- Salt and black pepper to taste
- 2 cloves garlic, crushed
- 1 bay leaf, cut in 6 pieces
- 1 tbsp olive oil

Directions:

1. Place the turnips, onion, and zucchini in a bowl. Toss with olive oil, salt, and pepper.
2. Preheat on Air Fry function to 380 F. Place the veggies into a baking pan. Slip the bay leaves in the different parts of the slices and tuck the garlic cloves in between the slices. Cook for 15 minutes. Serve warm with as a side to a meat dish or salad.

363. Cheesy Asparagus And Potato Platter

Servings: 5
Cooking Time: 26 Minutes
Ingredients:

- 4 medium potatoes, cut into wedges
- Cooking spray
- 1 bunch asparagus, trimmed
- 2 tablespoons olive oil
- Salt and pepper, to taste
- Cheese Sauce:
- ¼ cup crumbled cottage cheese

- ¼ cup buttermilk
- 1 tablespoon whole-grain mustard
- Salt and black pepper, to taste

Directions:

1. Spritz the air fryer basket with cooking spray.
2. Put the potatoes in the air fryer basket.
3. Put the air fryer basket on the baking pan and slide into Rack Position 2, select Roast, set temperature to 400ºF (205ºC) and set time to 20 minutes.
4. Stir the potatoes halfway through.
5. When cooking is complete, the potatoes should be golden brown.
6. Remove the potatoes from the oven to a platter. Cover the potatoes with foil to keep warm. Set aside.
7. Place the asparagus in the air fryer basket and drizzle with the olive oil. Sprinkle with salt and pepper.
8. Put the air fryer basket on the baking pan and slide into Rack Position 2, select Roast, set temperature to 400ºF (205ºC) and set time to 6 minutes. Stir the asparagus halfway through.
9. When cooking is complete, the asparagus should be crispy.
10. Meanwhile, make the cheese sauce by stirring together the cottage cheese, buttermilk, and mustard in a small bowl. Season as needed with salt and pepper.
11. Transfer the asparagus to the platter of potatoes and drizzle with the cheese sauce. Serve immediately.

364. Stuffed Portobellos With Peppers And Cheese

Servings: 4
Cooking Time: 15 Minutes
Ingredients:

- 4 tablespoons sherry vinegar or white wine vinegar
- 6 garlic cloves, minced, divided
- 1 tablespoon fresh thyme leaves
- 1 teaspoon Dijon mustard
- 1 teaspoon kosher salt, divided
- ¼ cup plus 3¼ teaspoons extra-virgin olive oil, divided
- 8 portobello mushroom caps, each about 3 inches across, patted dry
- 1 small red or yellow bell pepper, thinly sliced
- 1 small green bell pepper, thinly sliced
- 1 small onion, thinly sliced
- ¼ teaspoon red pepper flakes
- Freshly ground black pepper, to taste
- 4 ounces (113 g) shredded Fontina cheese

Directions:

1. Stir together the vinegar, 4 minced garlic cloves, thyme, mustard, and ½ teaspoon of kosher salt in a small bowl. Slowly pour in ¼ cup of olive oil, whisking constantly, or until an emulsion is formed. Reserve 2 tablespoons of the marinade and set aside.
2. Put the mushrooms in a resealable plastic bag and pour in the marinade. Seal and shake the bag, coating the mushrooms in the marinade. Transfer the mushrooms to the baking pan, gill-side down.
3. Put the remaining 2 minced garlic cloves, bell peppers, onion, red pepper flakes, remaining ½ teaspoon of salt, and black pepper in a medium bowl. Drizzle with the remaining 3¼ teaspoons of olive oil and toss well. Transfer the bell pepper mixture to the pan.
4. Slide the baking pan into Rack Position 2, select Roast, set temperature to 375ºF (190ºC), and set time to 12 minutes.
5. After 7 minutes, remove the pan and stir the peppers and flip the mushrooms. Return the pan to the oven and continue cooking for 5 minutes.
6. Remove from the oven and place the pepper mixture onto a cutting board and coarsely chop.
7. Brush both sides of the mushrooms with the reserved 2 tablespoons marinade. Stuff the caps evenly with the pepper mixture. Scatter the cheese on top.
8. Select Convection Broil, set temperature to High, and set time to 3 minutes.
9. When done, the mushrooms should be tender and the cheese should be melted.
10. Serve warm.

365.Cauliflower Momo's Recipe

Servings:x
Cooking Time:x
Ingredients:
- 2 tsp. ginger-garlic paste
- 2 tsp. soya sauce
- 2 tsp. vinegar
- 1 ½ cup all-purpose flour
- ½ tsp. salt
- 5 tbsp. water
- 2 cups grated cauliflower
- 2 tbsp. oil

Directions:
1. Squeeze the dough and cover it with plastic wrap and set aside. Next, cook the ingredients for the filling and try to ensure that the cauliflower is covered well with the sauce.
2. Roll the dough and cut it into a square. Place the filling in the center. Now, wrap the dough to cover the filling and pinch the edges together.

3. Pre heat the oven at 200° F for 5 minutes. Place the gnocchi's in the fry basket and close it. Let them cook at the same temperature for another 20 minutes. Recommended sides are chili sauce or ketchup

366.Cheese And Bean Enchiladas

Servings:x
Cooking Time:x
Ingredients:
- A pinch of salt or to taste
- A few red chili flakes to sprinkle
- 1 tsp. of oregano
- 2 tbsp. oil
- 2 tsp. chopped garlic
- 2 onions chopped finely
- 2 capsicums chopped finely
- 2 cups of readymade baked beans
- Flour tortillas (as many as required)
- 4 tbsp. of olive oil
- A pinch of salt
- 1 tsp. oregano
- ½ tsp. pepper
- 1 ½ tsp. red chili flakes or to taste
- 1 tbsp. of finely chopped jalapenos
- 1 cup grated pizza cheese (mix mozzarella and cheddar cheeses)
- 1 ½ tsp. of garlic that has been chopped
- 1 ½ cups of readymade tomato puree
- 3 medium tomatoes. Puree them in a mixer
- 1 tsp. of sugar
- A few drops of Tabasco sauce
- 1 cup crumbled or roughly mashed cottage cheese (cottage cheese)
- 1 cup grated cheddar cheese

Directions:
1. Prepare the flour tortillas. Now move on to making the red sauce. In a pan, pour around 2 tbsp. of oil and heat. Add some garlic. Add the rest of the ingredients mentioned under the heading "For the sauce".
2. Keep stirring. Cook until the sauce reduces and becomes thick. For the filling, heat one tbsp. of oil in another pan. Add onions and garlic and cook until the onions are caramelized or attain a golden-brown color. Add the rest of the ingredients required for the filling and cook for two to three minutes.
3. Take the pan off the flame and grate some cheese over the sauce. Mix it well and let it sit for a while. Let us start assembling the dish. Take a tortilla and spread some of the sauce on the surface. Now place the filling at the center in a line. Roll up the tortilla carefully. Do the same for all the tortillas. Now place all the tortillas in a tray and sprinkle them with grated cheese. Cover this with an aluminum foil. Pre heat the

oven at 160° C for 4-5 minutes. Open the basket and place the tray inside.

4. Keep the fryer at the same temperature for another 15 minutes. Turn the tortillas over in between to get a uniform cook.

367.Cabbage Flat Cakes

Servings:x
Cooking Time:x
Ingredients:
- 2 or 3 green chilies finely chopped
- 1 ½ tbsp. lemon juice
- Salt and pepper to taste
- 2 tbsp. garam masala
- 2 cups halved cabbage leaves
- 3 tsp. ginger finely chopped
- 1-2 tbsp. fresh coriander leaves

Directions:
1. Mix the ingredients in a clean bowl and add water to it. Make sure that the paste is not too watery but is enough to apply on the cabbage.
2. Pre heat the oven at 160 degrees Fahrenheit for 5 minutes. Place the French Cuisine Galettes in the fry basket and let them cook for another 25 minutes at the same temperature. Keep rolling them over to get a uniform cook. Serve either with mint sauce or ketchup.

368.Tortellini With Veggies And Parmesan

Servings:4
Cooking Time: 16 Minutes
Ingredients:
- 8 ounces (227 g) sugar snap peas, trimmed
- ½ pound (227 g) asparagus, trimmed and cut into 1-inch pieces
- 2 teaspoons kosher salt or 1 teaspoon fine salt, divided
- 1 tablespoon extra-virgin olive oil
- 1½ cups water
- 1 (20-ounce / 340-g) package frozen cheese tortellini
- 2 garlic cloves, minced
- 1 cup heavy (whipping) cream
- 1 cup cherry tomatoes, halved
- ½ cup grated Parmesan cheese
- ¼ cup chopped fresh parsley or basil
- Add the peas and asparagus to a large bowl. Add ½ teaspoon of kosher salt and the olive oil and toss until well coated. Place the veggies in the baking pan.

Directions:
1. Slide the baking pan into Rack Position 1, select Convection Bake, set the temperature to 450ºF (235ºC), and set the time for 4 minutes.
2. Meanwhile, dissolve 1 teaspoon of kosher salt in the water.

3. Once cooking is complete, remove the pan from the oven and place the tortellini in the pan. Pour the salted water over the tortellini. Put the pan back to the oven.
4. Slide the baking pan into Rack Position 1, select Convection Bake, set temperature to 450ºF (235ºC), and set time for 7 minutes.
5. Meantime, stir together the garlic, heavy cream, and remaining ½ teaspoon of kosher salt in a small bowl.
6. Once cooking is complete, remove the pan from the oven. Blot off any remaining water with a paper towel. Gently stir the ingredients. Drizzle the cream over and top with the tomatoes.
7. Slide the baking pan into Rack Position 2, select Roast, set the temperature to 375ºF (190ºC), and set the time for 5 minutes.
8. After 4 minutes, remove from the oven.
9. Add the Parmesan cheese and stir until the cheese is melted
10. Serve topped with the parsley.

369.Roasted Vegetables With Basil

Servings:2
Cooking Time: 20 Minutes
Ingredients:
- 1 small eggplant, halved and sliced
- 1 yellow bell pepper, cut into thick strips
- 1 red bell pepper, cut into thick strips
- 2 garlic cloves, quartered
- 1 red onion, sliced
- 1 tablespoon extra-virgin olive oil
- Salt and freshly ground black pepper, to taste
- ½ cup chopped fresh basil, for garnish
- Cooking spray

Directions:
1. Grease the baking pan with cooking spray.
2. Place the eggplant, bell peppers, garlic, and red onion in the greased baking pan. Drizzle with the olive oil and toss to coat well. Spritz any uncoated surfaces with cooking spray.
3. Slide the baking pan into Rack Position 1, select Convection Bake, set temperature to 350ºF (180ºC), and set time to 20 minutes.
4. Flip the vegetables halfway through the cooking time.
5. When done, remove from the oven and sprinkle with salt and pepper.
6. Sprinkle the basil on top for garnish and serve.

370.Parmesan Breaded Zucchini Chips

Servings: 5
Cooking Time: 20 Minutes
Ingredients:
- For the zucchini chips:

- 2 medium zucchini
- 2 eggs
- ⅓ cup bread crumbs
- ⅓ cup grated Parmesan cheese
- Salt
- Pepper
- Cooking oil
- For the lemon aioli:
- ½ cup mayonnaise
- ½ tablespoon olive oil
- Juice of ½ lemon
- 1 teaspoon minced garlic
- Salt
- Pepper

Directions:
1. Preparing the Ingredients. To make the zucchini chips:
2. Slice the zucchini into thin chips (about ⅛ inch thick) using a knife or mandoline.
3. In a small bowl, beat the eggs. In another small bowl, combine the bread crumbs, Parmesan cheese, and salt and pepper to taste.
4. Spray the Oven rack/basket with cooking oil.
5. Dip the zucchini slices one at a time in the eggs and then the bread crumb mixture. You can also sprinkle the bread crumbs onto the zucchini slices with a spoon.
6. Place the zucchini chips in the Oven rack/basket, but do not stack. Place the Rack on the middle-shelf of the air fryer oven.
7. Air Frying. Cook in batches. Spray the chips with cooking oil from a distance (otherwise, the breading may fly off). Cook for 10 minutes.
8. Remove the cooked zucchini chips from the air fryer oven, then repeat step 5 with the remaining zucchini.
9. To make the lemon aioli:
10. While the zucchini is cooking, combine the mayonnaise, olive oil, lemon juice, and garlic in a small bowl, adding salt and pepper to taste. Mix well until fully combined.
11. Cool the zucchini and serve alongside the aioli.
- **Nutrition Info:** CALORIES: 192; FAT: 13G; PROTEIN: 6

371.Cilantro Roasted Carrots With Cumin Seeds

Servings:4
Cooking Time: 15 Minutes
Ingredients:
- 1 lb carrots, julienned
- 1 tbsp olive oil
- 1 tsp cumin seeds
- 2 tbsp fresh cilantro, chopped

Directions:
1. Preheat on AirFry function to 350 F. In a bowl, mix oil, carrots, and cumin seeds. Gently stir to coat the carrots well. Place the carrots in a baking tray and press Star. Cook for 10 minutes. Scatter fresh coriander over the carrots and serve.

372.Veggie Mix Fried Chips

Servings:4
Cooking Time: 45 Minutes
Ingredients:
- 1 large eggplant, cut into strips
- 5 potatoes, peeled and cut into strips
- 3 zucchinis, cut into strips
- ½ cup cornstarch
- ½ cup olive oil
- Salt to taste

Directions:
1. Preheat on AirFry function to 390 F. In a bowl, stir cornstarch, ½ cup of water, salt, pepper, olive oil, eggplants, zucchini, and potatoes. Place the veggie mixture in the basket and press Start. Cook for 12 minutes. Serve warm.

373.Crispy Tofu Sticks

Servings:4
Cooking Time: 14 Minutes
Ingredients:
- 2 tablespoons olive oil, divided
- ½ cup flour
- ½ cup crushed cornflakes
- Salt and black pepper, to taste
- 14 ounces (397 g) firm tofu, cut into ½-inch-thick strips

Directions:
1. Grease the air fryer basket with 1 tablespoon of olive oil.
2. Combine the flour, cornflakes, salt, and pepper on a plate.
3. Dredge the tofu strips in the flour mixture until they are completely coated. Transfer the tofu strips to the greased basket.
4. Drizzle the remaining 1 tablespoon of olive oil over the top of tofu strips.
5. Put the air fryer basket on the baking pan and slide into Rack Position 2, select Air Fry, set temperature to 360ºF (182ºC), and set time to 14 minutes.
6. Flip the tofu strips halfway through the cooking time.
7. When cooking is complete, the tofu strips should be crispy. Remove from the oven and serve warm.

374.Simple Ratatouille

Servings:2

Cooking Time: 16 Minutes
Ingredients:

- 2 Roma tomatoes, thinly sliced
- 1 zucchini, thinly sliced
- 2 yellow bell peppers, sliced
- 2 garlic cloves, minced
- 2 tablespoons olive oil
- 2 tablespoons herbes de Provence
- 1 tablespoon vinegar
- Salt and black pepper, to taste

Directions:

1. Place the tomatoes, zucchini, bell peppers, garlic, olive oil, herbes de Provence, and vinegar in a large bowl and toss until the vegetables are evenly coated. Sprinkle with salt and pepper and toss again. Pour the vegetable mixture into the baking pan.
2. Slide the baking pan into Rack Position 2, select Roast, set temperature to 390ºF (199ºC) and set time to 16 minutes.
3. Stir the vegetables halfway through.
4. When cooking is complete, the vegetables should be tender.
5. Let the vegetable mixture stand for 5 minutes in the oven before removing and serving.

375.Potato Club Sandwich

Servings:x
Cooking Time:x
Ingredients:

- ¼ tbsp. Worcestershire sauce
- ½ tsp. olive oil
- ½ flake garlic crushed
- ¼ cup chopped onion
- ¼ tbsp. red chili sauce
- ½ cup water
- 2 slices of white bread
- 1 tbsp. softened butter
- 1 cup mashed potato
- 1 small capsicum

Directions:

1. Take the slices of bread and remove the edges. Now cut the slices horizontally.
2. Cook the ingredients for the sauce and wait till it thickens. Now, add the potato to the sauce and stir till it obtains the flavors. Roast the capsicum and peel the skin off. Cut the capsicum into slices. Apply the sauce on the slices.
3. Pre-heat the oven for 5 minutes at 300 Fahrenheit. Open the basket of the Fryer and place the prepared Classic Sandwiches in it such that no two Classic Sandwiches are touching each other. Now keep the fryer at 250 degrees for around 15 minutes. Turn the Classic Sandwiches in between the cooking process to cook both slices.

376.Cottage Cheese Fried Baked Pastry

Servings:x
Cooking Time:x
Ingredients:

- 1 or 2 green chilies that are finely chopped or mashed
- ½ tsp. cumin
- 1 tsp. coarsely crushed coriander
- 1 dry red chili broken into pieces
- A small amount of salt (to taste)
- ½ tsp. dried mango powder
- ½ tsp. red chili power
- 1-2 tbsp. coriander
- 2 tbsp. unsalted butter
- 1 ½ cup all-purpose flour
- A pinch of salt to taste
- Water
- 2 cups mashed cottage cheese
- ¼ cup boiled peas
- 1 tsp. powdered ginger

Directions:

1. Mix the dough for the outer covering and make it stiff and smooth. Leave it to rest in a container while making the filling.
2. Cook the ingredients in a pan and stir them well to make a thick paste. Roll the paste out.
3. Roll the dough into balls and flatten them. Cut them in halves and add the filling. Use water to help you fold the edges to create the shape of a cone.
4. Pre-heat the oven for around 5 to 6 minutes at 300 Fahrenheit. Place all the samosas in the fry basket and close the basket properly. Keep the oven at 200 degrees for another 20 to 25 minutes. Around the halfway point, open the basket and turn the samosas over for uniform cooking. After this, fry at 250 degrees for around 10 minutes in order to give them the desired golden-brown color. Serve hot. Recommended sides are tamarind or mint sauce.

377.Cauliflower Bites

Servings: 4
Cooking Time: 18 Minutes
Ingredients:

- 1 Head Cauliflower, cut into small florets
- Tsps Garlic Powder
- Pinch of Salt and Pepper
- 1 Tbsp Butter, melted
- 1/2 Cup Chili Sauce
- Olive Oil

Directions:

1. Preparing the Ingredients. Place cauliflower into a bowl and pour oil over florets to lightly cover.

2. Season florets with salt, pepper, and the garlic powder and toss well.
3. Air Frying. Place florets into the air fryer oven at 350 degrees for 14 minutes.
4. Remove cauliflower from the Air fryer oven.
5. Combine the melted butter with the chili sauce
6. Pour over the florets so that they are well coated.
7. Return to the air fryer oven and cook for additional 3 to 4 minutes
8. Serve as a side or with ranch or cheese dip as a snack.

378.Yam Spicy Lemon Kebab

Servings:x
Cooking Time:x
Ingredients:
- 2 tsp. garam masala
- 4 tbsp. chopped coriander
- 3 tbsp. cream
- 3 tbsp. chopped capsicum
- 3 eggs
- 2 ½ tbsp. white sesame seeds
- 2 cups sliced yam
- 3 onions chopped
- 5 green chilies-roughly chopped
- 1 ½ tbsp. ginger paste
- 1 ½ tsp. garlic paste
- 1 ½ tsp. salt
- 3 tsp. lemon juice

Directions:
1. Grind the ingredients except for the egg and form a smooth paste. Coat the yam in the paste. Now, beat the eggs and add a little salt to it.
2. Dip the coated vegetables in the egg mixture and then transfer to the sesame seeds and coat the yam well. Place the vegetables on a stick.
3. Pre heat the oven at 160 degrees Fahrenheit for around 5 minutes. Place the sticks in the basket and let them cook for another 25 minutes at the same temperature. Turn the sticks over in between the cooking process to get a uniform cook.

379.Spicy Kung Pao Tofu

Servings:4
Cooking Time: 10 Minutes
Ingredients:
- $^1/_3$ cup Asian-Style sauce
- 1 teaspoon cornstarch
- ½ teaspoon red pepper flakes, or more to taste
- 1 pound (454 g) firm or extra-firm tofu, cut into 1-inch cubes
- 1 small carrot, peeled and cut into ¼-inch-thick coins
- 1 small green bell pepper, cut into bite-size pieces
- 3 scallions, sliced, whites and green parts separated
- 3 tablespoons roasted unsalted peanuts

Directions:
1. In a large bowl, whisk together the sauce, cornstarch, and red pepper flakes. Fold in the tofu, carrot, pepper, and the white parts of the scallions and toss to coat. Spread the mixture evenly in the baking pan.
2. Slide the baking pan into Rack Position 2, select Roast, set temperature to 375ºF (190ºC), and set time to 10 minutes.
3. Stir the ingredients once halfway through the cooking time.
4. When done, remove from the oven. Serve sprinkled with the peanuts and scallion greens.

380.Rosemary Roasted Squash With Cheese

Servings:2
Cooking Time: 20 Minutes
Ingredients:
- 1 pound (454 g) butternut squash, cut into wedges
- 2 tablespoons olive oil
- 1 tablespoon dried rosemary
- Salt, to salt
- 1 cup crumbled goat cheese
- 1 tablespoon maple syrup

Directions:
1. Toss the squash wedges with the olive oil, rosemary, and salt in a large bowl until well coated.
2. Transfer the squash wedges to the air fryer basket, spreading them out in as even a layer as possible.
3. Put the air fryer basket on the baking pan and slide into Rack Position 2, select Air Fry, set temperature to 350ºF (180ºC), and set time to 20 minutes.
4. After 10 minutes, remove from the oven and flip the squash. Return the pan to the oven and continue cooking for 10 minutes.
5. When cooking is complete, the squash should be golden brown. Remove from the oven. Sprinkle the goat cheese on top and serve drizzled with the maple syrup.

381.Tofu, Carrot And Cauliflower Rice

Servings:4
Cooking Time: 22 Minutes
Ingredients:
- ½ block tofu, crumbled
- 1 cup diced carrot

- ½ cup diced onions
- 2 tablespoons soy sauce
- 1 teaspoon turmeric
- Cauliflower:
- 3 cups cauliflower rice
- ½ cup chopped broccoli
- ½ cup frozen peas
- 2 tablespoons soy sauce
- 1 tablespoon minced ginger
- 2 garlic cloves, minced
- 1 tablespoon rice vinegar
- 1½ teaspoons toasted sesame oil

Directions:
1. Mix the tofu, carrot, onions, soy sauce, and turmeric in a baking pan and stir until well incorporated.
2. Slide the baking pan into Rack Position 2, select Roast, set temperature to 370ºF (188ºC) and set time to 10 minutes.
3. Flip the tofu and carrot halfway through the cooking time.
4. When cooking is complete, the tofu should be crisp.
5. Meanwhile, in a large bowl, combine all the ingredients for the cauliflower and toss well.
6. Remove the pan from the oven and add the cauliflower mixture to the tofu and stir to combine.
7. Return to the oven and set time to 12 minutes on Roast.
8. When cooking is complete, the vegetables should be tender.
9. Cool for 5 minutes before serving.

382.Pineapple Spicy Lemon Kebab

Servings:x
Cooking Time:x
Ingredients:
- 4 tbsp. chopped coriander
- 3 tbsp. cream
- 3 tbsp. chopped capsicum
- 3 eggs
- 2 ½ tbsp. white sesame seeds
- 2 cups cubed pineapples
- 3 onions chopped
- 5 green chilies-roughly chopped
- 1 ½ tbsp. ginger paste
- 1 ½ tsp. garlic paste
- 1 ½ tsp. salt
- 3 tsp. lemon juice
- 2 tsp. garam masala

Directions:
1. Grind the ingredients except for the egg and form a smooth paste. Coat the pineapples in the paste. Now, beat the eggs and add a little salt to it.
2. Dip the coated vegetables in the egg mixture and then transfer to the sesame seeds and

coat the pineapples well. Place the vegetables on a stick.
3. Pre heat the oven at 160 degrees Fahrenheit for around 5 minutes. Place the sticks in the basket and let them cook for another 25 minutes at the same temperature. Turn the sticks over in between the cooking process to get a uniform cook.

383.Potato Flat Cakes

Servings:x
Cooking Time:x
Ingredients:
- 2 or 3 green chilies finely chopped
- 1 ½ tbsp. lemon juice
- Salt and pepper to taste
- 2 tbsp. garam masala
- 2 cups sliced potato
- 3 tsp. ginger finely chopped
- 1-2 tbsp. fresh coriander leaves

Directions:
1. Mix the ingredients in a clean bowl and add water to it. Make sure that the paste is not too watery but is enough to apply on the potato slices.
2. Pre heat the oven at 160 degrees Fahrenheit for 5 minutes. Place the French Cuisine Galettes in the fry basket and let them cook for another 25 minutes at the same temperature. Keep rolling them over to get a uniform cook. Serve either with mint sauce or ketchup.

384.Roasted Vegetables With Rice

Servings:4
Cooking Time: 12 Minutes
Ingredients:
- 2 teaspoons melted butter
- 1 cup chopped mushrooms
- 1 cup cooked rice
- 1 cup peas
- 1 carrot, chopped
- 1 red onion, chopped
- 1 garlic clove, minced
- Salt and black pepper, to taste
- 2 hard-boiled eggs, grated
- 1 tablespoon soy sauce

Directions:
1. Coat the baking pan with melted butter.
2. Stir together the mushrooms, cooked rice, peas, carrot, onion, garlic, salt, and pepper in a large bowl until well mixed. Pour the mixture into the prepared baking pan.
3. Slide the baking pan into Rack Position 2, select Roast, set temperature to 380ºF (193ºC), and set time to 12 minutes.
4. When cooking is complete, remove from the oven. Divide the mixture among four plates.

Serve warm with a sprinkle of grated eggs and a drizzle of soy sauce.

385.Beetroot Chips

Servings: 3
Cooking Time: 25 Minutes
Ingredients:
- 1lb golden beetroots, sliced
- 2 tbsp olive oil
- 1 tbsp yeast flakes
- 1 tsp vegan seasoning
- Salt to taste

Directions:
1. In a bowl, add the olive oil, beetroots, vegan seasoning, and yeast and mix well. Dump the coated chips in the basket.
2. Fit in the baking tray and cook in your for 15 minutes at 370 F on Air Fry function, shaking once halfway through. Serve.

386.Cottage Cheese Best Homemade Croquette(1)

Servings:x
Cooking Time:x
Ingredients:
- 2 tbsp. dry fenugreek leaves
- 1 tsp. black salt
- 1 tsp. chat masala
- 1 tsp. garam masala powder
- 1 tsp. red chili powder
- 1 tsp. salt
- 3 drops of red color
- 2 packets cottage cheese cubed
- 3 tbsp. vinegar or lemon juice
- 2 or 3 tsp. paprika
- 1 tsp. black pepper
- 1 tsp. salt
- 3 tsp. ginger-garlic paste
- 1 cup yogurt
- 4 tsp. tandoori masala

Directions:
1. Make the first marinade and soak the cubed cottage cheese in it for four hours. While this is happening, make the second marinade and soak the cottage cheese in it overnight to let the flavors blend.
2. Pre heat the oven at 160 degrees Fahrenheit for 5 minutes. Place the Oregano Fingers in the fry basket and close it. Let them cook at the same temperature for another 15 minutes or so. Toss the Oregano Fingers well so that they are cooked uniformly. Serve them with mint sauce.

387.Cornflakes French Toast

Servings:x
Cooking Time:x
Ingredients:
- 1 tsp. sugar for every 2 slices
- Crushed cornflakes
- Bread slices (brown or white)
- 1 egg white for every 2 slices

Directions:
1. Put two slices together and cut them along the diagonal.
2. In a bowl, whisk the egg whites and add some sugar.
3. Dip the bread triangles into this mixture and then coat them with the crushed cornflakes.
4. Pre heat the oven at 180° C for 4 minutes. Place the coated bread triangles in the fry basket and close it. Let them cook at the same temperature for another 20 minutes at least. Halfway through the process, turn the triangles over so that you get a uniform cook. Serve these slices with chocolate sauce.

388.Cauliflower Gnocchi's

Servings:x
Cooking Time:x
Ingredients:
- 2 tbsp. oil
- 2 tsp. ginger-garlic paste
- 2 tsp. soya sauce
- 2 tsp. vinegar
- 1 ½ cup all-purpose flour
- ½ tsp. salt
- 5 tbsp. water
- 2 cups grated cauliflower

Directions:
1. Squeeze the dough and cover it with plastic wrap and set aside. Next, cook the ingredients for the filling and try to ensure that the cauliflower is covered well with the sauce.
2. Roll the dough and place the filling in the center. Now, wrap the dough to cover the filling and pinch the edges together.
3. Pre heat the oven at 200° F for 5 minutes. Place the gnocchi's in the fry basket and close it. Let them cook at the same temperature for another 20
4. minutes. Recommended sides are chili sauce or ketchup.

389.Vegetable Skewer

Servings:x
Cooking Time:x
Ingredients:
- 3 tbsp. cream
- 3 eggs
- 2 cups mixed vegetables
- 3 onions chopped
- 5 green chilies
- 1 ½ tbsp. ginger paste
- 1 ½ tsp. garlic paste

- 1 ½ tsp. salt
- 2 ½ tbsp. white sesame seeds

Directions:
1. Grind the ingredients except for the egg and form a smooth paste. Coat the vegetables in the paste. Now, beat the eggs and add a little salt to it.
2. Dip the coated vegetables in the egg mixture and then transfer to the sesame seeds and coat the vegetables well. Place the vegetables on a stick.
3. Pre heat the oven at 160 degrees Fahrenheit for around 5 minutes. Place the sticks in the basket and let them cook for another 25 minutes at the same temperature. Turn the sticks over in between the cooking process to get a uniform cook.

390.Baked Turnip And Zucchini

Servings:4
Cooking Time: 18 Minutes
Ingredients:
- 3 turnips, sliced
- 1 large zucchini, sliced
- 1 large red onion, cut into rings
- 2 cloves garlic, crushed
- 1 tablespoon olive oil
- Salt and black pepper, to taste

Directions:
1. Put the turnips, zucchini, red onion, and garlic in the baking pan. Drizzle the olive oil over the top and sprinkle with the salt and pepper.
2. Slide the baking pan into Rack Position 1, select Convection Bake, set temperature to 330ºF (166ºC), and set time to 18 minutes.
3. When cooking is complete, the vegetables should be tender. Remove from the oven and serve on a plate.

391.Chickpea & Carrot Balls

Servings: 3
Cooking Time: 25 Minutes
Ingredients:
- 2 tbsp olive oil
- 2 tbsp soy sauce
- 1 tbsp flax meal
- 2 cups cooked chickpeas
- ½ cup sweet onions
- ½ cup grated carrots
- ½ cup roasted cashews
- Juice of 1 lemon
- ½ tsp turmeric
- 1 tsp cumin
- 1 tsp garlic powder
- 1 cup rolled oats

Directions:

1. Combine the olive oil, onions, and carrots into the Air Fryer baking pan and cook them on Air Fry function for 6 minutes at 350 F. Ground the oats and cashews in a food processor. Place in a large bowl. Mix in the chickpeas, lemon juice, and soy sauce.
2. Add onions and carrots to the bowl with chickpeas. Stir in the remaining ingredients; mix until fully incorporated. Make meatballs out of the mixture. Increase the temperature to 370 F and cook for 12 minutes.

392.Veg Momo's Recipe

Servings:x
Cooking Time:x
Ingredients:
- 2 tsp. ginger-garlic paste
- 2 tsp. soya sauce
- 2 tsp. vinegar
- 1 ½ cup all-purpose flour
- ½ tsp. salt or to taste
- 5 tbsp. water
- 2 cup carrots grated
- 2 cup cabbage grated
- 2 tbsp. oil

Directions:
1. Squeeze the dough and cover it with plastic wrap and set aside. Next, cook the ingredients for the filling and try to ensure that the vegetables are covered well with the sauce.
2. Roll the dough and cut it into a square. Place the filling in the center. Now, wrap the dough to cover the filling and pinch the edges together.
3. Pre heat the oven at 200° F for 5 minutes. Place the gnocchi's in the fry basket and close it. Let them cook at the same temperature for another 20 minutes. Recommended sides are chili sauce or ketchup.

393.Vegetarian Meatballs

Servings:3
Cooking Time: 18 Minutes
Ingredients:
- ½ cup grated carrots
- ½ cup sweet onions
- 2 tablespoons olive oil
- 1 cup rolled oats
- ½ cup roasted cashews
- 2 cups cooked chickpeas
- Juice of 1 lemon
- 2 tablespoons soy sauce
- 1 tablespoon flax meal
- 1 teaspoon garlic powder
- 1 teaspoon cumin
- ½ teaspoon turmeric

Directions:

1. Mix the carrots, onions, and olive oil in the baking pan and stir to combine.
2. Slide the baking pan into Rack Position 2, select Roast, set temperature to 350ºF (180ºC) and set time to 6 minutes.
3. Stir the vegetables halfway through.
4. When cooking is complete, the vegetables should be tender.
5. Meanwhile, put the oats and cashews in a food processor or blender and pulse until coarsely ground. Transfer the mixture to a large bowl. Add the chickpeas, lemon juice, and soy sauce to the food processor and pulse until smooth. Transfer the chickpea mixture to the bowl of oat and cashew mixture.
6. Remove the carrots and onions from the oven to the bowl of chickpea mixture. Add the flax meal, garlic powder, cumin, and turmeric and stir to incorporate.
7. Scoop tablespoon-sized portions of the veggie mixture and roll them into balls with your hands. Transfer the balls to the air fryer basket.
8. Increase the temperature to 370ºF (188ºC) and set time to 12 minutes on Bake. Flip the balls halfway through the cooking time.
9. When cooking is complete, the balls should be golden brown.
10. Serve warm.

394.Cottage Cheese Spicy Lemon Kebab

Servings:x
Cooking Time:x
Ingredients:

- 3 tsp. lemon juice
- 2 tbsp. coriander powder
- 3 tbsp. chopped capsicum
- 2 tbsp. peanut flour
- 2 cups cubed cottage cheese
- 3 onions chopped
- 5 green chilies-roughly chopped
- 1 ½ tbsp. ginger paste
- 1 ½ tsp. garlic paste
- 1 ½ tsp. salt
- 3 eggs

Directions:

1. Coat the cottage cheese cubes with the corn flour and mix the other ingredients in a bowl. Make the mixture into a smooth paste and coat the cheese cubes with the mixture. Beat the eggs in a bowl and add a little salt to them.
2. Dip the cubes in the egg mixture and coat them with sesame seeds and leave them in the refrigerator for an hour.
3. Pre heat the oven at 290 Fahrenheit for around 5 minutes. Place the kebabs in the basket and let them cook for another 25

minutes at the same temperature. Turn the kebabs over in between the cooking process to get a uniform cook. Serve the kebabs with mint sauce.

395.Tofu & Pea Cauli Rice

Servings:4
Cooking Time: 30 Minutes
Ingredients:

- Tofu:
- ½ block tofu
- ½ cup onions, chopped
- 2 tbsp soy sauce
- 1 tsp turmeric
- 1 cup carrots, chopped
- Cauliflower:
- 3 cups cauliflower rice
- 2 tbsp soy sauce
- ½ cup broccoli, chopped
- 2 garlic cloves, minced
- 1 ½ tsp toasted sesame oil
- 1 tbsp fresh ginger, minced
- ½ cup frozen peas
- 1 tbsp rice vinegar

Directions:

1. Preheat on AirFry function to 370 F. Crumble the tofu and combine it with all tofu ingredients. Place in a baking dish and cook for 10 minutes.
2. Meanwhile, place all cauliflower ingredients in a large bowl; mix to combine. Add the cauliflower mixture to the tofu and stir to combine. Press Start and cook for 12 minutes. Serve.

396.Caucasia Gnocchi's

Servings:x
Cooking Time:x
Ingredients:

- 2 cups minced colas Asia
- 2 tbsp. oil
- 2 tsp. ginger-garlic paste
- 2 tsp. soya sauce
- 2 tsp. vinegar
- 1 ½ cup all-purpose flour
- ½ tsp. salt
- 5 tbsp. water

Directions:

1. Squeeze the dough and cover it with plastic wrap and set aside. Next, cook the ingredients for the filling and try to ensure that the colas Asia is covered well with the sauce.
2. Roll the dough and place the filling in the center. Now, wrap the dough to cover the filling and pinch the edges together.
3. Pre heat the oven at 200° F for 5 minutes. Place the gnocchi's in the fry basket and close it. Let them cook at the same

temperature for another 20 minutes. Recommended sides are chili sauce or ketchup.

397.Classic Ratatouille

Servings: 2
Cooking Time: 30 Minutes
Ingredients:
- 1 tbsp olive oil
- 3 roma tomatoes, thinly sliced
- 2 garlic cloves, minced
- 1 zucchini, thinly sliced
- 2 yellow bell peppers, sliced
- 1 tbsp red wine vinegar
- 2 tbsp herbs de Provence
- Salt and black pepper to taste

Directions:
1. Preheat on Air Fry function to 390 F. In a bowl, mix together olive oil, garlic, vinegar, herbs, salt, and pepper. Add in tomatoes, zucchini, and bell peppers and toss to coat.
2. Arrange the vegetables in a baking dish and cook for 15 minutes, shaking occasionally. Let sit for 5 more minutes after the timer goes off. Serve.

398.Zucchini Fried Baked Pastry

Servings:x
Cooking Time:x
Ingredients:
- 1 or 2 green chilies that are finely chopped or mashed
- ½ tsp. cumin
- 1 tsp. coarsely crushed coriander
- 1 dry red chili broken into pieces
- A small amount of salt (to taste)
- ½ tsp. dried mango powder
- ½ tsp. red chili power.
- 2 tbsp. unsalted butter
- 1 ½ cup all-purpose flour
- A pinch of salt to taste
- Add as much water as required to make the dough stiff and firm
- 3 medium zucchinis (mashed)
- ¼ cup boiled peas
- 1 tsp. powdered ginger
- 1-2 tbsp. coriander.

Directions:

1. Mix the dough for the outer covering and make it stiff and smooth. Leave it to rest in a container while making the filling.
2. Cook the ingredients in a pan and stir them well to make a thick paste. Roll the paste out.
3. Roll the dough into balls and flatten them. Cut them in halves and add the
4. filling. Use water to help you fold the edges to create the shape of a cone.
5. Pre-heat the oven for around 5 to 6 minutes at 300 Fahrenheit. Place all the samosas in the fry basket and close the basket properly. Keep the oven at 200 degrees for another 20 to 25 minutes. Around the halfway point, open the basket and turn the samosas over for uniform cooking. After this, fry at 250 degrees for around 10 minutes in order to give them the desired golden-brown color. Serve hot. Recommended sides are tamarind or mint sauce.

399.Green Chili Taquitos

Servings: 3
Cooking Time: 10 Minutes
Ingredients:
- Nonstick cooking spray
- 6 corn tortillas
- ¾ cup vegan cream cheese
- 1 cup vegan cheddar cheese, grated
- 4 oz. green chilies, diced & drained

Directions:
1. Place baking pan in position 2. Lightly spray fryer basket with cooking spray.
2. Wrap tortillas in paper towels and microwave 1 minute.
3. Spread the cream cheese over tortillas. Top with cheddar cheese and chilies. Roll up tightly. Place, seam side down, in fryer basket.
4. Place the basket on the baking pan and set oven to air fry on 350°F for 10 minutes or until tortillas are browned and crispy. Turn taquitos over halfway through cooking time. Serve immediately.
- **Nutrition Info:** Calories 706, Total Fat 34g, Saturated Fat 18g, Total Carbs 51g, Net Carbs 35g, Protein 24g, Sugar 11g, Fiber 16g, Sodium 2371mg, Potassium 1074mg, Phosphorus 850mg

SNACKS AND DESSERTS RECIPES

400.Cinnamon Fried Bananas

Servings: 2-3
Cooking Time: 10 Minutes
Ingredients:

- 1 C. panko breadcrumbs
- 3 tbsp. cinnamon
- ½ C. almond flour
- 3 egg whites
- 8 ripe bananas
- 3 tbsp. vegan coconut oil

Directions:

1. Preparing the Ingredients. Heat coconut oil and add breadcrumbs. Mix around 2-3 minutes until golden. Pour into bowl.
2. Peel and cut bananas in half. Roll each bananas half into flour, eggs, and crumb mixture.
3. Air Frying. Place into the air fryer oven. Cook 10 minutes at 280 degrees.
4. A great addition to a healthy banana split!
- **Nutrition Info:** CALORIES: 219; FAT:10G; PROTEIN:3G; SUGAR:5G

401.Cheesy Roasted Jalapeño Poppers

Servings:8
Cooking Time: 15 Minutes
Ingredients:

- 6 ounces (170 g) cream cheese, at room temperature
- 4 ounces (113 g) shredded Cheddar cheese
- 1 teaspoon chili powder
- 12 large jalapeño peppers, deseeded and sliced in half lengthwise
- 2 slices cooked bacon, chopped
- ¼ cup panko bread crumbs
- 1 tablespoon butter, melted

Directions:

1. In a medium bowl, whisk together the cream cheese, Cheddar cheese and chili powder. Spoon the cheese mixture into the jalapeño halves and arrange them in the baking pan.
2. In a small bowl, stir together the bacon, bread crumbs and butter. Sprinkle the mixture over the jalapeño halves.
3. Slide the baking pan into Rack Position 2, select Roast, set temperature to 375ºF (190ºC) and set time to 15 minutes.
4. When cooking is complete, remove from the oven. Let the poppers cool for 5 minutes before serving.

402.Roasted Veggie Bowl

Servings: 2
Cooking Time: 35 Minutes
Ingredients:

- ¼ medium white onion; peeled.and sliced ¼-inch thick
- ½ medium green bell pepper; seeded and sliced ¼-inch thick
- 1 cup broccoli florets
- 1 cup quartered Brussels sprouts
- ½ cup cauliflower florets
- 1 tbsp. coconut oil
- ½ tsp. garlic powder.
- ½ tsp. cumin
- 2 tsp. chili powder

Directions:

1. Toss all ingredients together in a large bowl until vegetables are fully coated with oil and seasoning. Pour vegetables into the air fryer basket.
2. Adjust the temperature to 360 Degrees F and set the timer for 15 minutes. Shake two- or three-times during cooking. Serve warm.
- **Nutrition Info:** Calories: 121; Protein: 4.3g; Fiber: 5.2g; Fat: 7.1g; Carbs: 13.1g

403.Radish Chips

Servings: 6
Cooking Time: 18 Minutes
Ingredients:

- Garlic powder
- Avocado oil
- Radish slices, 1 lb.
- Pepper
- Onion powder
- Salt

Directions:

1. Toss the washed radish slices with oil, salt, pepper, onion powder, and garlic powder.
2. Spread these slices in the air fryer basket and return the basket to the fryer.
3. Air fry them for 5 minutes at 370 degrees F then toss them well.
4. Air fry the slices again for 5 more minutes.
5. Adjust seasoning with more spices and cooking oil.
6. Air fry these slices again for 5 minutes then toss them.
7. Cook for another 3 minutes and serve.
- **Nutrition Info:** Calories: 72 Fat: 6.6 g Carbs: 3.6 g Protein: 0.8 g

404.Almond Peanut Butter Bars

Servings: 8
Cooking Time: 30 Minutes
Ingredients:

- 2 eggs
- 1/2 cup erythritol
- 1/2 cup butter softened
- 1/2 cup peanut butter
- 1 tbsp coconut flour

- 1/2 cup almond flour

Directions:
1. Fit the oven with the rack in position
2. In a bowl, beat together butter, eggs, and peanut butter until well combined.
3. Add dry ingredients and mix until a smooth batter is formed.
4. Spread batter evenly in greased baking pan.
5. Set to bake at 350 F for 35 minutes. After 5 minutes place the baking pan in the preheated oven.
6. Slice and serve.

- **Nutrition Info:** Calories 168 Fat 12.5 g Carbohydrates 9.7 g Sugar 1.8 g Protein 6.5 g Cholesterol 41 mg

405.Margherita Pizza

Servings: 4
Cooking Time: 18 Minutes
Ingredients:
- 1 whole-wheat pizza crust
- 1/2 cup mozzarella cheese, grated
- 1/2 cup can tomatoes
- 2 tbsp olive oil
- 3 Roma tomatoes, sliced
- 10 basil leaves

Directions:
1. Fit the oven with the rack in position
2. Roll out whole wheat pizza crust using a rolling pin. Make sure the crust is ½-inch thick.
3. Sprinkle olive oil on top of pizza crust.
4. Spread can tomatoes over pizza crust.
5. Arrange sliced tomatoes and basil on pizza crust. Sprinkle grated cheese on top.
6. Place pizza on top of the oven rack and set to bake at 425 F for 23 minutes.
7. Slice and serve.

- **Nutrition Info:** Calories 126 Fat 7.9 g Carbohydrates 11.3 g Sugar 4.2 g Protein 3.6 g Cholesterol 2 mg

406.Buffalo Style Cauliflower

Servings:x
Cooking Time:x
Ingredients:
- ¼ cup Frank's red-hot sauce
- 1 Tbsp fresh lime juice
- Chopped parsley or cilantro
- 2 Tbsp olive oil
- 1 head cauliflower
- Salt and pepper, to taste
- 2 Tbsp unsalted butter

Directions:
1. Preheat oven to 375°F.
2. Chop off tough flower part at the base of the cauliflower. Break into
3. small to medium sized florets.
4. In a microwave-safe bowl, melt butter.

5. Add hot sauce and lime juice to butter and stir.
6. Heat oven to medium-low heat.
7. Add oil and cauliflower florets. Saute until nicely browned, 4-5 minutes.
8. Pour in hot sauce mixture and stir to coat evenly.
9. Place in oven for 15-20 minutes, until cauliflower is softened.
10. Remove from oven and sprinkle with parsley or cilantro.

407.Autumn Walnut Crisp

Servings: 8
Cooking Time: 15 Minutes
Ingredients:
- 1 cup walnuts
- 1/2 cup swerve
- Topping:
- 1 ½ cups almond flour
- 1/2 cup coconut flour
- 1/2 cup swerve
- 1 teaspoon crystallized ginger
- 1/2 teaspoon ground cardamom
- A pinch of salt
- 1 stick butter, cut into pieces

Directions:
1. Place walnuts and 1/2 cup of swerve in a baking pan lightly greased with nonstick cooking spray.
2. In a mixing dish, thoroughly combine all the topping ingredients. Sprinkle the topping ingredients over the walnut layer.
3. Bake in the preheated Air Fryer at 330 degrees F for 35 minutes.

- **Nutrition Info:** 288 Calories; 25g Fat; 2g Carbs; 6g Protein; 3g Sugars; 4g Fiber

408.Blueberry Lemon Muffins

Servings: 12
Cooking Time: 10 Minutes
Ingredients:
- 1 tsp. vanilla
- Juice and zest of 1 lemon
- 2 eggs
- 1 C. blueberries
- ½ C. cream
- ¼ C. avocado oil
- ½ C. monk fruit
- 2 ½ C. almond flour

Directions:
1. Preparing the Ingredients. Mix monk fruit and flour together.
2. In another bowl, mix vanilla, egg, lemon juice, and cream together. Add mixtures together and blend well.
3. Spoon batter into cupcake holders.

4. Air Frying. Place in the air fryer oven. Bake 10 minutes at 320 degrees, checking at 6 minutes to ensure you don't overbake them.

- **Nutrition Info:** CALORIES: 317; FAT:11G; PROTEIN:3G; SUGAR:5G

409.Hush Puppies

Servings:12
Cooking Time: 10 Minutes
Ingredients:

- 1 cup self-rising yellow cornmeal
- ½ cup all-purpose flour
- 1 teaspoon sugar
- 1 teaspoon salt
- 1 teaspoon freshly ground black pepper
- 1 large egg
- $^1/_3$ cup canned creamed corn
- 1 cup minced onion
- 2 teaspoons minced jalapeño pepper
- 2 tablespoons olive oil, divided

Directions:

1. Thoroughly combine the cornmeal, flour, sugar, salt, and pepper in a large bowl.
2. Whisk together the egg and corn in a small bowl. Pour the egg mixture into the bowl of cornmeal mixture and stir to combine. Stir in the minced onion and jalapeño. Cover the bowl with plastic wrap and place in the refrigerator for 30 minutes.
3. Line the air fryer basket with parchment paper and lightly brush it with 1 tablespoon of olive oil.
4. Scoop out the cornmeal mixture and form into 24 balls, about 1 inch.
5. Arrange the balls on the parchment, leaving space between each ball.
6. Put the air fryer basket on the baking pan and slide into Rack Position 2, select Air Fry, set temperature to 375ºF (190ºC), and set time to 10 minutes.
7. After 5 minutes, remove from the oven. Flip the balls and brush them with the remaining 1 tablespoon of olive oil. Return to the oven and continue cooking for 5 minutes until golden brown.
8. When cooking is complete, remove the balls (hush puppies) from the oven and serve on a plate.

410.Sweet Cherry Clafouti

Servings:x
Cooking Time:x
Ingredients:

- 2 Tbsp butter, melted
- ½ cup all-purpose flour
- 2 cups cherries, pitted and sliced
- Powdered sugar
- 1 cup whole milk
- ¼ cup whipping cream

- 3 eggs
- ½ cup granulated sugar
- 1 tsp almond extract

Directions:

1. Preheat the oven to 350°F.
2. Whisk together milk, cream, eggs, sugar, extract and butter.
3. Add the flour and whisk gently until incorporated.
4. Lightly grease oven and heat in oven for 5 minutes.
5. Remove from heat and pour in batter.
6. Scatter cherries all around batter and place in oven.
7. Bake until golden and puffed, about 35 minutes.
8. Dust with powdered sugar.

411.Easy Ricotta Cake

Servings: 8
Cooking Time: 45 Minutes
Ingredients:

- 2 eggs
- 1/2 cup erythritol
- 1/4 cup coconut flour
- 15 oz ricotta
- Pinch of salt

Directions:

1. Fit the oven with the rack in position
2. In a bowl whisk eggs.
3. Add remaining ingredients and mix until well combined.
4. Transfer batter in greased cake pan.
5. Set to bake at 350 F for 50 minutes. After 5 minutes place the cake pan in the preheated oven.
6. Slice and serve.

- **Nutrition Info:** Calories 91 Fat 5.4 g Carbohydrates 3.1 g Sugar 0.3 g Protein 7.5 g Cholesterol 57 mg

412.Coconut Pineapple Sticks

Servings:4
Cooking Time: 10 Minutes
Ingredients:

- ½ fresh pineapple, cut into sticks
- ¼ cup desiccated coconut

Directions:

1. Place the desiccated coconut on a plate and roll the pineapple sticks in the coconut until well coated.
2. Lay the pineapple sticks in the air fryer basket.
3. Put the air fryer basket on the baking pan and slide into Rack Position 2, select Air Fry, set temperature to 400ºF (205ºC), and set time to 10 minutes.
4. When cooking is complete, the pineapple sticks should be crisp-tender.

5. Serve warm.

413.Apple-peach Crisp With Oatmeal

Servings:4
Cooking Time: 10 To 12 Minutes
Ingredients:
- 2 peaches, peeled, pitted, and chopped
- 1 apple, peeled and chopped
- 2 tablespoons honey
- 3 tablespoons packed brown sugar
- 2 tablespoons unsalted butter, at room temperature
- ½ cup quick-cooking oatmeal
- $^1/_3$ cup whole-wheat pastry flour
- ½ teaspoon ground cinnamon

Directions:
1. Place the peaches, apple, and honey in the baking pan and toss until thoroughly combined.
2. Mix together the brown sugar, butter, oatmeal, pastry flour, and cinnamon in a medium bowl and stir until crumbly. Sprinkle this mixture generously on top of the peaches and apples.
3. Slide the baking pan into Rack Position 1, select Convection Bake, set temperature to 380ºF (193ºC), and set the time to 10 minutes.
4. Bake until the fruit is bubbling and the topping is golden brown.
5. Once cooking is complete, remove from the oven and allow to cool for 5 minutes before serving.

414.Caramel Apple Cake

Servings: 12
Cooking Time: 55 Minutes
Ingredients:
- 1 cup coconut oil, melted
- 2 cups sugar
- 3 eggs
- 1 ½ tsp vanilla
- 2 cups flour
- 1 tsp salt
- 1 tsp baking soda
- 3 cups apples, peeled & chopped
- ½ cup butter
- 1 cup brown sugar
- ¼ cup milk

Directions:
1. Place rack in position Spray an 8x11-inch pan with cooking spray.
2. In a large bowl, beat oil, sugar, eggs, and vanilla until smooth.
3. Add flour, salt, and baking soda and stir to combine. Fold in apples.
4. Set oven to bake on 350°F for 60 minutes.
5. Pour batter in prepared pan. After oven has preheated for 5 minutes, put cake in oven and bake 55-60 minutes, or until it passes the toothpick test. Let cool completely.
6. In a saucepan, over medium heat, combine butter, brown sugar, and milk. Stirring constantly, bring to a boil. Let boil, without stirring, 3 minutes. Remove from heat and spread over top of cake. Let sit 1 hour before serving.
- **Nutrition Info:** Calories 553, Total Fat 27g, Saturated Fat 21g, Total Carbs 71g, Net Carbs 70g, Protein 4g, Sugar 54g, Fiber 1g, Sodium 385mg, Potassium 99mg, Phosphorus 58mg

415.Lemon-raspberry Muffins

Servings:6
Cooking Time: 15 Minutes
Ingredients:
- 2 cups almond flour
- ¾ cup Swerve
- 1¼ teaspoons baking powder
- $^1/_3$ teaspoon ground allspice
- $^1/_3$ teaspoon ground anise star
- ½ teaspoon grated lemon zest
- ¼ teaspoon salt
- 2 eggs
- 1 cup sour cream
- ½ cup coconut oil
- ½ cup raspberries

Directions:
1. Line a muffin pan with 6 paper liners.
2. In a mixing bowl, mix the almond flour, Swerve, baking powder, allspice, anise, lemon zest, and salt.
3. In another mixing bowl, beat the eggs, sour cream, and coconut oil until well mixed. Add the egg mixture to the flour mixture and stir to combine. Mix in the raspberries.
4. Scrape the batter into the prepared muffin cups, filling each about three-quarters full.
5. Put the muffin pan into Rack Position 1, select Convection Bake, set temperature to 345ºF (174ºC), and set time to 15 minutes.
6. When cooking is complete, the tops should be golden and a toothpick inserted in the middle should come out clean.
7. Allow the muffins to cool for 10 minutes in the muffin pan before removing and serving.

416.Roasted Chickpeas

Servings: 4
Cooking Time: 10 Minutes
Ingredients:
- 3 cup boiled chickpeas
- ¼ tsp. rosemary
- ¼ tsp. dry mango powder
- 1 tsp. olive oil
- ½ tsp. cinnamon powder
- ¼ tsp. cumin powder

- 1 tsp. salt
- ½ tsp. chili powder
- ¼ tsp. dry coriander powder

Directions:
1. Preheat your Air Fryer to a temperature of 370°F (190°C).
2. Transfer chickpeas with olive oil in fryer basket and cook for 8 minutes.
3. Shake fryer basket after every 2 minutes.
4. In a bowl add chickpeas with all spices and toss to combine.
5. Serve!
- **Nutrition Info:** Calories: 214 Protein: 10.98 g Fat: 4.4 g Carbs: 34.27 g

417.Vanilla-lemon Cupcakes With Lemon Glaze

Servings:6
Cooking Time: 30 Minutes
Ingredients:

- 1 cup flour
- ½ cup sugar
- 1 small egg
- 1 tsp lemon zest
- ¾ tsp baking powder
- ¼ tsp baking soda
- ½ tsp salt
- 2 tbsp vegetable oil
- ½ cup milk
- ½ tsp vanilla extract
- Glaze:
- ½ cup powdered sugar
- 2 tsp lemon juice

Directions:
1. Preheat on Bake function to 350 F. In a bowl, combine all dry muffin ingredients. In another bowl, whisk together the wet ingredients. Gently combine the two mixtures.
2. Divide the batter between 6 greased muffin tins. Place the tins in the oven and cook for 13 to 16 minutes. Whisk the powdered sugar with the lemon juice. Spread the glaze over the muffins.

418.Keto Mixed Berry Crumble Pots

Servings: 6
Cooking Time: 15 Minutes
Ingredients:

- 2 ounces unsweetened mixed berries
- 1/2 cup granulated swerve
- 2 tablespoons golden flaxseed meal
- 1/4 teaspoon ground star anise
- 1/2 teaspoon ground cinnamon
- 1 teaspoon xanthan gum
- 2/3 cup almond flour
- 1 cup powdered swerve
- 1/2 teaspoon baking powder

- 1/3 cup unsweetened coconut, finely shredded
- 1/2 stick butter, cut into small pieces

Directions:
1. Toss the mixed berries with the granulated swerve, golden flaxseed meal, star anise, cinnamon, and xanthan gum. Divide between six custard cups coated with cooking spray.
2. In a mixing dish, thoroughly combine the remaining ingredients. Sprinkle over the berry mixture.
3. Bake in the preheated Air Fryer at 330 degrees F for 35 minutes. Work in batches if needed.
- **Nutrition Info:** 155 Calories; 13g Fat; 1g Carbs; 1g Protein; 8g Sugars; 6g Fiber

419.Crab Stuffed Mushrooms

Servings: 16
Cooking Time: 8 Minutes
Ingredients:

- 16 mushrooms, clean and chop stems
- 2 oz crab meat, chopped
- 8 oz cream cheese, softened
- 1/4 tsp chili powder
- 1/4 cup mozzarella cheese, shredded

Directions:
1. Fit the oven with the rack in position 2.
2. In a bowl, mix chopped stems, chili powder, cheese, crabmeat, and cream cheese.
3. Stuff cheese mixture in mushrooms and place in air fryer basket then place air fryer basket in baking pan.
4. Place a baking pan on the oven rack. Set to air fry at 370 F for 8 minutes.
5. Serve and enjoy.
- **Nutrition Info:** Calories 59 Fat 5.1 g Carbohydrates 1.2 g Sugar 0.4 g Protein 2.2 g Cholesterol 18 mg

420.Creamy Chicken Dip

Servings: 6
Cooking Time: 20 Minutes
Ingredients:

- 2 cups chicken, cooked and shredded
- 8 oz cream cheese, softened
- 3 tbsp hot sauce
- 1/4 tsp garlic powder
- 3/4 cup sour cream
- 1/4 tsp onion powder

Directions:
1. Fit the oven with the rack in position 2.
2. Add all ingredients in a large bowl and mix until well combined.
3. Transfer mixture in air fryer baking dish.
4. Set to bake at 325 F for 25 minutes. After 5 minutes place the baking dish in the preheated oven.

5. Serve and enjoy.

- **Nutrition Info:** Calories 265 Fat 20.7 g Carbohydrates 2.5 g Sugar 0.3 g Protein 17.4 g Cholesterol 90 mg

421.Simple Cinnamon Rolls

Servings: 8
Cooking Time: 10 Minutes
Ingredients:
- Nonstick cooking spray
- 1 tbsp. cinnamon
- ¾ stick butter, soft
- 6 tbsp. brown sugar
- 1 sheet puff pastry, thawed
- ½ cup powdered sugar
- 1 tbsp. milk
- 2 tsp fresh lemon juice

Directions:
1. Place baking pan in position 2. Lightly spray fryer basket with cooking spray.
2. In a small bowl, stir together cinnamon, butter, and sugar.
3. Gently roll out pastry and spread with cinnamon mixture covering it completely.
4. Carefully roll up the pastry, starting at the short end. Use a serrated knife to cut the pastry in 1-inch pieces.
5. Place them in the fryer basket, these will need to be cooked in 2 batches. Place the basket on the baking pan and set oven to air fry on 400°F for 8 minutes. Cook cinnamon rolls until puffed and golden brown. Repeat with remaining rolls.
6. Let cool slightly. In a small bowl, whisk together powdered sugar, milk, and lemon juice, drizzle over cinnamon rolls and serve.

- **Nutrition Info:** Calories 155, Total Fat 11g, Saturated Fat 6g, Total Carbs 13g, Net Carbs 12g, Protein 1g, Sugar 10g, Fiber 1g, Sodium 85mg, Potassium 19mg, Phosphorus 9mg

422.Peanut Butter Cookies

Servings: 8
Cooking Time: 30 Minutes
Ingredients:
- 1 large egg.
- ⅓ cup granular erythritol.
- 1 cup no-sugar-added smooth peanut butter.
- 1 tsp. vanilla extract.

Directions:
1. Take a large bowl, mix all ingredients until smooth. Continue stirring for 2 additional minutes and the mixture will begin to thicken.
2. Roll the mixture into eight balls and press gently down to flatten into 2-inch round disks.
3. Cut a piece of parchment to fit your air fryer and place it into the basket. Place the cookies onto the parchment, working in batches as necessary.
4. Adjust the temperature to 320 Degrees F and set the timer for 8 minutes.
5. Flip the cookies at the 6-minute mark. Serve completely cooled.

- **Nutrition Info:** Calories: 210; Protein: 8.8g; Fiber: 2.0g; Fat: 17.5g; Carbs: 14.1g

423.Yogurt Pumpkin Bread

Servings: 4
Cooking Time: 15 Minutes
Ingredients:
- 2 large eggs
- 8 tablespoons pumpkin puree
- 6 tablespoons banana flour
- 4 tablespoons honey
- 4 tablespoons plain Greek yogurt
- 2 tablespoons vanilla essence
- Pinch of ground nutmeg 6 tablespoons oats

Directions:
1. In a bowl, add in all the ingredients except oats and with a hand mixer, mix until smooth.
2. Add the oats and with a fork, mix well.
3. Grease and flour a loaf pan.
4. Place the mixture into the prepared loaf pan.
5. Press "Power Button" of Air Fry Oven and turn the dial to select the "Air Crisp" mode.
6. Press the Time button and again turn the dial to set the cooking time to 15 minutes.
7. Now push the Temp button and rotate the dial to set the temperature at 360 degrees F.
8. Press "Start/Pause" button to start.
9. When the unit beeps to show that it is preheated, open the lid.
10. Arrange the pan in "Air Fry Basket" and insert in the oven.
11. Carefully, invert the bread onto wire rack to cool completely before slicing.
12. Cut the bread into desired-sized slices and serve.

- **Nutrition Info:** Calories 232 Total Fat 8.33 g Saturated Fat 1.5 g Cholesterol 94 mg Sodium 53 mg Total Carbs 29.3 g Fiber 2.8 g Sugar 20.5 g Protein 7.7 g

424.Tasty Sweet Potato Fries

Servings: 2
Cooking Time: 20 Minutes
Ingredients:
- 2 small sweet potatoes, peel and cut into fries shape
- 2 tbsp olive oil
- 1/4 tsp sea salt
- 1/4 tsp coriander
- 1/2 tsp curry powder

Directions:
1. Fit the oven with the rack in position 2.

2. Add all ingredients into the large mixing bowl and toss well.
3. Spray air fryer basket with cooking spray.
4. Transfer sweet potato fries in the air fryer basket then place the air fryer basket in the baking pan.
5. Place a baking pan on the oven rack. Set to air fry at 370 F for 20 minutes.
6. Serve and enjoy.
- **Nutrition Info:** Calories 240 Fat 14.2 g Carbohydrates 28.3 g Sugar 0.5 g Protein 1.6 g Cholesterol 0 mg

425.Cheesy Quesadillas

Servings:x
Cooking Time:x
Ingredients:
- 1 teaspoon dried oregano
- 1 tablespoon olive oil
- 10 (10-inch) flour tortillas
- 1 cup oil-packed sun-dried tomatoes
- 1 cup grated sharp Cheddar cheese
- 2 cups grated pepper jack cheese
- ½ cup grated Parmesan cheese

Directions:
1. Preheat oven to 400ºF. Chop sun-dried tomatoes and reserve oil. In medium bowl, combine cheeses, oregano, olive oil, and chopped tomatoes and mix well. Place cheese mixture on 5 tortillas and cover with the other 5. Brush stuffed tortillas on both sides with reserved oil and place on baking sheets. Bake at 400ºF for 25 to 35 minutes or until tortillas are golden and cheese is melted.
2. Cool completely in refrigerator, then cut each stuffed tortilla into six wedges. Wrap, label, and freeze.
3. To reheat: Place frozen wedges on cookie sheet and bake at 400ºF for 7 to 12 minutes, until quesadillas are hot and cheese is melted.

426.Homemade Bbq Chicken Pizza

Servings:1
Cooking Time: 8 Minutes
Ingredients:
- 1 piece naan bread
- ¼ cup Barbecue sauce
- ¼ cup shredded Monterrey Jack cheese
- ¼ cup shredded Mozzarella cheese
- ½ chicken herby sausage, sliced
- 2 tablespoons red onion, thinly sliced
- Chopped cilantro or parsley, for garnish
- Cooking spray

Directions:
1. Spritz the bottom of naan bread with cooking spray, then transfer to the air fryer basket.

2. Brush with the Barbecue sauce. Top with the cheeses, sausage, and finish with the red onion.
3. Put the air fryer basket on the baking pan and slide into Rack Position 2, select Air Fry, set temperature to 400ºF (205ºC), and set time to 8 minutes.
4. When cooking is complete, the cheese should be melted. Remove from the oven. Garnish with the chopped cilantro or parsley before slicing to serve.

427.Chocolate Coffee Cake

Servings: 8
Cooking Time: 15 Minutes
Ingredients:
- 1 ½ cups almond flour
- 1/2 cup coconut meal
- 2/3 cup swerve
- 1 teaspoon baking powder
- 1/4 teaspoon salt
- 1 stick butter, melted
- 1/2 cup hot strongly brewed coffee
- 1/2 teaspoon vanilla
- 1 egg
- Topping:
- 1/4 cup coconut flour
- 1/2 cup confectioner's swerve
- 1/2 teaspoon ground cardamom
- 1 teaspoon ground cinnamon
- 3 tablespoons coconut oil

Directions:
1. Mix all dry ingredients for your cake; then, mix in the wet ingredients. Mix until everything is well incorporated.
2. Spritz a baking pan with cooking spray. Scrape the batter into the baking pan.
3. Then, make the topping by mixing all ingredients. Place on top of the cake.Smooth the top with a spatula.
4. Bake at 330 degrees F for 30 minutes or until the top of the cake springs back when gently pressed with your fingers. Serve with your favorite hot beverage.
- **Nutrition Info:** 285 Calories; 21g Fat; 6g Carbs; 8g Protein; 3g Sugars; 1g Fiber

428.Coconut Cookies With Pecans

Servings:10
Cooking Time: 25 Minutes
Ingredients:
- 1½ cups coconut flour
- 1½ cups extra-fine almond flour
- ½ teaspoon baking powder
- $^{1}/_{3}$ teaspoon baking soda
- 3 eggs plus an egg yolk, beaten
- ¾ cup coconut oil, at room temperature
- 1 cup unsalted pecan nuts, roughly chopped
- ¾ cup monk fruit

- ¼ teaspoon freshly grated nutmeg
- $^1/_3$ teaspoon ground cloves
- ½ teaspoon pure vanilla extract
- ½ teaspoon pure coconut extract
- ⅛ teaspoon fine sea salt

Directions:
1. Line the baking pan with parchment paper.
2. Mix the coconut flour, almond flour, baking powder, and baking soda in a large mixing bowl.
3. In another mixing bowl, stir together the eggs and coconut oil. Add the wet mixture to the dry mixture.
4. Mix in the remaining ingredients and stir until a soft dough forms.
5. Drop about 2 tablespoons of dough on the parchment paper for each cookie and flatten each biscuit until it's 1 inch thick.
6. Slide the baking pan into Rack Position 1, select Convection Bake, set temperature to 370ºF (188ºC), and set time to 25 minutes.
7. When cooking is complete, the cookies should be golden and firm to the touch.
8. Remove from the oven to a plate. Let the cookies cool to room temperature and serve.

429.Deep-dish Giant Double Chocolate Chip Cookie

Servings:x
Cooking Time:x
Ingredients:
- 1 large egg
- 1 cup all-purpose flour
- ½ tsp baking powder
- ½ tsp salt
- 1 cup chocolate chip
- ½ cup unsalted butter
- ½ cup light brown sugar
- ½ cup white sugar
- 1 tsp vanilla
- ½ cup chocolate chunks

Directions:
1. Preheat oven to 350°F.
2. Melt butter in oven over low heat.
3. Add sugars and stir well.
4. Incorporate vanilla and egg, and beat quickly to make sure eggs do not cook.
5. Stir in flour, baking soda and salt.
6. Fold in chocolate chips and chunks and spread dough out in oven lightly with a spatula to flatten.
7. Bake for 25 minutes until cookie appears browned on top.

430.Handmade Donuts

Servings:4
Cooking Time: 25 Minutes
Ingredients:
- 8 oz self-rising flour

- 1 tsp baking powder
- ½ cup milk
- 2 ½ tbsp butter
- 1 egg
- 2 oz brown sugar

Directions:
1. Preheat on Bake function to 350 F. In a bowl, beat the butter with sugar until smooth. Whisk in egg and milk. In another bowl, combine the flour with the baking powder.
2. Fold the flour into the butter mixture. Form donut shapes and cut off the center with cookie cutters. Arrange on a lined baking sheet and cook for 15 minutes. Serve with whipped cream.

431.Cardamom Cakes

Servings:x
Cooking Time:x
Ingredients:
- 2 tbsp. butter
- 2 tbsp. sugar
- Muffin cups
- 2 cups All-purpose flour
- 1 ½ cup milk
- 1 tbsp. cardamom powder
- ½ tsp. baking powder
- ½ tsp. baking soda

Directions:
1. Mix the ingredients together and use your Oregano Fingers to get a crumbly mixture.
2. Add the baking soda and the vinegar to the milk and mix continuously. Add this milk to the mixture and create a batter, which you will need to transfer to the muffin cups.
3. Preheat the fryer to 300 Fahrenheit for five minutes. You will need to place the muffin cups in the basket and cover it. Cook the muffins for fifteen minutes and check whether or not the muffins are cooked using a toothpick. Remove the cups and serve hot.

432.Cripsy Artichoke Bites

Servings:4
Cooking Time: 8 Minutes
Ingredients:
- 14 whole artichoke hearts packed in water
- ½ cup all-purpose flour
- 1 egg
- $^1/_3$ cup panko bread crumbs
- 1 teaspoon Italian seasoning
- Cooking spray

Directions:
1. Drain the artichoke hearts and dry thoroughly with paper towels.
2. Place the flour on a plate. Beat the egg in a shallow bowl until frothy. Thoroughly

combine the bread crumbs and Italian seasoning in a separate shallow bowl.

3. Dredge the artichoke hearts in the flour, then in the beaten egg, and finally roll in the bread crumb mixture until evenly coated.
4. Place the artichoke hearts in the air fryer basket and mist them with cooking spray.
5. Put the air fryer basket on the baking pan and slide into Rack Position 2, select Air Fry, set temperature to 375ºF (190ºC), and set time to 8 minutes.
6. Flip the artichoke hearts halfway through the cooking time.
7. When cooking is complete, the artichoke hearts should start to brown and the edges should be crispy. Remove from the oven and let the artichoke hearts sit for 5 minutes before serving.

433.Almond Milk

Servings:x
Cooking Time:x
Ingredients:
- 2 tbsp. custard powder
- 3 tbsp. powdered sugar
- 3 tbsp. unsalted butter
- 2 cups almond powder
- 2 cups milk
- 1 tsp. gelatin

Directions:
1. Boil the milk and the sugar in a pan and add the custard powder followed by the almond powder and stir till you get a thick mixture. Add the gelatin and mix the ingredients well.
2. Preheat the fryer to 300 Fahrenheit for five minutes. Place the dish in the basket and reduce the temperature to 250 Fahrenheit. Cook for ten minutes and set aside to cool.

434.Sago Payada

Servings:x
Cooking Time:x
Ingredients:
- 3 tbsp. powdered sugar
- 3 tbsp. unsalted butter
- 2 cups milk
- 2 cups-soaked sago
- 2 tbsp. custard powder

Directions:
1. Boil the milk and the sugar in a pan and add the custard powder followed by the sago and stir till you get a thick mixture.
2. Preheat the fryer to 300 Fahrenheit for five minutes. Place the dish in the basket and reduce the temperature to 250 Fahrenheit. Cook for ten minutes and set aside to cool.

435.Parmesan Zucchini Fries

Servings: 4

Cooking Time: 10 Minutes
Ingredients:
- 2 medium zucchini, cut into fries shape
- 1/2 cup breadcrumbs
- 1 egg, lightly beaten
- 1/2 tsp garlic powder
- 1 tsp Italian seasoning
- 1/2 cup parmesan cheese, grated
- Pepper
- Salt

Directions:
1. Fit the oven with the rack in position 2.
2. Add egg in a bowl and whisk well.
3. In a shallow bowl, mix together breadcrumbs, spices, parmesan cheese, pepper, and salt.
4. Dip zucchini in egg then coat with breadcrumb mixture and place in air fryer basket then place air fryer basket in baking pan.
5. Place a baking pan on the oven rack. Set to air fry at 400 F for 10 minutes.
6. Serve and enjoy.
- **Nutrition Info:** Calories 126 Fat 4.8 g Carbohydrates 13.9 g Sugar 2.8 g Protein 8.1 g Cholesterol 50 mg

436.Egg Rolls

Servings:x
Cooking Time:x
Ingredients:
- 1 cup shredded Napa cabbage
- 2 tablespoons soy sauce
- 1 tablespoon oyster sauce
- 2 tablespoons cornstarch 1 tablespoon water
- 1 package egg roll wrappers
- 3 cups peanut oil
- ½ pound ground pork
- ½ pound ground shrimp
- 1 carrot, shredded
- 2 cloves garlic, minced
- 1 bunch green onions, finely chopped

Directions:
1. In a large skillet, brown ground pork until almost done. Add ground shrimp, carrot, and garlic; cook and stir for 4 to 6 minutes or until pork is cooked. Remove from heat, drain well, and add green onions, cabbage, soy sauce, and oyster sauce.
2. Combine cornstarch and water in a small bowl and blend well.
3. To form egg rolls, place one wrapper, point-side down, on work surface. Place 1 tablespoon filling 1 inch from corner. Brush all edges of the egg roll wrapper with cornstarch mixture. Fold point over filling, then fold in sides and roll up egg roll, using cornstarch mixture to seal as necessary.
4. At this point, egg rolls may be flash frozen, or you can flash freeze them after frying.

Once frozen, pack, label, and freeze in rigid containers.

5. To reheat untried egg rolls: Fry the frozen rolls in peanut oil heated to 375ºF for 2 to 3 minutes, turning once, or until deep golden brown. To reheat fried egg rolls: Place frozen egg rolls on baking sheet. Bake at 375ºF for 8 to 10 minutes or until crisp and hot.

437.Spicy Chicken Wings

Servings: 6
Cooking Time: 16 Minutes
Ingredients:
- 1/2 lb chicken wings
- 2 tsp ginger powder
- 1 tsp paprika
- 1/3 cup hot sauce
- 2 tsp garlic powder
- Pepper
- Salt

Directions:
1. Fit the oven with the rack in position 2.
2. Toss chicken wings with paprika, garlic powder, pepper, ginger powder, and salt.
3. Add chicken wings to the air fryer basket then place an air fryer basket in the baking pan.
4. Place a baking pan on the oven rack. Set to air fry at 360 F for 16 minutes.
5. Serve with hot sauce.
- **Nutrition Info:** Calories 104 Fat 2.9 g Carbohydrates 5.8 g Sugar 3.9 g Protein 11.2 g Cholesterol 34 mg

438.Easy Cheese Dip

Servings: 12
Cooking Time: 30 Minutes
Ingredients:
- 1/2 cup mayonnaise
- 1 small onion, diced
- 1 1/2 cups mozzarella cheese, shredded
- 4 oz cream cheese, cubed
- 1 1/2 cups cheddar cheese, shredded

Directions:
1. Fit the oven with the rack in position
2. Add all ingredients into the mixing bowl and mix until well combined.
3. Pour mixture into the prepared baking dish.
4. Set to bake at 400 F for 35 minutes. After 5 minutes place the baking dish in the preheated oven.
5. Serve and enjoy.
- **Nutrition Info:** Calories 140 Fat 11.9 g Carbohydrates 3.4 g Sugar 1 g Protein 5.4 g Cholesterol 30 mg

439.Old Bay Chicken Wings

Servings:4
Cooking Time: 13 Minutes
Ingredients:
- 2 tablespoons Old Bay seasoning
- 2 teaspoons baking powder
- 2 teaspoons salt
- 2 pounds (907 g) chicken wings, patted dry
- Cooking spray

Directions:
1. Combine the Old Bay seasoning, baking powder, and salt in a large zip-top plastic bag. Add the chicken wings, seal, and shake until the wings are thoroughly coated in the seasoning mixture.
2. Lightly spray the air fryer basket with cooking spray. Lay the chicken wings in the basket in a single layer and lightly mist them with cooking spray.
3. Put the air fryer basket on the baking pan and slide into Rack Position 2, select Air Fry, set temperature to 400ºF (205ºC), and set time to 13 minutes.
4. Flip the wings halfway through the cooking time.
5. When cooking is complete, the wings should reach an internal temperature of 165ºF (74ºC) on a meat thermometer. Remove from the oven to a plate and serve hot.

440.Apple Fritters

Servings:6
Cooking Time: 7 Minutes
Ingredients:
- 1 cup chopped, peeled Granny Smith apple
- ½ cup granulated sugar
- 1 teaspoon ground cinnamon
- 1 cup all-purpose flour
- 1 teaspoon baking powder
- 1 teaspoon salt
- 2 tablespoons milk
- 2 tablespoons butter, melted
- 1 large egg, beaten
- Cooking spray

Directions:
1. ¼ cup confectioners' sugar (optional)
2. Mix together the apple, granulated sugar, and cinnamon in a small bowl. Allow to sit for 30 minutes.
3. Combine the flour, baking powder, and salt in a medium bowl. Add the milk, butter, and egg and stir to incorporate.
4. Pour the apple mixture into the bowl of flour mixture and stir with a spatula until a dough forms.
5. Make the fritters: On a clean work surface, divide the dough into 12 equal portions and shape into 1-inch balls. Flatten them into patties with your hands.
6. Line the baking pan with parchment paper and spray it with cooking spray.
7. Transfer the apple fritters onto the parchment paper, evenly spaced but not too close together. Spray the fritters with cooking spray.
8. Slide the baking pan into Rack Position 1, select Convection Bake, set temperature to 350ºF (180ºC), and set time to 7 minutes.

9. Flip the fritters halfway through the cooking time.
10. When cooking is complete, the fritters should be lightly browned.
11. Remove from the oven to a plate and serve with the confectioners' sugar sprinkled on top, if desired.

441.Easy Spanish Churros

Servings: 4
Cooking Time: 15 Minutes
Ingredients:
- 3/4 cup water
- 1 tablespoon swerve
- 1/4 teaspoon sea salt
- 1/4 teaspoon grated nutmeg
- 1/4 teaspoon ground cloves
- 6 tablespoons butter
- 3/4 cup almond flour
- 2 eggs

Directions:
1. To make the dough, boil the water in a pan over medium-high heat; now, add the swerve, salt, nutmeg, and cloves; cook until dissolved.
2. Add the butter and turn the heat to low. Gradually stir in the almond flour, whisking continuously, until the mixture forms a ball.
3. Remove from the heat; fold in the eggs one at a time, stirring to combine well.
4. Pour the mixture into a piping bag with a large star tip. Squeeze 4-inch strips of dough into the greased Air Fryer pan.
5. Cook at 410 degrees F for 6 minutes, working in batches.
- **Nutrition Info:** 321 Calories; 31g Fat; 4g Carbs; 4g Protein; 1g Sugars; 3g Fiber

442.Baked Cream

Servings:x
Cooking Time:x
Ingredients:
- 1 cup fresh blueberries
- 1 cup blackberries
- Handful of mint leaves
- 3 tsp. sugar
- 2 cups condensed milk
- 2 cups fresh cream
- 1 cup fresh strawberries
- 4 tsp. water

Directions:
1. Blend the cream and add the milk to it. Whisk the ingredients well together and transfer this mixture into small baking bowls ensuring you do not overfill the bowls.
2. Preheat the fryer to 300 Fahrenheit for five minutes. You will need to place the bowls in the basket and cover it. Cook it for fifteen minutes. When you shake the bowls, the mixture should just shake but not break. Leave it in the refrigerator to set and then arrange the fruits, garnish and serve.

443.Healthy Broccoli Tots

Servings: 4
Cooking Time: 12 Minutes
Ingredients:
- 1 lb broccoli, cooked & chopped
- 1/2 tsp garlic powder
- 1/2 cup almond flour
- 1/4 cup ground flaxseed
- 1 tsp salt

Directions:
1. Fit the oven with the rack in position 2.
2. Add broccoli into the food processor and process until it looks like rice.
3. Transfer broccoli to a large mixing bowl.
4. Add remaining ingredients into the bowl and mix until well combined.
5. Make tots from broccoli mixture and place in the air fryer basket then place an air fryer basket in the baking pan.
6. Place a baking pan on the oven rack. Set to air fry at 375 F for 12 minutes.
7. Serve and enjoy.
- **Nutrition Info:** Calories 97 Fat 4.3 g Carbohydrates 10.5 g Sugar 2.3 g Protein 5.3 g Cholesterol 0 mg

444.Crusted Mozzarella Sticks

Servings: 12
Cooking Time: 5 Minutes
Ingredients:
- Halved mozzarella sticks string cheese, 12.
- Italian seasoning, 1 tsp.
- Large eggs, 2.
- Garlic salt, ½ tsp.
- Parmesan cheese, ½ cup
- Almond flour, ½ cup

Directions:
1. Mix almond flour with Italian seasoning, garlic salt, and parmesan cheese.
2. Whisk eggs in a separate bowl and keep them aside.
3. Dip the mozzarella sticks in eggs then coat with cheese mixture.
4. Arrange them on a well-lined baking tray with wax paper.
5. Freeze the sticks for 30 minutes then place them in the air fryer basket.
6. Return the basket to the fryer than air fry them for 5 minutes at 400 ºF.
7. Let them sit for 1 minute then transfer to a plate.
8. Serve.
- **Nutrition Info:** Calories: 362 Fat: 15.9 g Carbs: 4.1 g Protein: 23.3 g

445.Spicy Crab Dip

Servings: 4
Cooking Time: 10 Minutes
Ingredients:
- 1 cup crabmeat
- 2 cups cheese, grated
- 1/4 cup mayonnaise

- 2 tbsp parsley, chopped
- 2 tbsp fresh lemon juice
- 2 tbsp hot sauce
- 1/2 cup green onion, sliced
- 1/4 tsp pepper
- 1/2 tsp salt

Directions:
1. Fit the oven with the rack in position
2. Add all ingredients into the mixing bowl and mix well.
3. Pour mixture into the greased baking dish.
4. Set to bake at 400 F for 15 minutes. After 5 minutes place the baking dish in the preheated oven.
5. Serve and enjoy.
- **Nutrition Info:** Calories 313 Fat 23.9 g Carbohydrates 8.8 g Sugar 3.1 g Protein 16.2 g Cholesterol 67 mg

446.Mini Crab Cakes

Servings:x
Cooking Time:x
Ingredients:
- ½ cup dried bread crumbs
- ½ cup mayonnaise
- ¼ cup minced green onions
- 3 tablespoons olive oil
- 1-pound canned lump crabmeat
- 1 cup fresh cilantro leaves
- ½ cup chopped walnuts
- ½ cup grated Romano cheese
- 2 tablespoons olive oil

Directions:
1. Drain crabmeat well and pick over to remove any cartilage. Set aside in large bowl. In food processor or blender, combine cilantro, walnuts, cheese, and 2 tablespoons olive oil (6 tablespoons for triple batch). Process or blend until mixture forms a paste. Stir into crabmeat.
2. Add bread crumbs, mayonnaise, and green onions to crab mixture. Stir to combine. Form into 2- inch patties about ½-inch thick. Flash freeze on baking sheet. When frozen solid, pack crab cakes in rigid containers, with waxed paper between the layers. Label crab cakes and freeze. Reserve remaining olive oil in pantry.
3. To thaw and reheat: Thaw crab cakes in refrigerator overnight. Heat 3 tablespoons olive oil (9 for triple batch) in large, heavy skillet over medium heat. Fry crab cakes until golden and hot, turning once, about 3 to 5 minutes on each side.

447.Cherry Apple Risotto

Servings: 4
Cooking Time: 12 Minutes
Ingredients:
- 1 tablespoon of butter
- ¼ cup of brown sugar
- ½ cup of apple juice

- 1½ cups of milk
- ¾ cup of Arborio rice, boiled
- 1 apple, diced
- 2 pinches salt
- ¾ teaspoon of cinnamon powder
- ¼ cup of dried cherries
- 1½ tablespoons of almonds, roasted and sliced
- ¼ cup of whipped cream

Directions:
1. Set the Instant Vortex on Air fryer to 375 degrees F for 12 minutes. Combine rice with butter, sugar, apple juice, milk, apple, salt, and cinnamon in a bowl. Pour the rice mixture into the cooking tray. Insert the cooking tray in the Vortex when it displays "Add Food". Toss the food when it displays "Turn Food". Remove from the oven when cooking time is complete. Top with the dried cherries, almonds, and whipped cream to serve.
- **Nutrition Info:** Calories: 317 Cal Total Fat: 8.5 g Saturated Fat: 0 g Cholesterol: 0 mg Sodium: 0 mg Total Carbs: 54.8 g Fiber: 0 g Sugar: 0 g Protein: 6.2 g

448.Green Chiles Nachos

Servings:6
Cooking Time: 10 Minutes
Ingredients:
- 8 ounces (227 g) tortilla chips
- 3 cups shredded Monterey Jack cheese, divided
- 2 (7-ounce / 198-g) cans chopped green chiles, drained
- 1 (8-ounce / 227-g) can tomato sauce
- ¼ teaspoon dried oregano
- ¼ teaspoon granulated garlic
- ¼ teaspoon freshly ground black pepper
- Pinch cinnamon
- Pinch cayenne pepper

Directions:
1. Arrange the tortilla chips close together in a single layer in the baking pan. Sprinkle 1½ cups of the cheese over the chips. Arrange the green chiles over the cheese as evenly as possible. Top with the remaining 1½ cups of the cheese.
2. Slide the baking pan into Rack Position 2, select Roast, set temperature to 375ºF (190ºC) and set time to 10 minutes.
3. Meanwhile, stir together the remaining ingredients in a bowl.
4. When cooking is complete, the cheese will be melted and starting to crisp around the edges of the pan. Remove from the oven. Drizzle the sauce over the nachos and serve warm.

449.Strawberry And Rhubarb Crumble

Servings:6
Cooking Time: 12 To 17 Minutes

Ingredients:

- 1½ cups sliced fresh strawberries
- $^1/_3$ cup sugar
- ¾ cup sliced rhubarb
- $^2/_3$ cup quick-cooking oatmeal
- ¼ cup packed brown sugar
- ½ cup whole-wheat pastry flour
- ½ teaspoon ground cinnamon
- 3 tablespoons unsalted butter, melted

Directions:

1. Place the strawberries, sugar, and rhubarb in the baking pan and toss to coat.
2. Combine the oatmeal, brown sugar, pastry flour, and cinnamon in a medium bowl.
3. Add the melted butter to the oatmeal mixture and stir until crumbly. Sprinkle this generously on top of the strawberries and rhubarb.
4. Slide the baking pan into Rack Position 1, select Convection Bake, set temperature to 370ºF (188ºC), and set the time to 12 minutes.
5. Bake until the fruit is bubbly and the topping is golden brown. Continue cooking for an additional 2 to 5 minutes if needed.
6. When cooking is complete, remove from the oven and serve warm.

450.Gluten-free Fried Bananas

Servings: 8
Cooking Time: 15 Minutes
Ingredients:

- 8 bananas
- 3 tbsp vegetable oil
- 3 tbsp cornflour
- 1 egg white
- ¾ cup breadcrumbs

Directions:

1. Preheat on Toast function to 350 F. Combine the oil and breadcrumbs in a small bowl. Coat the bananas with the corn flour first, brush them with egg white, and dip them in the breadcrumb mixture. Arrange on a lined baking sheet and cook for 8-12 minutes. Serve.

451.Apple Hand Pies

Servings: 6
Cooking Time: 8 Minutes
Ingredients:

- 15-ounces no-sugar-added apple pie filling
- 1 store-bought crust

Directions:

1. Preparing the Ingredients. Lay out pie crust and slice into equal-sized squares.
2. Place 2 tbsp. filling into each square and seal crust with a fork.
3. Air Frying. Place into the air fryer oven. Cook 8 minutes at 390 degrees until golden in color.
- **Nutrition Info:** CALORIES: 278; FAT:10G; PROTEIN:5G; SUGAR:4G

452.Delicious Lemon Bars

Servings: 8
Cooking Time: 40 Minutes
Ingredients:

- 4 eggs
- 1 lemon zest
- 1/4 cup fresh lemon juice
- 1/2 cup butter softened
- 1/2 cup sour cream
- 1/3 cup erythritol
- 2 tsp baking powder
- 2 cups almond flour

Directions:

1. Fit the oven with the rack in position
2. In a bowl, beat eggs until frothy.
3. Add butter and sour cream and beat until well combined.
4. Add sweetener, lemon zest, and lemon juice and blend well.
5. Add baking powder and almond flour and mix until well combined.
6. Transfer batter in a greased baking pan and spread evenly.
7. Set to bake at 350 F for 45 minutes. After 5 minutes place the baking pan in the preheated oven.
8. Slice and serve.
- **Nutrition Info:** Calories 147 Fat 10.9 g Carbohydrates 8.8 g Sugar 0.8 g Protein 5.3 g Cholesterol 88 mg

453.Garlicky-lemon Zucchini

Servings:x
Cooking Time:x
Ingredients:

- Coarse salt and black pepper, to taste
- ½ tsp thyme, minced
- ½ lemon
- 4 small green zucchinis, any color, sliced about ¼-inch thick
- 1½ Tbsp extra virgin olive oil
- 1 Tbsp garlic, minced

Directions:

1. Heat oven over medium-low heat. Add oil and let heat for 1 minute.
2. Sprinkle zucchini with salt and pepper.
3. Add to the pan in a single layer. When zucchini is nicely browned, flip
4. and brown on other side.
5. Add garlic and saute for 1 minute.
6. Sprinkle thyme and additional salt if necessary.
7. Remove from pan and squeeze lemon juice on zucchini.

454.Easy Pumpkin Pie

Servings: 8
Cooking Time: 35 Minutes
Ingredients:

- Egg yolks, 3.
- Large egg, 1.
- Ground ginger, ½ tsp.

- Fine salt, ½ tsp.
- Chinese 5-spice powder, 1/8 tsp.
- Unbaked pie crust, 19-inch.
- Freshly grated nutmeg, ¼ tsp.
- Sweetened condensed milk, 14 oz.
- Pumpkin puree, 15 oz.
- Ground cinnamon, 1 tsp.

Directions:
1. Lightly grease a baking pan of air fryer with cooking spray. Press pie crust on bottom of pan, stretching all the way up to the sides of the pan. Pierce all over with a fork.
2. In blender, blend well egg, egg yolks, and pumpkin puree. Add Chinese 5-spice powder, nutmeg, salt, ginger, cinnamon, and condensed milk. Pour on top of pie crust.
3. Cover pan with foil.
4. For 15 minutes, cook on preheated 390 ºF air fryer.
5. Cook for 20 more minutes at 330 ºF without the foil until middle is set.
6. Allow to cool in air fryer completely.
7. Serve and enjoy.
- **Nutrition Info:** Calories: 326 Carbs: 41.9g Fat: 14.2g Protein: 7.6g

455.Crispy Shrimps

Servings: 2
Cooking Time: 8 Minutes
Ingredients:
- 1 egg
- ¼ pound nacho chips, crushed
- 10 shrimps, peeled and deveined
- 1 tablespoon olive oil
- Salt and black pepper, to taste

Directions:
1. Preheat the Air fryer to 365 ºF and grease an Air fryer basket.
2. Crack egg in a shallow dish and beat well.
3. Place the nacho chips in another shallow dish.
4. Season the shrimps with salt and black pepper, coat into egg and then roll into nacho chips.
5. Place the coated shrimps into the Air fryer basket and cook for about 8 minutes.
6. Dish out and serve warm.
- **Nutrition Info:** Calories: 514, Fat: 25.8g, Carbohydrates: 36.9g, Sugar: 2.3g, Protein: 32.5g, Sodium: 648mg

456.Dark Chocolate Lava Cakes

Servings: 4
Cooking Time: 20 Minutes
Ingredients:
- 3 ½ oz butter, melted
- 3 ½ tbsp sugar
- 1 ½ tbsp self-rising flour
- 3 ½ oz dark chocolate, melted
- 2 eggs

Directions:
1. Grease 4 ramekins with butter. Preheat on Bake function to 375 F. Beat the eggs and sugar until frothy. Stir in butter and chocolate; gently fold in the flour. Divide the mixture between the ramekins and bake for 10 minutes. Let cool for 2 minutes before turning the cakes upside down onto serving plates.

457.Easy Corn And Bell Pepper Casserole

Servings:4
Cooking Time: 20 Minutes
Ingredients:
- 1 cup corn kernels
- ¼ cup bell pepper, finely chopped
- ½ cup low-fat milk
- 1 large egg, beaten
- ½ cup yellow cornmeal
- ½ cup all-purpose flour
- ½ teaspoon baking powder
- 2 tablespoons melted unsalted butter
- 1 tablespoon granulated sugar
- Pinch of cayenne pepper
- ¼ teaspoon kosher salt
- Cooking spray

Directions:
1. Spritz the baking pan with cooking spray.
2. Combine all the ingredients in a large bowl. Stir to mix well. Pour the mixture into the baking pan.
3. Slide the baking pan into Rack Position 1, select Convection Bake, set temperature to 330ºF (166ºC) and set time to 20 minutes.
4. When cooking is complete, the casserole should be lightly browned and set.
5. Remove from the oven and serve immediately.

458.Pão De Queijo

Servings: 12 Balls
Cooking Time: 12 Minutes
Ingredients:
- 2 tablespoons butter, plus more for greasing
- ½ cup milk
- 1½ cups tapioca flour
- ½ teaspoon salt
- 1 large egg
- $^2/_3$ cup finely grated aged Asiago cheese

Directions:
1. Put the butter in a saucepan and pour in the milk, heat over medium heat until the liquid boils. Keep stirring.
2. Turn off the heat and mix in the tapioca flour and salt to form a soft dough. Transfer the dough in a large bowl, then wrap the bowl in plastic and let sit for 15 minutes.
3. Break the egg in the bowl of dough and whisk with a hand mixer for 2 minutes or until a sanity dough forms. Fold the cheese in the dough. Cover the bowl in plastic again and let sit for 10 more minutes.
4. Grease the baking pan with butter.
5. Scoop 2 tablespoons of the dough into the baking pan. Repeat with the remaining dough to make dough 12 balls. Keep a little distance between each two balls.
6. Slide the baking pan into Rack Position 1, select Convection Bake, set temperature to 375ºF (190ºC) and set time to 12 minutes.
7. Flip the balls halfway through the cooking time.
8. When cooking is complete, the balls should be golden brown and fluffy.
9. Remove the balls from the oven and allow to cool for 5 minutes before serving.

459.Milky Pecan Tart

Servings:8
Cooking Time: 26 Minutes
Ingredients:
- Tart Crust:
- ¼ cup firmly packed brown sugar
- $^1/_3$ cup butter, softened
- 1 cup all-purpose flour
- ¼ teaspoon kosher salt
- Filling:
- ¼ cup whole milk
- 4 tablespoons butter, diced
- ½ cup packed brown sugar
- ¼ cup pure maple syrup
- 1½ cups finely chopped pecans
- ¼ teaspoon pure vanilla extract
- ¼ teaspoon sea salt

Directions:
1. Line the baking pan with aluminum foil, then spritz the pan with cooking spray.
2. Stir the brown sugar and butter in a bowl with a hand mixer until puffed, then add the flour and salt and stir until crumbled.
3. Pour the mixture in the prepared baking pan and tilt the pan to coat the bottom evenly.
4. Slide the baking pan into Rack Position 1, select Convection Bake, set temperature to 350ºF (180ºC) and set time to 13 minutes.
5. When done, the crust will be golden brown.
6. Meanwhile, pour the milk, butter, sugar, and maple syrup in a saucepan. Stir to mix well. Bring to a simmer, then cook for 1 more minute. Stir constantly.
7. Turn off the heat and mix the pecans and vanilla into the filling mixture.
8. Pour the filling mixture over the golden crust and spread with a spatula to coat the crust evenly.
9. Select Bake and set time to 12 minutes. When cooked, the filling mixture should be set and frothy.
10. Remove the baking pan from the oven and sprinkle with salt. Allow to sit for 10 minutes or until cooled.

11. Transfer the pan to the refrigerator to chill for at least 2 hours, then remove the aluminum foil and slice to serve.

460.Sweet Air Fried Pecans

Servings: 4 Cups
Cooking Time: 10 Minutes
Ingredients:
- 2 egg whites
- 1 tablespoon cumin
- 2 teaspoons smoked paprika
- ½ cup brown sugar
- 2 teaspoons kosher salt
- 1 pound (454 g) pecan halves
- Cooking spray

Directions:
1. Spritz the air fryer basket with cooking spray.
2. Combine the egg whites, cumin, paprika, sugar, and salt in a large bowl. Stir to mix well. Add the pecans to the bowl and toss to coat well.
3. Transfer the pecans to the basket.
4. Put the air fryer basket on the baking pan and slide into Rack Position 2, select Air Fry, set temperature to 300ºF (150ºC) and set time to 10 minutes.
5. Stir the pecans at least two times during the cooking.
6. When cooking is complete, the pecans should be lightly caramelized. Remove from the oven and serve immediately.

461.Classic Worcestershire Poutine

Servings:2
Cooking Time: 33 Minutes
Ingredients:
- 2 russet potatoes, scrubbed and cut into ½-inch sticks
- 2 teaspoons vegetable oil
- 2 tablespoons butter
- ¼ onion, minced
- ¼ teaspoon dried thyme
- 1 clove garlic, smashed
- 3 tablespoons all-purpose flour
- 1 teaspoon tomato paste
- 1½ cups beef stock
- 2 teaspoons Worcestershire sauce
- Salt and freshly ground black pepper, to taste
- $^2/_3$ cup chopped string cheese

Directions:
1. Bring a pot of water to a boil, then put in the potato sticks and blanch for 4 minutes.
2. Drain the potato sticks and rinse under running cold water, then pat dry with paper towels.
3. Transfer the sticks in a large bowl and drizzle with vegetable oil. Toss to coat well.

Place the potato sticks in the air fryer basket.
4. Put the air fryer basket on the baking pan and slide into Rack Position 2, select Air Fry, set temperature to 400ºF (205ºC) and set time to 25 minutes.
5. Stir the potato sticks at least three times during cooking.
6. Meanwhile, make the gravy: Heat the butter in a saucepan over medium heat until melted.
7. Add the onion, thyme, and garlic and sauté for 5 minutes or until the onion is translucent.
8. Add the flour and sauté for an additional 2 minutes. Pour in the tomato paste and beef stock and cook for 1 more minute or until lightly thickened.
9. Drizzle the gravy with Worcestershire sauce and sprinkle with salt and ground black pepper. Reduce the heat to low to keep the gravy warm until ready to serve.
10. When done, the sticks should be golden brown. Remove from the oven. Transfer the fried potato sticks onto a plate, then sprinkle with salt and ground black pepper. Scatter with string cheese and pour the gravy over. Serve warm.

462.Spicy Air Fried Old Bay Shrimp

Servings: 2 Cups
Cooking Time: 10 Minutes
Ingredients:
- ½ teaspoon Old Bay Seasoning
- 1 teaspoon ground cayenne pepper
- ½ teaspoon paprika
- 1 tablespoon olive oil
- ⅛ teaspoon salt
- ½ pound (227 g) shrimps, peeled and deveined
- Juice of half a lemon

Directions:
1. Combine the Old Bay Seasoning, cayenne pepper, paprika, olive oil, and salt in a large bowl, then add the shrimps and toss to coat well.
2. Put the shrimps in the air fryer basket.
3. Put the air fryer basket on the baking pan and slide into Rack Position 2, select Air Fry, set temperature to 390ºF (199ºC) and set time to 10 minutes.
4. Flip the shrimps halfway through the cooking time.
5. When cooking is complete, the shrimps should be opaque. Serve the shrimps with lemon juice on top.

463.Bartlett Pears With Lemony Ricotta

Servings:4
Cooking Time: 8 Minutes

Ingredients:

- 2 large Bartlett pears, peeled, cut in half, cored
- 3 tablespoons melted butter
- ½ teaspoon ground ginger
- ¼ teaspoon ground cardamom
- 3 tablespoons brown sugar
- ½ cup whole-milk ricotta cheese
- 1 teaspoon pure lemon extract
- 1 teaspoon pure almond extract
- 1 tablespoon honey, plus additional for drizzling

Directions:

1. Toss the pears with butter, ginger, cardamom, and sugar in a large bowl. Toss to coat well. Arrange the pears in the baking pan, cut side down.
2. Put the air fryer basket on the baking pan and slide into Rack Position 2, select Air Fry, set temperature to 375ºF (190ºC) and set time to 8 minutes.
3. After 5 minutes, remove the pan and flip the pears. Return to the oven and continue cooking.
4. When cooking is complete, the pears should be soft and browned. Remove from the oven.
5. In the meantime, combine the remaining ingredients in a separate bowl. Whip for 1 minute with a hand mixer until the mixture is puffed.
6. Divide the mixture into four bowls, then put the pears over the mixture and drizzle with more honey to serve.

464.Potato Chips With Lemony Cream Dip

Servings:2 To 4
Cooking Time: 15 Minutes
Ingredients:

- 2 large russet potatoes, sliced into ⅛-inch slices, rinsed
- Sea salt and freshly ground black pepper, to taste
- Cooking spray
- Lemony Cream Dip:
- ½ cup sour cream
- ¼ teaspoon lemon juice
- 2 scallions, white part only, minced
- 1 tablespoon olive oil
- ¼ teaspoon salt
- Freshly ground black pepper, to taste

Directions:

1. Soak the potato slices in water for 10 minutes, then pat dry with paper towels.
2. Transfer the potato slices in the air fryer basket. Spritz the slices with cooking spray.
3. Put the air fryer basket on the baking pan and slide into Rack Position 2, select Air Fry, set temperature to 300ºF (150ºC) and set time to 15 minutes.
4. Stir the potato slices three times during cooking. Sprinkle with salt and ground black pepper in the last minute.
5. Meanwhile, combine the ingredients for the dip in a small bowl. Stir to mix well.
6. When cooking is complete, the potato slices will be crispy and golden brown. Remove from the oven and serve the potato chips immediately with the dip.

465.Spanakopita

Servings:6
Cooking Time: 8 Minutes
Ingredients:

- ½ (10-ounce / 284-g) package frozen spinach, thawed and squeezed dry
- 1 egg, lightly beaten
- ¼ cup pine nuts, toasted
- ¼ cup grated Parmesan cheese
- ¾ cup crumbled feta cheese
- ⅛ teaspoon ground nutmeg
- ½ teaspoon salt
- Freshly ground black pepper, to taste
- 6 sheets phyllo dough
- ½ cup butter, melted

Directions:

1. Combine all the ingredients, except for the phyllo dough and butter, in a large bowl. Whisk to combine well. Set aside.
2. Place a sheet of phyllo dough on a clean work surface. Brush with butter then top with another layer sheet of phyllo. Brush with butter, then cut the layered sheets into six 3-inch-wide strips.
3. Top each strip with 1 tablespoon of the spinach mixture, then fold the bottom left corner over the mixture towards the right strip edge to make a triangle. Keep folding triangles until each strip is folded over.
4. Brush the triangles with butter and repeat with remaining strips and phyllo dough.
5. Place the triangles in the baking pan.
6. Put the air fryer basket on the baking pan and slide into Rack Position 2, select Air Fry, set temperature to 350ºF (180ºC) and set time to 8 minutes.
7. Flip the triangles halfway through the cooking time.
8. When cooking is complete, the triangles should be golden brown. Remove from the oven and serve immediately.

466.Chocolate Buttermilk Cake

Servings:8
Cooking Time: 20 Minutes
Ingredients:

- 1 cup all-purpose flour
- ²/₃ cup granulated white sugar
- ¼ cup unsweetened cocoa powder

- ¾ teaspoon baking soda
- ¼ teaspoon salt
- $^2/_3$ cup buttermilk
- 2 tablespoons plus 2 teaspoons vegetable oil
- 1 teaspoon vanilla extract
- Cooking spray

Directions:
1. Spritz the baking pan with cooking spray.
2. Combine the flour, cocoa powder, baking soda, sugar, and salt in a large bowl. Stir to mix well.
3. Mix in the buttermilk, vanilla, and vegetable oil. Keep stirring until it forms a grainy and thick dough.
4. Scrape the chocolate batter from the bowl and transfer to the pan, level the batter in an even layer with a spatula.
5. Slide the baking pan into Rack Position 1, select Convection Bake, set temperature to 325ºF (163ºC) and set time to 20 minutes.
6. After 15 minutes, remove the pan from the oven. Check the doneness. Return the pan to the oven and continue cooking.
7. When done, a toothpick inserted in the center should come out clean.
8. Invert the cake on a cooling rack and allow to cool for 15 minutes before slicing to serve.

467.Creamy Pork Gratin

Servings:4
Cooking Time: 21 Minutes
Ingredients:
- 2 tablespoons olive oil
- 2 pounds (907 g) pork tenderloin, cut into serving-size pieces
- 1 teaspoon dried marjoram
- ¼ teaspoon chili powder
- 1 teaspoon coarse sea salt
- ½ teaspoon freshly ground black pepper
- 1 cup Ricotta cheese
- 1½ cups chicken broth
- 1 tablespoon mustard
- Cooking spray

Directions:
1. Spritz the baking pan with cooking spray.
2. Heat the olive oil in a nonstick skillet over medium-high heat until shimmering.
3. Add the pork and sauté for 6 minutes or until lightly browned.
4. Transfer the pork to the prepared baking pan and sprinkle with marjoram, chili powder, salt, and ground black pepper.
5. Combine the remaining ingredients in a large bowl. Stir to mix well. Pour the mixture over the pork in the pan.

6. Slide the baking pan into Rack Position 1, select Convection Bake, set temperature to 350ºF (180ºC) and set time to 15 minutes.
7. Stir the mixture halfway through.
8. When cooking is complete, the mixture should be frothy and the cheese should be melted.
9. Serve immediately.

468.Shrimp With Sriracha And Worcestershire Sauce

Servings:4
Cooking Time: 10 Minutes
Ingredients:
- 1 tablespoon Sriracha sauce
- 1 teaspoon Worcestershire sauce
- 2 tablespoons sweet chili sauce
- ¾ cup mayonnaise
- 1 egg, beaten
- 1 cup panko bread crumbs
- 1 pound (454 g) raw shrimp, shelled and deveined, rinsed and drained
- Lime wedges, for serving
- Cooking spray

Directions:
1. Spritz the air fryer basket with cooking spray.
2. Combine the Sriracha sauce, Worcestershire sauce, chili sauce, and mayo in a bowl. Stir to mix well. Reserve $^1/_3$ cup of the mixture as the dipping sauce.
3. Combine the remaining sauce mixture with the beaten egg. Stir to mix well. Put the panko in a separate bowl.
4. Dredge the shrimp in the sauce mixture first, then into the panko. Roll the shrimp to coat well. Shake the excess off.
5. Place the shrimp in the basket, then spritz with cooking spray.
6. Put the air fryer basket on the baking pan and slide into Rack Position 2, select Air Fry, set temperature to 360ºF (182ºC) and set time to 10 minutes.
7. Flip the shrimp halfway through the cooking time.
8. When cooking is complete, the shrimp should be opaque.
9. Remove the shrimp from the oven and serve with reserve sauce mixture and squeeze the lime wedges over.

469.Oven Grits

Servings: About 4 Cups
Cooking Time: 1 Hour 5 Minutes
Ingredients:
- 1 cup grits or polenta (not instant or quick cook)
- 2 cups chicken or vegetable stock
- 2 cups milk

- 2 tablespoons unsalted butter, cut into 4 pieces
- 1 teaspoon kosher salt or ½ teaspoon fine salt

Directions:
1. Add the grits to the baking pan. Stir in the stock, milk, butter, and salt.
2. Select Bake, set the temperature to 325ºF (163ºC), and set the time for 1 hour and 5 minutes. Select Start to begin preheating.
3. Once the unit has preheated, place the pan in the oven.
4. After 15 minutes, remove the pan from the oven and stir the polenta. Return the pan to the oven and continue cooking.
5. After 30 minutes, remove the pan again and stir the polenta again. Return the pan to the oven and continue cooking for 15 to 20 minutes, or until the polenta is soft and creamy and the liquid is absorbed.
6. When done, remove the pan from the oven.
7. Serve immediately.

470.Goat Cheese And Asparagus Frittata

Servings:2 To 4
Cooking Time: 25 Minutes
Ingredients:
- 1 cup asparagus spears, cut into 1-inch pieces
- 1 teaspoon vegetable oil
- 1 tablespoon milk
- 6 eggs, beaten
- 2 ounces (57 g) goat cheese, crumbled
- 1 tablespoon minced chives, optional
- Kosher salt and pepper, to taste
- Add the asparagus spears to a small bowl and drizzle with the vegetable oil. Toss until well coated and transfer to the air fryer basket.

Directions:
1. Put the air fryer basket on the baking pan and slide into Rack Position 2, select Air Fry, set temperature to 400ºF (205ºC) and set time to 5 minutes.
2. Flip the asparagus halfway through.
3. When cooking is complete, the asparagus should be tender and slightly wilted.
4. Remove from the oven to the baking pan.
5. Stir together the milk and eggs in a medium bowl. Pour the mixture over the asparagus in the pan. Sprinkle with the goat cheese and the chives (if using) over the eggs. Season with salt and pepper.
6. Slide the baking pan into Rack Position 1, select Convection Bake, set temperature to 320ºF (160ºC) and set time to 20 minutes.
7. When cooking is complete, the top should be golden and the eggs should be set.
8. Transfer to a serving dish. Slice and serve.

471.Riced Cauliflower Casserole

Servings:4
Cooking Time: 12 Minutes
Ingredients:
- 1 head cauliflower, cut into florets
- 1 cup okra, chopped
- 1 yellow bell pepper, chopped
- 2 eggs, beaten
- ½ cup chopped onion
- 1 tablespoon soy sauce
- 2 tablespoons olive oil
- Salt and ground black pepper,
- to taste Spritz the baking pan with cooking spray.

Directions:
1. Put the cauliflower in a food processor and pulse to rice the cauliflower.
2. Pour the cauliflower rice in the baking pan and add the remaining ingredients. Stir to mix well.
3. Slide the baking pan into Rack Position 1, select Convection Bake, set temperature to 380ºF (193ºC) and set time to 12 minutes.
4. When cooking is complete, the eggs should be set.
5. Remove from the oven and serve immediately.

472.Jewish Blintzes

Servings: 8 Blintzes
Cooking Time: 10 Minutes
Ingredients:
- 2 (7½-ounce / 213-g) packages farmer cheese, mashed
- ¼ cup cream cheese
- ¼ teaspoon vanilla extract
- ¼ cup granulated white sugar
- 8 egg roll wrappers
- 4 tablespoons butter, melted

Directions:
1. Combine the farmer cheese, cream cheese, vanilla extract, and sugar in a bowl. Stir to mix well.
2. Unfold the egg roll wrappers on a clean work surface, spread ¼ cup of the filling at the edge of each wrapper and leave a ½-inch edge uncovering.
3. Wet the edges of the wrappers with water and fold the uncovered edge over the filling. Fold the left and right sides in the center, then tuck the edge under the filling and fold to wrap the filling.
4. Brush the wrappers with melted butter, then arrange the wrappers in a single layer in the air fryer basket, seam side down. Leave a little space between each two wrappers.
5. Put the air fryer basket on the baking pan and slide into Rack Position 2, select Air Fry,

set temperature to 375ºF (190ºC) and set time to 10 minutes.
6. When cooking is complete, the wrappers will be golden brown.
7. Serve immediately.

473.Supplì Al Telefono (risotto Croquettes)

Servings:6
Cooking Time: 54 Minutes
Ingredients:
- Risotto Croquettes:
- 4 tablespoons unsalted butter
- 1 small yellow onion, minced
- 1 cup Arborio rice
- 3½ cups chicken stock
- ½ cup dry white wine
- 3 eggs
- Zest of 1 lemon
- ½ cup grated Parmesan cheese
- 2 ounces (57 g) fresh Mozzarella cheese
- ¼ cup peas
- 2 tablespoons water
- ½ cup all-purpose flour
- 1½ cups panko bread crumbs
- Kosher salt and ground black pepper, to taste
- Cooking spray
- Tomato Sauce:
- 2 tablespoons extra-virgin olive oil
- 4 cloves garlic, minced
- ¼ teaspoon red pepper flakes
- 1 (28-ounce / 794-g) can crushed tomatoes
- 2 teaspoons granulated sugar
- Kosher salt and ground black pepper, to taste

Directions:
1. Melt the butter in a pot over medium heat, then add the onion and salt to taste. Sauté for 5 minutes or until the onion in translucent.
2. Add the rice and stir to coat well. Cook for 3 minutes or until the rice is lightly browned. Pour in the chicken stock and wine.
3. Bring to a boil. Then cook for 20 minutes or until the rice is tender and liquid is almost absorbed.
4. Make the risotto: When the rice is cooked, break the egg into the pot. Add the lemon zest and Parmesan cheese. Sprinkle with salt and ground black pepper. Stir to mix well.
5. Pour the risotto in a baking sheet, then level with a spatula to spread the risotto evenly. Wrap the baking sheet in plastic and refrigerate for1 hour.
6. Meanwhile, heat the olive oil in a saucepan over medium heat until shimmering.
7. Add the garlic and sprinkle with red pepper flakes. Sauté for a minute or until fragrant.
8. Add the crushed tomatoes and sprinkle with sugar. Stir to mix well. Bring to a boil. Reduce the heat to low and simmer for 15 minutes or until lightly thickened. Sprinkle with salt and pepper to taste. Set aside until ready to serve.
9. Remove the risotto from the refrigerator. Scoop the risotto into twelve 2-inch balls, then flatten the balls with your hands.
10. Arrange a about ½-inch piece of Mozzarella and 5 peas in the center of each flattened ball, then wrap them back into balls.
11. Transfer the balls to a baking sheet lined with parchment paper, then refrigerate for 15 minutes or until firm.
12. Whisk the remaining 2 eggs with 2 tablespoons of water in a bowl. Pour the flour in a second bowl and pour the panko in a third bowl.
13. Dredge the risotto balls in the bowl of flour first, then into the eggs, and then into the panko. Shake the excess off.
14. Transfer the balls to the baking pan and spritz with cooking spray.
15. Slide the baking pan into Rack Position 1, select Convection Bake, set temperature to 400ºF (205ºC) and set time to 10 minutes.
16. Flip the balls halfway through the cooking time.
17. When cooking is complete, the balls should be until golden brown.
18. Serve the risotto balls with the tomato sauce.

474.Garlicky Olive Stromboli

Servings:8
Cooking Time: 25 Minutes
Ingredients:
- 4 large cloves garlic, unpeeled
- 3 tablespoons grated Parmesan cheese
- ½ cup packed fresh basil leaves
- ½ cup marinated, pitted green and black olives
- ¼ teaspoon crushed red pepper
- ½ pound (227 g) pizza dough, at room temperature
- 4 ounces (113 g) sliced provolone cheese (about 8 slices)
- Cooking spray

Directions:
1. Spritz the air fryer basket with cooking spray. Put the unpeeled garlic in the basket.
2. Put the air fryer basket on the baking pan and slide into Rack Position 2, select Air Fry, set temperature to 370ºF (188ºC) and set time to 10 minutes.

3. When cooked, the garlic will be softened completely. Remove from the oven and allow to cool until you can handle.
4. Peel the garlic and place into a food processor with 2 tablespoons of Parmesan, basil, olives, and crushed red pepper. Pulse to mix well. Set aside.
5. Arrange the pizza dough on a clean work surface, then roll it out with a rolling pin into a rectangle. Cut the rectangle in half.
6. Sprinkle half of the garlic mixture over each rectangle half, and leave ½-inch edges uncover. Top them with the provolone cheese.
7. Brush one long side of each rectangle half with water, then roll them up. Spritz the basket with cooking spray. Transfer the rolls to the basket. Spritz with cooking spray and scatter with remaining Parmesan.
8. Select Air Fry and set time to 15 minutes.
9. Flip the rolls halfway through the cooking time. When done, the rolls should be golden brown.
10. Remove the rolls from the oven and allow to cool for a few minutes before serving.

475.Chicken Ham Casserole

Servings:4 To 6
Cooking Time: 15 Minutes
Ingredients:
- 2 cups diced cooked chicken
- 1 cup diced ham
- ¼ teaspoon ground nutmeg
- ½ cup half-and-half
- ½ teaspoon ground black pepper
- 6 slices Swiss cheese
- Cooking spray

Directions:
1. Spritz the baking pan with cooking spray.
2. Combine the chicken, ham, nutmeg, half-and-half, and ground black pepper in a large bowl. Stir to mix well.
3. Pour half of the mixture into the baking pan, then top the mixture with 3 slices of Swiss cheese, then pour in the remaining mixture and top with remaining cheese slices.
4. Slide the baking pan into Rack Position 1, select Convection Bake, set temperature to 350ºF (180ºC) and set time to 15 minutes.
5. When cooking is complete, the egg should be set and the cheese should be melted.
6. Serve immediately.

476.Roasted Mushrooms

Servings: About 1½ Cups
Cooking Time: 30 Minutes
Ingredients:
- 1 pound (454 g) button or cremini mushrooms, washed, stems trimmed, and cut into quarters or thick slices
- ¼ cup water
- 1 teaspoon kosher salt or ½ teaspoon fine salt
- 3 tablespoons unsalted butter, cut into pieces, or extra-virgin olive oil

Directions:
1. Place a large piece of aluminum foil on the sheet pan. Place the mushroom pieces in the middle of the foil. Spread them out into an even layer. Pour the water over them, season with the salt, and add the butter. Wrap the mushrooms in the foil.
2. Select Roast, set the temperature to 325ºF (163ºC), and set the time for 15 minutes. Select Start to begin preheating.
3. Once the unit has preheated, place the pan in the oven.
4. After 15 minutes, remove the pan from the oven. Transfer the foil packet to a cutting board and carefully unwrap it. Pour the mushrooms and cooking liquid from the foil onto the sheet pan.
5. Select Roast, set the temperature to 350ºF (180ºC), and set the time for 15 minutes. Return the pan to the oven. Select Start to begin.
6. After about 10 minutes, remove the pan from the oven and stir the mushrooms. Return the pan to the oven and continue cooking for anywhere from 5 to 15 more minutes, or until the liquid is mostly gone and the mushrooms start to brown.
7. Serve immediately.

477.Lush Seafood Casserole

Servings:2
Cooking Time: 22 Minutes
Ingredients:
- 1 tablespoon olive oil
- 1 small yellow onion, chopped
- 2 garlic cloves, minced
- 4 ounces (113 g) tilapia pieces
- 4 ounces (113 g) rockfish pieces
- ½ teaspoon dried basil
- Salt and ground white pepper, to taste
- 4 eggs, lightly beaten
- 1 tablespoon dry sherry
- 4 tablespoons cheese, shredded

Directions:
1. Heat the olive oil in a nonstick skillet over medium-high heat until shimmering.
2. Add the onion and garlic and sauté for 2 minutes or until fragrant.
3. Add the tilapia, rockfish, basil, salt, and white pepper to the skillet. Sauté to combine well and transfer them into the baking pan.
4. Combine the eggs, sherry and cheese in a large bowl. Stir to mix well. Pour the

mixture in the baking pan over the fish mixture.

5. Slide the baking pan into Rack Position 1, select Convection Bake, set temperature to 360ºF (182ºC) and set time to 20 minutes.
6. When cooking is complete, the eggs should be set and the casserole edges should be lightly browned.
7. Serve immediately.

478.Classic Churros

Servings: 12 Churros
Cooking Time: 10 Minutes
Ingredients:
- 4 tablespoons butter
- ¼ teaspoon salt
- ½ cup water
- ½ cup all-purpose flour
- 2 large eggs
- 2 teaspoons ground cinnamon
- ¼ cup granulated white sugar
- Cooking spray

Directions:
1. Put the butter, salt, and water in a saucepan. Bring to a boil until the butter is melted on high heat. Keep stirring.
2. Reduce the heat to medium and fold in the flour to form a dough. Keep cooking and stirring until the dough is dried out and coat the pan with a crust.
3. Turn off the heat and scrape the dough in a large bowl. Allow to cool for 15 minutes.
4. Break and whisk the eggs into the dough with a hand mixer until the dough is sanity and firm enough to shape.
5. Scoop up 1 tablespoon of the dough and roll it into a ½-inch-diameter and 2-inch-long cylinder. Repeat with remaining dough to make 12 cylinders in total.
6. Combine the cinnamon and sugar in a large bowl and dunk the cylinders into the cinnamon mix to coat.
7. Arrange the cylinders on a plate and refrigerate for 20 minutes.
8. Spritz the air fryer basket with cooking spray. Place the cylinders in the basket and spritz with cooking spray.
9. Put the air fryer basket on the baking pan and slide into Rack Position 2, select Air Fry, set temperature to 375ºF (190ºC) and set time to 10 minutes.
10. Flip the cylinders halfway through the cooking time.
11. When cooked, the cylinders should be golden brown and fluffy.
12. Serve immediately.

479.Oven Baked Rice

Servings: About 4 Cups
Cooking Time: 35 Minutes
Ingredients:
- 1 cup long-grain white rice, rinsed and drained
- 1 tablespoon unsalted butter, melted, or 1 tablespoon extra-virgin olive oil
- 2 cups water
- 1 teaspoon kosher salt or ½ teaspoon fine salt

Directions:
1. Add the butter and rice to the baking pan and stir to coat. Pour in the water and sprinkle with the salt. Stir until the salt is dissolved.
2. Select Bake, set the temperature to 325ºF (163ºC), and set the time for 35 minutes. Select Start to begin preheating.
3. Once the unit has preheated, place the pan in the oven.
4. After 20 minutes, remove the pan from the oven. Stir the rice. Transfer the pan back to the oven and continue cooking for 10 to 15 minutes, or until the rice is mostly cooked through and the water is absorbed.
5. When done, remove the pan from the oven and cover with aluminum foil. Let stand for 10 minutes. Using a fork, gently fluff the rice.
6. Serve immediately.

480.Golden Salmon And Carrot Croquettes

Servings:6
Cooking Time: 10 Minutes
Ingredients:
- 2 egg whites
- 1 cup almond flour
- 1 cup panko bread crumbs
- 1 pound (454 g) chopped salmon fillet
- $^2/_3$ cup grated carrots
- 2 tablespoons minced garlic cloves
- ½ cup chopped onion
- 2 tablespoons chopped chives
- Cooking spray

Directions:
1. Spritz the air fryer basket with cooking spray.
2. Whisk the egg whites in a bowl. Put the flour in a second bowl. Pour the bread crumbs in a third bowl. Set aside.
3. Combine the salmon, carrots, garlic, onion, and chives in a large bowl. Stir to mix well.
4. Form the mixture into balls with your hands. Dredge the balls into the flour, then egg, and then bread crumbs to coat well.
5. Arrange the salmon balls on the basket and spritz with cooking spray.
6. Put the air fryer basket on the baking pan and slide into Rack Position 2, select Air Fry, set temperature to 350ºF (180ºC) and set time to 10 minutes.

7. Flip the salmon balls halfway through cooking.
8. When cooking is complete, the salmon balls will be crispy and browned. Remove from the oven and serve immediately.

481.Traditional Latkes

Servings: 4 Latkes
Cooking Time: 10 Minutes
Ingredients:
- 1 egg
- 2 tablespoons all-purpose flour
- 2 medium potatoes, peeled and shredded, rinsed and drained
- ¼ teaspoon granulated garlic
- ½ teaspoon salt
- Cooking spray

Directions:
1. Spritz the air fryer basket with cooking spray.
2. Whisk together the egg, flour, potatoes, garlic, and salt in a large bowl. Stir to mix well.
3. Divide the mixture into four parts, then flatten them into four circles. Arrange the circles onto the basket and spritz with cooking spray.
4. Put the air fryer basket on the baking pan and slide into Rack Position 2, select Air Fry, set temperature to 380ºF (193ºC) and set time to 10 minutes.
5. Flip the latkes halfway through.
6. When cooked, the latkes will be golden brown and crispy. Remove from the oven and serve immediately.

482.Parsnip Fries With Garlic-yogurt Dip

Servings:4
Cooking Time: 10 Minutes
Ingredients:
- 3 medium parsnips, peeled, cut into sticks
- ¼ teaspoon kosher salt
- 1 teaspoon olive oil
- 1 garlic clove, unpeeled
- Cooking spray
- Dip:
- ¼ cup plain Greek yogurt
- ⅛ teaspoon garlic powder
- 1 tablespoon sour cream
- ¼ teaspoon kosher salt
- Freshly ground black pepper, to taste

Directions:
1. Spritz the air fryer basket with cooking spray.
2. Put the parsnip sticks in a large bowl, then sprinkle with salt and drizzle with olive oil.
3. Transfer the parsnip into the basket and add the garlic.
4. Put the air fryer basket on the baking pan and slide into Rack Position 2, select Air Fry, set temperature to 360ºF (182ºC) and set time to 10 minutes.
5. Stir the parsnip halfway through the cooking time.
6. Meanwhile, peel the garlic and crush it. Combine the crushed garlic with the ingredients for the dip. Stir to mix well.
7. When cooked, the parsnip sticks should be crisp. Remove the parsnip fries from the oven and serve with the dipping sauce.

483.Simple Air Fried Okra Chips

Servings:6
Cooking Time: 16 Minutes
Ingredients:
- 2 pounds (907 g) fresh okra pods, cut into 1-inch pieces
- 2 tablespoons canola oil
- 1 teaspoon coarse sea salt

Directions:
1. Stir the oil and salt in a bowl to mix well. Add the okra and toss to coat well. Place the okra in the air fryer basket.
2. Put the air fryer basket on the baking pan and slide into Rack Position 2, select Air Fry, set temperature to 400ºF (205ºC) and set time to 16 minutes.
3. Flip the okra at least three times during cooking.
4. When cooked, the okra should be lightly browned. Remove from the oven and serve immediately.

484.Simple Cheesy Shrimps

Servings:4 To 6
Cooking Time: 8 Minutes
Ingredients:
- ⅔ cup grated Parmesan cheese
- 4 minced garlic cloves
- 1 teaspoon onion powder
- ½ teaspoon oregano
- 1 teaspoon basil
- 1 teaspoon ground black pepper
- 2 tablespoons olive oil
- 2 pounds (907 g) cooked large shrimps, peeled and deveined
- Lemon wedges, for topping
- Cooking spray

Directions:
1. Spritz the air fryer basket with cooking spray.
2. Combine all the ingredients, except for the shrimps, in a large bowl. Stir to mix well.
3. Dunk the shrimps in the mixture and toss to coat well. Shake the excess off. Arrange the shrimps in the basket.
4. Put the air fryer basket on the baking pan and slide into Rack Position 2, select Air Fry, set temperature to 350ºF (180ºC) and set time to 8 minutes.

5. Flip the shrimps halfway through the cooking time.
6. When cooking is complete, the shrimps should be opaque. Transfer the cooked shrimps onto a large plate and squeeze the lemon wedges over before serving.

485.Cauliflower And Pumpkin Casserole

Servings:6
Cooking Time: 50 Minutes
Ingredients:
- 1 cup chicken broth
- 2 cups cauliflower florets
- 1 cup canned pumpkin purée
- ¼ cup heavy cream
- 1 teaspoon vanilla extract
- 2 large eggs, beaten
- $^1/_3$ cup unsalted butter, melted, plus more for greasing the pan
- ¼ cup sugar
- 1 teaspoon fine sea salt
- Chopped fresh parsley leaves, for garnish
- TOPPING:
- ½ cup blanched almond flour
- 1 cup chopped pecans
- $^1/_3$ cup unsalted butter, melted
- ½ cup sugar

Directions:
1. Pour the chicken broth in the baking pan, then add the cauliflower.
2. Slide the baking pan into Rack Position 1, select Convection Bake, set temperature to 350ºF (180ºC) and set time to 20 minutes.
3. When cooking is complete, the cauliflower should be soft.
4. Meanwhile, combine the ingredients for the topping in a large bowl. Stir to mix well.
5. Pat the cauliflower dry with paper towels, then place in a food processor and pulse with pumpkin purée, heavy cream, vanilla extract, eggs, butter, sugar, and salt until smooth.
6. Clean the baking pan and grease with more butter, then pour the purée mixture in the pan. Spread the topping over the mixture.
7. Put the baking pan back to the oven. Select Bake and set time to 30 minutes.
8. When baking is complete, the topping of the casserole should be lightly browned.
9. Remove the casserole from the oven and serve with fresh parsley on top.

486.Air Fried Crispy Brussels Sprouts

Servings:4
Cooking Time: 20 Minutes
Ingredients:
- ¼ teaspoon salt
- ⅛ teaspoon ground black pepper
- 1 tablespoon extra-virgin olive oil
- 1 pound (454 g) Brussels sprouts, trimmed and halved
- Lemon wedges, for garnish

Directions:
1. Combine the salt, black pepper, and olive oil in a large bowl. Stir to mix well.
2. Add the Brussels sprouts to the bowl of mixture and toss to coat well. Arrange the Brussels sprouts in the air fryer basket.
3. Put the air fryer basket on the baking pan and slide into Rack Position 2, select Air Fry, set temperature to 350ºF (180ºC) and set time to 20 minutes.
4. Stir the Brussels sprouts two times during cooking.
5. When cooked, the Brussels sprouts will be lightly browned and wilted. Transfer the cooked Brussels sprouts to a large plate and squeeze the lemon wedges on top to serve.

487.Lemony And Garlicky Asparagus

Servings: 10 Spears
Cooking Time: 10 Minutes
Ingredients:
- 10 spears asparagus (about ½ pound / 227 g in total), snap the ends off
- 1 tablespoon lemon juice
- 2 teaspoons minced garlic
- ½ teaspoon salt
- ¼ teaspoon ground black pepper
- Cooking spray

Directions:
1. Line the air fryer basket with parchment paper.
2. Put the asparagus spears in a large bowl. Drizzle with lemon juice and sprinkle with minced garlic, salt, and ground black pepper. Toss to coat well.
3. Transfer the asparagus to the basket and spritz with cooking spray.
4. Put the air fryer basket on the baking pan and slide into Rack Position 2, select Air Fry, set temperature to 400ºF (205ºC) and set time to 10 minutes.
5. Flip the asparagus halfway through cooking.
6. When cooked, the asparagus should be wilted and soft. Remove from the oven and serve immediately.

488.Keto Cheese Quiche

Servings:8
Cooking Time: 1 Hour
Ingredients:
- Crust:
- 1¼ cups blanched almond flour
- 1 large egg, beaten
- 1¼ cups grated Parmesan cheese
- ¼ teaspoon fine sea salt
- Filling:
- 4 ounces (113 g) cream cheese
- 1 cup shredded Swiss cheese
- $^1/_3$ cup minced leeks
- 4 large eggs, beaten
- ½ cup chicken broth
- ⅛ teaspoon cayenne pepper

- ¾ teaspoon fine sea salt
- 1 tablespoon unsalted butter, melted
- Chopped green onions, for garnish
- Cooking spray

Directions:
1. Spritz the baking pan with cooking spray.
2. Combine the flour, egg, Parmesan, and salt in a large bowl. Stir to mix until a satiny and firm dough forms.
3. Arrange the dough between two grease parchment papers, then roll the dough into a $^1/_{16}$-inch thick circle.
4. Make the crust: Transfer the dough into the prepared pan and press to coat the bottom.
5. Slide the baking pan into Rack Position 1, select Convection Bake, set temperature to 325ºF (163ºC) and set time to 12 minutes.
6. When cooking is complete, the edges of the crust should be lightly browned.
7. Meanwhile, combine the ingredient for the filling, except for the green onions in a large bowl.
8. Pour the filling over the cooked crust and cover the edges of the crust with aluminum foil.
9. Slide the baking pan into Rack Position 1, select Convection Bake, set time to 15 minutes.
10. When cooking is complete, reduce the heat to 300ºF (150ºC) and set time to 30 minutes.
11. When cooking is complete, a toothpick inserted in the center should come out clean.
12. Remove from the oven and allow to cool for 10 minutes before serving.

489.Banana Cake

Servings:8
Cooking Time: 20 Minutes
Ingredients:
- 1 cup plus 1 tablespoon all-purpose flour
- ¼ teaspoon baking soda
- ¾ teaspoon baking powder
- ¼ teaspoon salt
- 9½ tablespoons granulated white sugar
- 5 tablespoons butter, at room temperature
- 2½ small ripe bananas, peeled
- 2 large eggs
- 5 tablespoons buttermilk
- 1 teaspoon vanilla extract
- Cooking spray

Directions:
1. Spritz the baking pan with cooking spray.
2. Combine the flour, baking soda, baking powder, and salt in a large bowl. Stir to mix well.
3. Beat the sugar and butter in a separate bowl with a hand mixer on medium speed for 3 minutes.
4. Beat in the bananas, eggs, buttermilk, and vanilla extract into the sugar and butter mix with a hand mixer.
5. Pour in the flour mixture and whip with hand mixer until sanity and smooth.
6. Scrape the batter into the pan and level the batter with a spatula.
7. Slide the baking pan into Rack Position 1, select Convection Bake, set temperature to 325ºF (163ºC) and set time to 20 minutes.
8. After 15 minutes, remove the pan from the oven. Check the doneness. Return the pan to the oven and continue cooking.
9. When done, a toothpick inserted in the center should come out clean.
10. Invert the cake on a cooling rack and allow to cool for 15 minutes before slicing to serve.

490.Baked Cherry Tomatoes With Basil

Servings:2
Cooking Time: 5 Minutes
Ingredients:
- 2 cups cherry tomatoes
- 1 clove garlic, thinly sliced
- 1 teaspoon olive oil
- ⅛ teaspoon kosher salt
- 1 tablespoon freshly chopped basil, for topping
- Cooking spray

Directions:
1. Spritz the baking pan with cooking spray and set aside.
2. In a large bowl, toss together the cherry tomatoes, sliced garlic, olive oil, and kosher salt. Spread the mixture in an even layer in the prepared pan.
3. Slide the baking pan into Rack Position 1, select Convection Bake, set temperature to 360ºF (182ºC) and set time to 5 minutes.
4. When cooking is complete, the tomatoes should be the soft and wilted.
5. Transfer to a bowl and rest for 5 minutes. Top with the chopped basil and serve warm.

491.Greek Frittata

Servings:2
Cooking Time: 8 Minutes
Ingredients:
- 1 cup chopped mushrooms
- 2 cups spinach, chopped
- 4 eggs, lightly beaten
- 3 ounces (85 g) feta cheese, crumbled
- 2 tablespoons heavy cream
- A handful of fresh parsley, chopped
- Salt and ground black pepper, to taste
- Cooking spray

Directions:
1. Spritz the baking pan with cooking spray.
2. Whisk together all the ingredients in a large bowl. Stir to mix well.
3. Pour the mixture in the prepared baking pan.
4. Slide the baking pan into Rack Position 1, select Convection Bake, set temperature to 350ºF (180ºC) and set time to 8 minutes.

5. Stir the mixture halfway through.
6. When cooking is complete, the eggs should be set.
7. Serve immediately.

492.Parmesan Cauliflower Fritters

Servings:6
Cooking Time: 8 Minutes
Ingredients:
- 2 cups cooked cauliflower
- 1 cup panko bread crumbs
- 1 large egg, beaten
- ½ cup grated Parmesan cheese
- 1 tablespoon chopped fresh chives Spritz the air fryer basket with cooking spray
- Cooking spray.

Directions:
1. Put the cauliflower, panko bread crumbs, egg, Parmesan, and chives in a food processor, then pulse to lightly mash and combine the mixture until chunky and thick.
2. Shape the mixture into 6 flat patties, then arrange them in the basket and spritz with cooking spray.
3. Put the air fryer basket on the baking pan and slide into Rack Position 2, select Air Fry, set temperature to 390ºF (199ºC) and set time to 8 minutes.
4. Flip the patties halfway through the cooking time.
5. When done, the patties should be crispy and golden brown. Remove from the oven and serve immediately.

493.Asian Dipping Sauce

Servings: About 1 Cup
Cooking Time: 0 Minutes
Ingredients:
- ¼ cup rice vinegar
- ¼ cup hoisin sauce
- ¼ cup low-sodium chicken or vegetable stock
- 3 tablespoons soy sauce
- 1 tablespoon minced or grated ginger
- 1 tablespoon minced or pressed garlic
- 1 teaspoon chili-garlic sauce or sriracha (or more to taste)

Directions:
1. Stir together all the ingredients in a small bowl, or place in a jar with a tight-fitting lid and shake until well mixed.
2. Use immediately.

494.Chinese Pork And Mushroom Egg Rolls

Servings: 25 Egg Rolls
Cooking Time: 33 Minutes
Ingredients:
- Egg Rolls:
- 1 tablespoon mirin
- 3 tablespoons soy sauce, divided
- 1 pound (454 g) ground pork
- 3 tablespoons vegetable oil, plus more for brushing
- 5 ounces (142 g) shiitake mushrooms, minced
- 4 cups shredded Napa cabbage
- ¼ cup sliced scallions
- 1 teaspoon grated fresh ginger
- 1 clove garlic, minced
- ¼ teaspoon cornstarch
- 1 (1-pound / 454-g) package frozen egg roll wrappers, thawed
- Dipping Sauce:
- 1 scallion, white and light green parts only, sliced
- ¼ cup rice vinegar
- ¼ cup soy sauce
- Pinch sesame seeds
- Pinch red pepper flakes
- 1 teaspoon granulated sugar

Directions:
1. Line the air fryer basket with parchment paper. Set aside.
2. Combine the mirin and 1 tablespoon of soy sauce in a large bowl. Stir to mix well.
3. Dunk the ground pork in the mixture and stir to mix well. Wrap the bowl in plastic and marinate in the refrigerator for at least 10 minutes.
4. Heat the vegetable oil in a nonstick skillet over medium-high heat until shimmering. Add the mushrooms, cabbage, and scallions and sauté for 5 minutes or until tender.
5. Add the marinated meat, ginger, garlic, and remaining 2 tablespoons of soy sauce. Sauté for 3 minutes or until the pork is lightly browned. Turn off the heat and allow to cool until ready to use.
6. Put the cornstarch in a small bowl and pour in enough water to dissolve the cornstarch. Put the bowl alongside a clean work surface.
7. Put the egg roll wrappers in the basket.
8. Put the air fryer basket on the baking pan and slide into Rack Position 2, select Air Fry, set temperature to 400ºF (205ºC) and set time to 15 minutes.
9. Flip the wrappers halfway through the cooking time.
10. When cooked, the wrappers will be golden brown. Remove the egg roll wrappers from the oven and allow to cool for 10 minutes or until you can handle them with your hands.
11. Lay out one egg roll wrapper on the work surface with a corner pointed toward you. Place 2 tablespoons of the pork mixture on the egg roll wrapper and fold corner up over the mixture. Fold left and right corners toward the center and continue to roll. Brush a bit of the dissolved cornstarch on the last corner to help seal the egg wrapper. Repeat with remaining wrappers to make 25 egg rolls in total.
12. Arrange the rolls in the basket and brush the rolls with more vegetable oil.

13. Select Air Fry and set time to 10 minutes. Return to the oven. When done, the rolls should be well browned and crispy.
14. Meanwhile, combine the ingredients for the dipping sauce in a small bowl. Stir to mix well.
15. Serve the rolls with the dipping sauce immediately.

495.Teriyaki Shrimp Skewers

Servings: 12 Skewered Shrimp
Cooking Time: 6 Minutes
Ingredients:
- 1½ tablespoons mirin
- 1½ teaspoons ginger juice
- 1½ tablespoons soy sauce
- 12 large shrimp (about 20 shrimps per pound), peeled and deveined
- 1 large egg
- ¾ cup panko bread crumbs
- Cooking spray

Directions:
1. Combine the mirin, ginger juice, and soy sauce in a large bowl. Stir to mix well.
2. Dunk the shrimp in the bowl of mirin mixture, then wrap the bowl in plastic and refrigerate for 1 hour to marinate.
3. Spritz the air fryer basket with cooking spray.
4. Run twelve 4-inch skewers through each shrimp.
5. Whisk the egg in the bowl of marinade to combine well. Pour the bread crumbs on a plate.
6. Dredge the shrimp skewers in the egg mixture, then shake the excess off and roll over the bread crumbs to coat well.
7. Arrange the shrimp skewers in the basket and spritz with cooking spray.
8. Put the air fryer basket on the baking pan and slide into Rack Position 2, select Air Fry, set temperature to 400ºF (205ºC) and set time to 6 minutes.
9. Flip the shrimp skewers halfway through the cooking time.
10. When done, the shrimp will be opaque and firm.
11. Serve immediately.

496.Fried Dill Pickles With Buttermilk Dressing

Servings:6 To 8
Cooking Time: 8 Minutes
Ingredients:
- Buttermilk Dressing:
- ¼ cup buttermilk
- ¼ cup chopped scallions
- ¾ cup mayonnaise
- ½ cup sour cream
- ½ teaspoon cayenne pepper
- ½ teaspoon onion powder
- ½ teaspoon garlic powder
- 1 tablespoon chopped chives
- 2 tablespoons chopped fresh dill
- Kosher salt and ground black pepper, to taste
- Fried Dill Pickles:
- ¾ cup all-purpose flour
- 1 (2-pound / 907-g) jar kosher dill pickles, cut into 4 spears, drained
- 2½ cups panko bread crumbs
- 2 eggs, beaten with 2 tablespoons water
- Kosher salt and ground black pepper, to taste
- Cooking spray

Directions:
1. Combine the ingredients for the dressing in a bowl. Stir to mix well.
2. Wrap the bowl in plastic and refrigerate for 30 minutes or until ready to serve.
3. Pour the flour in a bowl and sprinkle with salt and ground black pepper. Stir to mix well. Put the bread crumbs in a separate bowl. Pour the beaten eggs in a third bowl.
4. Dredge the pickle spears in the flour, then into the eggs, and then into the panko to coat well. Shake the excess off.
5. Arrange the pickle spears in a single layer in the air fryer basket and spritz with cooking spray.
6. Put the air fryer basket on the baking pan and slide into Rack Position 2, select Air Fry, set temperature to 400ºF (205ºC) and set time to 8 minutes.
7. Flip the pickle spears halfway through the cooking time.
8. When cooking is complete, remove from the oven.
9. Serve the pickle spears with buttermilk dressing.

497.Herbed Cheddar Frittata

Servings:4
Cooking Time: 20 Minutes
Ingredients:
- ½ cup shredded Cheddar cheese
- ½ cup half-and-half
- 4 large eggs
- 2 tablespoons chopped scallion greens
- 2 tablespoons chopped fresh parsley
- ½ teaspoon kosher salt
- ½ teaspoon ground black pepper
- Cooking spray

Directions:
1. Spritz the baking pan with cooking spray.
2. Whisk together all the ingredients in a large bowl, then pour the mixture into the prepared baking pan.
3. Slide the baking pan into Rack Position 1, select Convection Bake, set temperature to 300ºF (150ºC) and set time to 20 minutes.
4. Stir the mixture halfway through.
5. When cooking is complete, the eggs should be set.
6. Serve immediately.

498.Crispy Cheese Wafer

Servings:2
Cooking Time: 5 Minutes
Ingredients:
- 1 cup shredded aged Manchego cheese
- 1 teaspoon all-purpose flour
- ½ teaspoon cumin seeds
- ¼ teaspoon cracked black pepper

Directions:
1. Line the air fryer basket with parchment paper.
2. Combine the cheese and flour in a bowl. Stir to mix well. Spread the mixture in the pan into a 4-inch round.
3. Combine the cumin and black pepper in a small bowl. Stir to mix well. Sprinkle the cumin mixture over the cheese round.
4. Put the air fryer basket on the baking pan and slide into Rack Position 2, select Air Fry, set temperature to 375ºF (190ºC) and set time to 5 minutes.
5. When cooked, the cheese will be lightly browned and frothy.
6. Use tongs to transfer the cheese wafer onto a plate and slice to serve.

499.Roasted Carrot Chips

Servings: 3 Cups
Cooking Time: 15 Minutes
Ingredients:
- 3 large carrots, peeled and sliced into long and thick chips diagonally
- 1 tablespoon granulated garlic
- 1 teaspoon salt
- ¼ teaspoon ground black pepper
- 1 tablespoon olive oil
- 1 tablespoon finely chopped fresh parsley

Directions:
1. Toss the carrots with garlic, salt, ground black pepper, and olive oil in a large bowl to coat well. Place the carrots in the air fryer basket.
2. Put the air fryer basket on the baking pan and slide into Rack Position 2, select Roast, set temperature to 360ºF (182ºC) and set time to 15 minutes.
3. Stir the carrots halfway through the cooking time.
4. When cooking is complete, the carrot chips should be soft. Remove from the oven. Serve the carrot chips with parsley on top.

500.Arancini

Servings: 10 Arancini
Cooking Time: 30 Minutes
Ingredients:
- $^2/_3$ cup raw white Arborio rice
- 2 teaspoons butter
- ½ teaspoon salt
- $1^1/_3$ cups water
- 2 large eggs, well beaten
- 1¼ cups seasoned Italian-style dried bread crumbs
- 10 ¾-inch semi-firm Mozzarella cubes
- Cooking spray

Directions:
1. Pour the rice, butter, salt, and water in a pot. Stir to mix well and bring a boil over medium-high heat. Keep stirring.
2. Reduce the heat to low and cover the pot. Simmer for 20 minutes or until the rice is tender.
3. Turn off the heat and let sit, covered, for 10 minutes, then open the lid and fluffy the rice with a fork. Allow to cool for 10 more minutes.
4. Pour the beaten eggs in a bowl, then pour the bread crumbs in a separate bowl.
5. Scoop 2 tablespoons of the cooked rice up and form it into a ball, then press the Mozzarella into the ball and wrap.
6. Dredge the ball in the eggs first, then shake the excess off the dunk the ball in the bread crumbs. Roll to coat evenly. Repeat to make 10 balls in total with remaining rice.
7. Transfer the balls in the air fryer basket and spritz with cooking spray.
8. Put the air fryer basket on the baking pan and slide into Rack Position 2, select Air Fry, set temperature to 375ºF (190ºC) and set time to 10 minutes.
9. When cooking is complete, the balls should be lightly browned and crispy.
10. Remove the balls from the oven and allow to cool before serving.

CPSIA information can be obtained
at www.ICGtesting.com
Printed in the USA
LVHW100545080321
680837LV00010B/211